THE GOOD GOLF COURSE GUIDE

CW01083783

THE
GOOD GOLF
COURSE
GUIDE

PETER ALLISS

Macdonald
Queen Anne Press

KEY TO SYMBOLS

🌳 PARKLAND

🚩 LINKS

🌿 MOORLAND

🌱 HEATHLAND

🏔 DOWNLAND

⛰ UPLAND

☎ TELEPHONE

✉ NEED TO BOOK
IN ADVANCE

£ APPROXIMATE COURSE FEE

Ⓜ MEMBERSHIP REQUIREMENTS
FOR VISITORS

✕ CATERING PROVIDED

🏨 ACCOMMODATION PROVIDED

Ⓛ RESTRICTIONS ON LADIES
AND/OR YOUTHS

🎯 OTHER SPORTING FACILITIES

🚗 DIRECTIONS

A QUEEN ANNE PRESS BOOK

© Text Peter Alliss and Michael Hobbs, 1986, 1991
Illustrations Technical Art Services
Cover picture by Phil Sheldon
First published in Great Britain in 1986 by
Queen Anne Press, a division of
Macdonald & Co (Publishers) Ltd
Orbit House
1 New Fetter Lane
London EC4A 1AR

A member of Maxwell Macmillan Pergamon Publishing Corporation

Reprinted 1987
This revised edition first published in 1991

A CIP catalogue record for this book is available from the British
Library

ISBN 0-356-19685-2

Typeset by Text Filmsetters
Printed and bound in Great Britain by BPCC Hazell Books Ltd,
Aylesbury, Bucks

CONTENTS

INTRODUCTION

The British Isles are full of excellent golf courses, from the north of Scotland to the south-east of England and the south-west of Ireland. At one time most golfers just had to dream of playing in surroundings remote from their home course, but modern transportation and the wander lust has meant that this unparalleled variety of course types and settings is now open to those who want to increase their golfing experience and enjoyment. The object of this book is to help you pick through the 2000 or so courses in England, Scotland, Wales and Ireland and to introduce you to the 10 per cent that in my opinion provide the best golf to be had.

My own experiences of playing the courses have come from a variety of sources. I have, for example, been attached as a professional to clubs in Dorset, Yorkshire and Hampshire and as a result played on a good proportion of courses in the surrounding areas. Although as a tournament professional, I played all over the world, the majority of my competitive golf took place in Great Britain and Ireland. I have also played in scores of exhibition matches and, of course, there have been so many friendly games and minor competitions all over the country. Finally, there have been visits to courses (sometimes perhaps playing no golf at all or just a few holes) for the *Around with Alliss* TV series, company days, clinics or even just a stroll around on a summer's evening.

Among the courses I have selected for this book you'll find most of our great championship and tournament courses, and also many others which will be unknown except to their own members and others who live fairly close by.

In deciding what makes the 'best' golf, various criteria have been applied. I opted against a rigid system of giving marks out of ten for different features, but I did ask myself questions about each club and course, most notably:
1 Is the course enjoyable for the average golfer and scratch player alike?
2 Does the club welcome visitors?
3 Is the course normally in good condition; are there times of year not to visit?
4 What are the clubhouse facilities like?

5 Is the course a good test of golf and, just as important for
me, a pleasant place to be?

Of course, there were many other factors, both major and
minor, but I'll leave these to emerge in my descriptions. But
by and large, how testing the features of the course are is an
important element in my choice, but is only one element,
and a good course also has to be attractive and offer decent
facilities.

My readers may find omissions that surprise them, even
protest that their own course is surely superior to course X or
Y that I have chosen. But, above all, this is my personal
choice. I have my likes and dislikes, too, and I'm prepared to
nail my colours to the mast. I'm a lover of silver birch, pine
and heather (the golfing country of my youth), less fond of
parkland and downs golf or a links that becomes bone hard
and dusty in summer and a chill monster in winter. Worse
still, the unfortunate clay courses that become a trudge
through the mud for much of the winter and rock-like in
summer. Even so, all of these can be a delight when the
weather is kind. But if you do think I've omitted a particularly fine course, write to me giving details and I'll consider it for
the next edition of this book.

Some clubs, they shall be nameless, preferred not to be
included in this book. There are a few which would rather
have no visitors at all unless the guests of members. Even
these clubs will usually let visitors on but, for a day out, a
warm welcome beats grudging permission every time.

To every club included in this book I've written for
up-to-date information on green fees, playing credentials,
practice facilities, food, accommodation and other facilities
and conditions. I should like to record my thanks to those
who have expended much time and enthusiasm in their
replies, the secretaries, captains, chairmen, green rangers,
historians, club professionals and others, without titles of
any kind, who have been so helpful in enabling me to make
this book as up to date as possible.

Finally, there are several points about the information in
this book that you should be aware of before using it.

Credentials

The basic credentials to be allowed to play are the membership card of your own club, a handicap certificate and a

7

letter of introduction from your home club secretary. However, even when specified by the club, you will seldom be asked for any of these. If you arrive respectably dressed for golf, enter the professional's shop and ask to pay a green fee, questions are hardly ever asked. Even so, an envelope containing your 'documentation' permanently in your car glove box will prevent a wasted journey. Other preparations before the day are also advisable.

The telephone

I have not generally specified restrictions on visitors at weekends in the entries because this is so much the norm. Never visit a golf club at the weekend without a prior telephone call. Visitors may be prohibited absolutely or there may be some limitation as regards tee-off times. Courses are also frequently closed except to competitors in club competitions. Although this usually applies to the main golfing season, it can happen in mid-winter as well. Be forwarned also that some clubs apply punitive green fees at the weekend, when they would much prefer to have no visiting players at all.

To take pot luck during the week is often safe enough, but a phone call is still a good idea. Your visit is quite likely to coincide with a society day or perhaps the club's ladies or seniors happen to have a regular event which will cramp your day out. Some clubs have an enormous number of visitors and others not. You are unlikely to know which is the case.

Green fees

These are normally the club's own estimate, given ahead of time, of what they expect the fees to be at the time of publication. My figures will occasionally be a pound or so out but there shouldn't be any severe shocks. I give the cost per day through the week, which is usually, though not always, the same as for a single round. Weekend rates are likely to be some 25 per cent higher, when weekend visitors are allowed.

Dress

This is mostly a matter of a few don'ts. On the course, avoid jeans, shorts, tee shirts and trainers. Often none of these are prohibited but there's little point in taking an unnecessary risk. On the other hand, just about any combination of trousers, shirt, pullover and golf shoes will do but a visitor is always more likely to be allowed to play the more he or she looks like a golfer.

In the clubhouse, jackets and ties aren't often required in daylight hours but they are in the evening and, quite frequently, the club dining room. Be prepared.

Food
As a rule, only small or remote clubs provide none at all. At worst, you should be able to get a snack meal at lunchtime and early evening. Always enquire, and book anything more substantial, before going out to play.

The standard of your golf
In my descriptions of the courses in this book, I have been writing with golfers of not much more than 18 handicap in mind, capable of a firm enough hit to carry the ball around 200 yards. In other words, a golfer who is looking to get up in two at short par 5s when conditions are reasonably favourable. Better golfers and shorter hitters (including ladies) should find no great difficulty in making adjustments.

Tees
The yardages quoted throughout are from the men's medal tees. These are the figures the architect had in mind when the course was designed, not the forward, ladies' or, possibly, back tournament tees.

Course condition and weather
Throughout I have written of individual holes when the ground is firm and the air still. It is obvious that, say, a 120 yard par 3 can need just a punched wedge with a gale at your back or a full driver into one. I do, however, refer to the prevailing wind quite frequently.

Stroke index
As first a young scratch golfer and then a tournament player these never affected my actual score. A visitor shouldn't take the index on the card too literally, mainly because many clubs have strange policies towards stroke indexing.

In an ideal world, I believe the index should be calculated in one of two ways. The first is to analyse score cards returned in club competitions in average weather. See what scores are actually made on each hole and produce a stroke index which will then be based on how difficult competitors find each hole.

Another suitable approach is to consider the length of shot into the green, assuming drives and second shots of 200 yards. The result here will usually be that the par 5s will come into the high numbers of the stroke index, and the long par 3s the low, quite the reverse of what so often occurs at our clubs where, say, four par 3 holes are automatically made stroke index 15 to 18 and par 5s are often rated as far more difficult than they actually are.

In general, when playing a strange course, if you look at the indexing on the card and find some of the par 3s rated as amongst the more difficult holes and the reverse for the par 5s, this is a good guide to how you will find the course yourself.

However, remember that the index has to alternate between first and second half and that, for club matchplay, howls are heard from those who find they have to give shots on the closing holes. The 18th, in particular, is seldom a stroke hole in these circumstances.

And now for the golf itself. We begin at Boat of Garten in the Scottish Highlands and end by the Atlantic at Waterville in Ireland. I do hope you enjoy our journey and add many of my choices to your list of golfing adventures.

KEY MAP

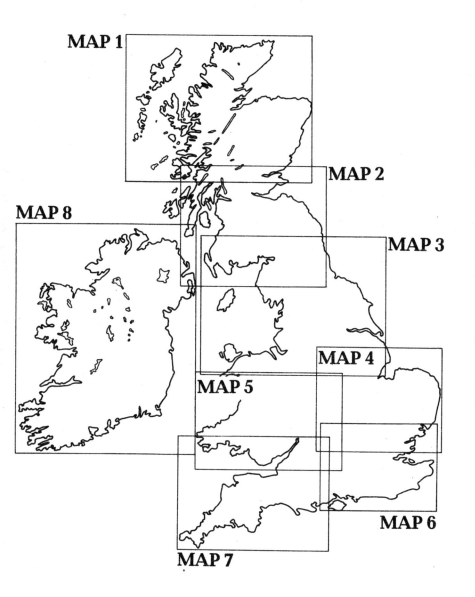

MAP 1

MAP 2

MAP 8

MAP 3

MAP 4

MAP 5

MAP 6

MAP 7

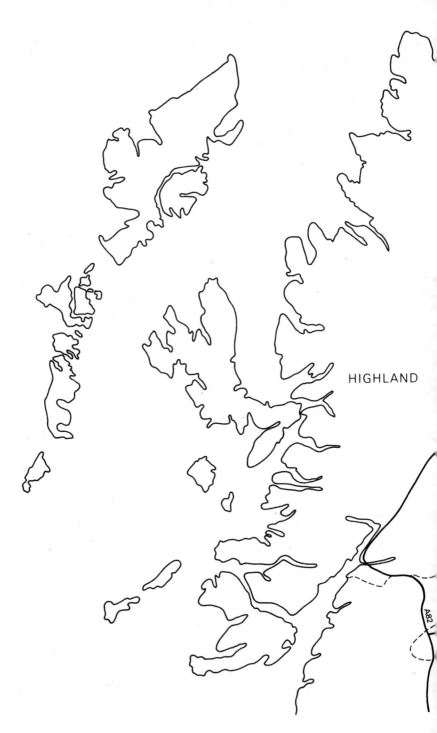

HIGHLAND

A82

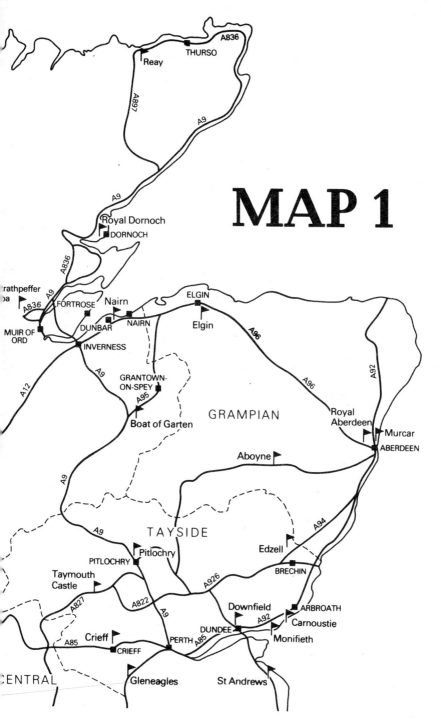

MAP 1

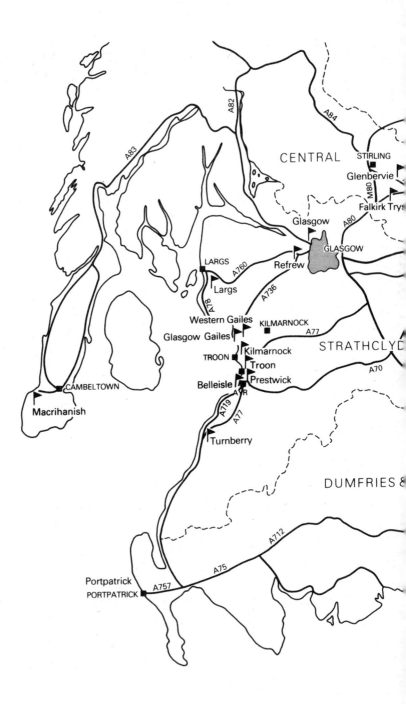

CENTRAL
STIRLING
Glenbervie
M80
Falkirk Trys

A82
A84

Glasgow
A80
GLASGOW
A760
Refrew

LARGS
Largs
A736

A78
Western Gailes
KILMARNOCK
Glasgow Gailes
A77
STRATHCLYD

TROON
Kilmarnock
Troon
A70
Belleisle
Prestwick
A R
A719
A77
Macrihanish
CAMBELTOWN

Turnberry

DUMFRIES &

A712

Portpatrick
A75
PORTPATRICK
A757

MAP 2

ST ANDREWS • St Andrews

FIFE

Lundin Links

Golf House

A915

DUNFERMLINE

Gullane

Honourable Company
of Edinburgh Golfers

North Berwick

A198

FALKIRK

Bruntsfield

Longniddry

Dunbar

Royal Burgess

DUNBAR

Dalmahoy

EDINBURGH

LOTHIAN

A71

A70

A7

BERWICK-UPON-TWEED

Peebles

PEEBLES

A72

BORDER

A7

A1

A68

GALLOWAY

A696

Dumfries and
County

NORTHUMBERLAND

A75

DUMFRIES

Northumberland

A710

A1(M)

Southerness

CUMBRIA

M6

DURHAM

15

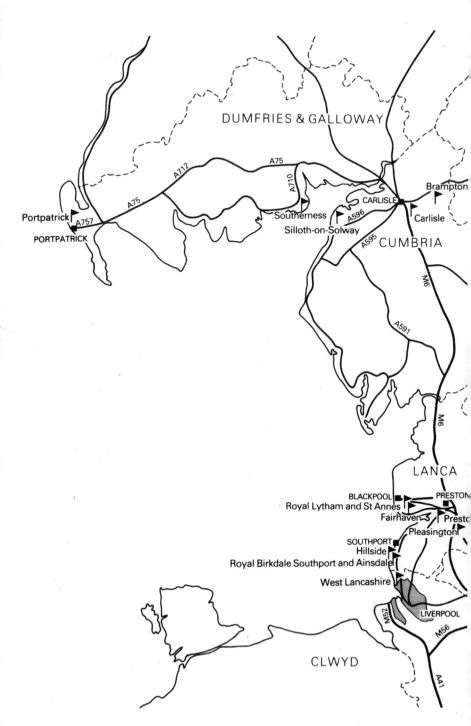

DUMFRIES & GALLOWAY

A712

A75

A710

A75

Portpatrick

A757

PORTPATRICK

Southerness

Silloth-on-Solway

CARLISLE

A596

Carlisle

Brampton

CUMBRIA

A595

M6

A591

M6

LANCA

BLACKPOOL

PRESTON

Royal Lytham and St Annes

Fairhaven

Presto

Pleasington

SOUTHPORT

Hillside

Royal Birkdale Southport and Ainsdale

West Lancashire

M52

LIVERPOOL

M56

CLWYD

A41

MAP 3

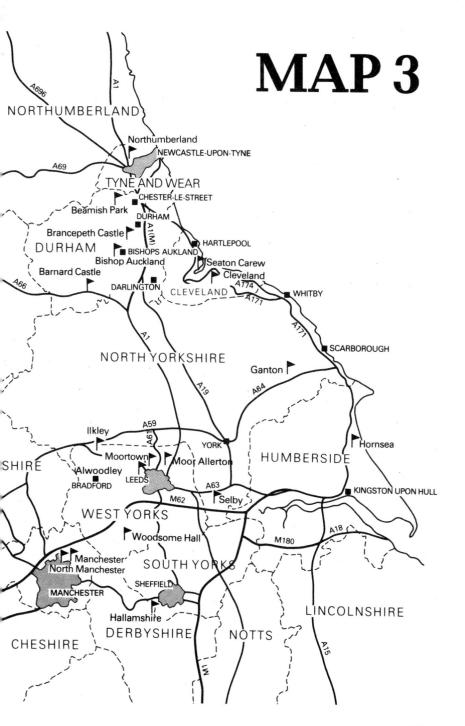

NORTHUMBERLAND

A696

A1

Northumberland

NEWCASTLE-UPON-TYNE

A69

TYNE AND WEAR

CHESTER-LE-STREET

Beamish Park

DURHAM

Brancepeth Castle

DURHAM

BISHOPS AUKLAND

Bishop Auckland

HARTLEPOOL

Barnard Castle

Seaton Carew

A66

DARLINGTON

Cleveland

A774

CLEVELAND

A171

WHITBY

A1

NORTH YORKSHIRE

A19

A171

SCARBOROUGH

Ganton

A64

Ilkley

A59

A61

YORK

Hornsea

Moortown

Moor Allerton

HUMBERSIDE

SHIRE

Alwoodley

LEEDS

BRADFORD

A63

Selby

KINGSTON UPON HULL

M62

WEST YORKS

Woodsome Hall

M180

A18

Manchester

North Manchester

SOUTH YORKS

MANCHESTER

SHEFFIELD

LINCOLNSHIRE

Hallamshire

DERBYSHIRE

NOTTS

A15

CHESHIRE

M1

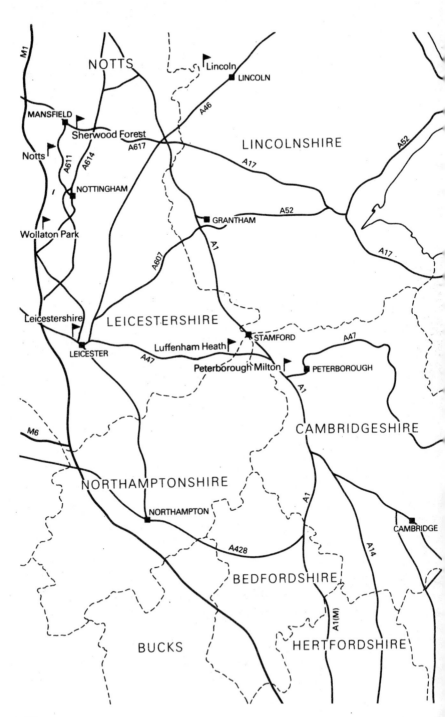

18

MAP 4

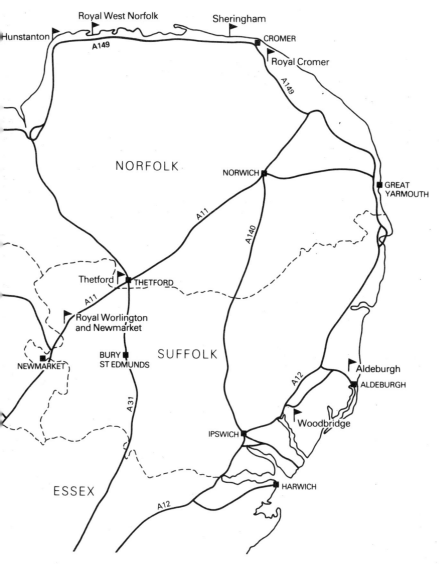

MAP 5

CLWYD

GWYNEDD

POWYS

ABERYSTWYTH ■

DYFED

PEMBROKE ■   Tenby   Ashburnham ⚑ A484   WEST   MID
                                                    GLAMORGAN GLAMORGAN
          A4118   Clyne ⚑   SWANSEA ■

          Pyle and Kenfig ⚑ SOUTH
                              GLAMORGAN
          Royal Porthcawl
          Southerndown   ⚑ BARRY ■

20

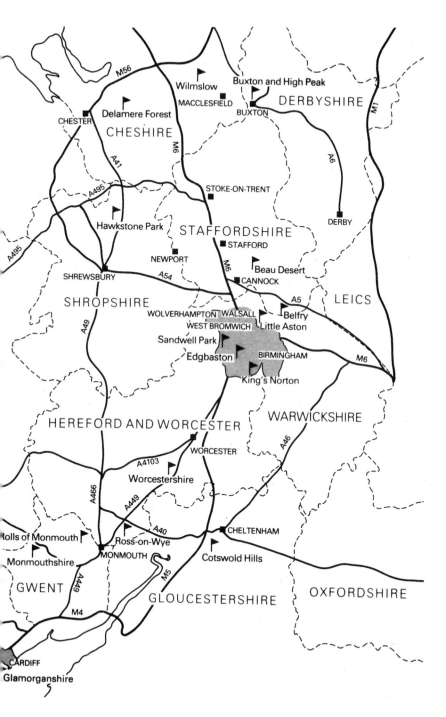

21

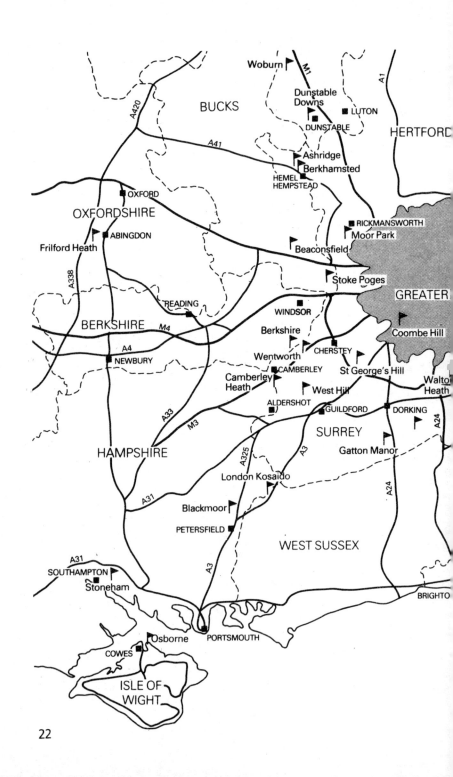

BISHOP'S ■)
STORTFORD (

ESSEX

■ COLCHESTER

SHIRE

A10

A12

CHELMSFORD ■

■ BRENTWOOD

Thorndon
Park

A13

LONDON

■ ROCHESTER

RAMSGATE

A299

Addington

M20

M2

CANTERBURY

Royal St
George's

Prince's
Sandwich

Croham Hurst

Royal Cinque
Ports

DEAL

Knole
Park

KENT

A20

A2

Tandridge

Royal Ashdown
Forest

TUNBRIDGE WELLS

A259

A22

A2070

M20

FOLKESTONE

EAST GRINSTEAD

A259

A26

Littlestone

A259

NEW ROMNEY

EAST SUSSEX

HASTINGS

A259

Seaford

EASTBOURNE

MAP 6

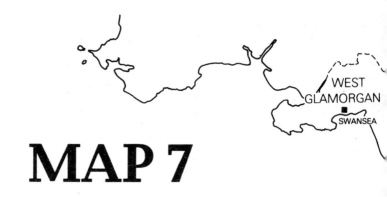

MAP 7

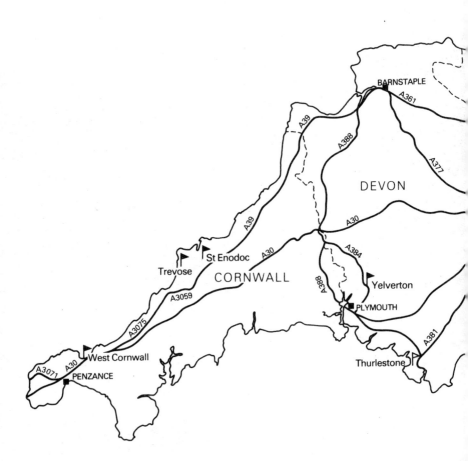

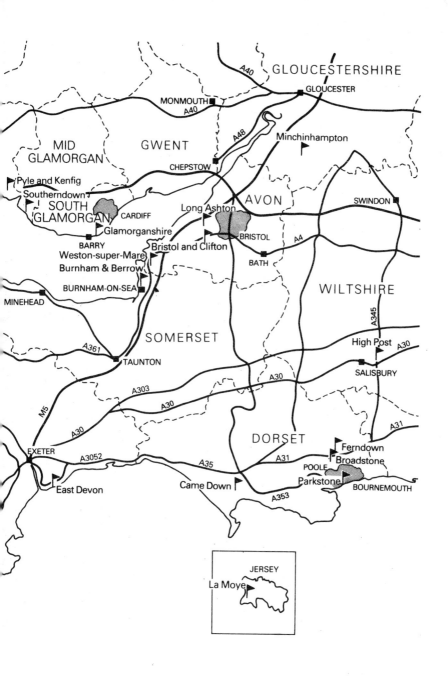

GLOUCESTERSHIRE

GLOUCESTER

MONMOUTH

A40

A40

A48

Minchinhampton

MID GLAMORGAN

GWENT

CHEPSTOW

AVON

SWINDON

Pyle and Kenfig

Southerndown

SOUTH GLAMORGAN

CARDIFF

Long Ashton

Glamorganshire

BRISTOL

A4

BARRY

Bristol and Clifton

Weston-super-Mare

Burnham & Berrow

BATH

BURNHAM-ON-SEA

MINEHEAD

WILTSHIRE

A345

SOMERSET

A361

TAUNTON

High Post

A30

SALISBURY

A303

A30

A30

M5

A30

DORSET

A31

A3052

Ferndown

Broadstone

POOLE

Parkstone

BOURNEMOUTH

EXETER

A35

A31

East Devon

Came Down

A353

JERSEY

La Moye

MAP 8

PORTRUSH
Royal Portrush
COLERAINE
LONDONDERRY
T7
LONDONDERRY
A6
DONEGAL
ANTRIM
N15 (T18)
TYRONE
Malone
BELFAST
LISBURN
T3
PORTADOWN
T2
LEITRIM
DOWN
SLIGO
FERMANAGH
ARMAGH
NEWCASTLE
SLIGO
MONAGHAN
NEWRY
Royal County Down
N4 (T3)
N3
DUNDALK
MAYO
ROSCOMMON
CAVAN
LOUTH
N3 (T35)
LONGFORD
MEATH
WESTMEATH
N3
Portmarnock
GALWAY
TULLAMORE
Royal Dublin
GALWAY
T44
Tullamore
DUBLIN
OFFALY
KILDARE
T6
N52 (T21)
T5
LAOIS
WICKLOW
CLARE
KILKENNY
CARLOW
N7 (T5)
LIMERICK
Kilkenny
KILKENNY
Ballybunion
Limerick
TIPPERARY
WEXFORD
LIMERICK
N24 (T13)
N9 (T14)
N25 (T7)
T68
N20 (T11)
WEXFORD
TRALEE
WATERFORD
Killarney
KILLARNEY
CORK
WATERFORD
KERRY
Waterville
T66
N25 (T12)
(T29)
CORK

THE HIGHLANDS

MAP 1

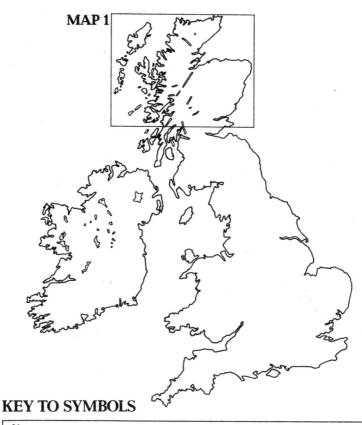

KEY TO SYMBOLS

PARKLAND	☎ TELEPHONE	✕ CATERING PROVIDED
LINKS	⊠ NEED TO BOOK IN ADVANCE	♙ ACCOMMODATION PROVIDED
MOORLAND	🄴 APPROXIMATE COURSE FEE	Ⓛ RESTRICTIONS ON LADIES AND/OR YOUTHS
HEATHLAND	🄼 MEMBERSHIP REQUIREMENTS FOR VISITORS	
DOWNLAND		▧ OTHER SPORTING FACILITIES
UPLAND		🚗 DIRECTIONS

BOAT OF GARTEN

Boat of Garten, Highland PH24 3BU
☎ *Boat of Garten (047 983) 351*

With scenery like this, does the golf really matter? From the course, there are superb views of nearby hills and the Cairngorm range, and the River Spey can also be seen from many of the holes. But if the golf does indeed matter, then this course is good enough to make you ignore the Highland surroundings. James Braid cut some holes out through birch wood, while others are more strictly moorland in type, and each has its own individual character and distinctive feel. As you'd expect, many of the fairways are quite narrow and there are also very distinct undulations. Power, if you're wild with it, won't get you far at Boat of Garten. Though only 5,720 yards or so in length, this course just can't be overpowered and instead is a test of accuracy of very high order.

You begin with quite a long par 3, a feature of many golf courses that can seem to hold up play rather a long time but which helps eventually because there is a bigger gap between games. The second, a medium-length par 4, with a slight dogleg, gives you a downhill drive, followed by the reverse for your second to a green surrounded by gorse.

Soon after, the birch closes in on you and your straightest hitting will be needed. The 6th is called the 'Avenue', an appropriate name. From a high tee you drive down between the birches and must reach the angle of the dogleg if you're going to have a sight of the green. This is set on a plateau and well guarded. Two good shots and you'll be putting but some think this one of the most teasing inland holes in Scottish golf. My advice is, be wary.

There is a fine finish to Boat of Garten. At the 15th, 'Gully', you may do better to play short of the obstacle that gives the hole its name rather than attempt to carry it, and the 16th is the best of the four par 3s, particularly heavily bunkered. The 18th, 435 yards, is quite a long par 4. An out of bounds menaces you on the right and your second will have to be a long carrying shot to a green high up above you. Yet you shouldn't dare to overclub – there's another out of bounds just through the back of the green.

£ £10, £12 at weekends   Ⓜ none

✗ snacks, lunch and dinner daily

🎾 two tennis courts, and Aviemore is just a few miles away

🚗 turn off the A95 at the signpost for Boat of Garten and, just through the village, take the B970 for Nethybridge for 50 yards

NAIRN

Seabank Road, Nairn, Highland
☎ *Nairn (0667) 53208*

Situated to the north-east of Inverness on the southern side of the Moray Firth, Nairn is very probably the best course between Aberdeen and Royal Dornoch. Its close-knit turf, the result of a probably unique combination of sea-washed turf and fine heathy grasses, is a special delight for iron play.

The course was first laid out in 1887 but a couple of years later the architect of the day, Old Tom Morris, was summoned from St Andrews to modify and extend it. His work was revised later by James Braid.

This is a course of championship standard, though not particularly long at 6,556 yards. It has been used by the Scottish Ladies for their championship on seven occasions, the British Ladies once and has been the scene of both Scottish Amateur and Professional Championships.

Famous for its fast and true greens – in a drying wind the slopes can make them too fast at times – Nairn is a flat course, with any real change of level coming only at the 13th and 14th. There are no sand dunes but a wealth of gorse and heather, through which the holes were originally carved.

You begin with a 400-yard par 4, taking the line for your tee shot on the extreme left peak of the Five Sisters of Kintail, some 60 miles in the distance. The sea is close at hand on your right for much of the outward nine.

The 2nd tee is just a stride or two away from the beach, a par 5 of about 500 yards. The main hazard is a dry ditch crossing the fairway, with bunkers along the right in the driving area and a well bunkered green. The next two holes are not difficult but at the par 3 4th, you'll be on the beach if your mid-iron is much left of the green.

The 5th is one of the great holes of Scottish golf. Too far right with your drive and you're in the Firth; left will put you in a bunker. Thereafter, the line to the green is barred by a fairway cross-bunker that'll catch anything rather short on this 378 yard hole, followed by a semi-circle of further bunkers around the front of the green. Good judgement of distance is needed to the two-tiered green.

The 6th is a difficult par 3, with heavy contouring and tends to throw off many shots. By this time, gorse and heather have become more of a threat and continue to be so for the rest of your round. The 8th should be easy enough at only 330 yards but the plateau green is crowned and tilts away from the player. There must be plenty of bite on your approach shot. It takes you back towards the clubhouse but you immediately turn away again for the 9th. You'll probably have been playing into the prevailing wind so far (except, of course, for the 8th) and if so, you may begin to fancy your chances of getting home in two at the 10th, which is 500 yards.

Both the 12th and 13th require firm hitting. The first of these has gorse on both sides of the fairway, which is, however, quite wide, and at the 13th you have a rare uphill shot to a two-level green. The 14th, 206 yards, is played from an elevated tee to an undulating green below, with a deep cleft.

At the 16th there's a good carry from the tee to reach the fairway and a dry ditch can catch a second shot. There's a similar barrier at the 17th, where the Alton Burn runs across, just short of the green. At the last, 516 yards, there's again a chance of getting home in two with a favourable wind but the fairway is heavily bunkered, particularly along the left.

Links golf can become rather too bouncy after a long spell of dry weather so May for Nairn Golf Week could be a good time to go. Details from the golf club or the Tourist Information Centre, King Street, Nairn or, in the winter months, 23 Church Street, Inverness.

£ £16	**✕** snacks, lunch and dinner daily
M a handicap certificate	**🚗** 1 mile to north of A96 just west of Nairn

REAY

Reay by Thurso, Highland KW14 7RE
☎ Reay (084781) 288

This is the most northerly golf club in mainland Scotland (there are still a few thriving in the Orkneys and Shetlands).

Reay overlooks Sandside Bay and that 'great green sea upon the north', the Pentland Firth, a wild stretch of water indeed. There are views of hills to the south and west and the Orkney Islands northwards. It is protected from the winds to some extent by heatherclad hills and the dunes that separate this gently undulating links from the beach.

The club was formed in 1893 by the local laird. Members of the parish could join for 2 shillings annually (small wonder golf is still expected to be cheap in Britain!). It could not be maintained during the Second World War but was revived in the early 1960s.

Hazards are mainly natural so there are few bunkers. A burn comes into play at a few holes. There are out of bounds left of the 2nd and 16th fairways.

The 4th is stroke index 1, a monster par 5 of 584 yards, apart from one or two championship tees the longest in this book. There is a good carry over rough from the tee. Another tester is the long par 3 7th, played to a plateau green over rough and the burn. The par 3s play a large part in making a good score on this course. There are six in all, ranging in length from the 240-yard 1st hole to the 138-yard 15th. This high number of par 3s is the main reason the course isn't longer than its 5,865 yards.

Reay is a simple club where the golf's the thing, and there's no professional.

£6	🚗 Some 10 miles from Thurso on the A836 just past the church before Reay village
✗ only occasional catering	

ROYAL DORNOCH

Golf Road, Dornoch, Highland IV25 3LW
☎ *Dornoch (0862) 810219*

This is a place of pilgrimage rather than just a golf course. It's not the most northerly in mainland Britain as there are some half dozen more in the far north-east of Scotland towards John o'Groats, including Reay, of course. But it is one of the great links courses of Britain and, indeed, the world, visited in recent years by such 'tourists' as Tom Watson and Ben Crenshaw. The latter, who came just before an Open Championship, said he'd found it difficult to leave for the great event.

Dornoch is a little more than 600 miles north of London and a couple of hundred from Edinburgh. Even Inverness, the most northerly city in Britain, is a drive of some 50 miles to the south. Though this little town of some 1,000 people has a course fit to host an Open Championship, such distances, even in days of easy air travel, prevent this being a real possibility. However, the Scottish Ladies' and Northern Open Championships come regularly, and the Home Internationals were held at Dornoch in 1980. More important, perhaps, the R and A gave the course overdue recognition when the Amateur Championship, won by Garth McGimpsey, came in 1985, bringing the course to a wider audience through newspaper reporting.

Royal Dornoch, however, has long been famous to those 'in the know', even if, for them also, it was often just too far away. When there's little time to spare, more golf rather than more travel often has to be the decision.

The first mention of golf at Dornoch was when the 13th Earl of Sutherland was recorded in household accounts as spending money on 'bows, arrows, golfclubs and balls'. This was in 1616. At this time Sir Robert Gordon described the links in the following terms: 'About this town along the sea coast are the fairest and largest links or green fields of any pairt of Scotland. Fitt for archery, golfing, riding and all other

31

THE HIGHLANDS/Royal Dornoch

exercises, they doe surpass the fields of Montrose or St Andrews.'

All this means that written records of golf at Dornoch follow only St Andrews and Leith – where golf was actually first played in Scotland will probably never be known. The written word is our only authority.

In the mid-nineteenth century the Sutherland Golfing Society used to play over the links at Dornoch and Golspie, a little to the north. This led to the formation of the club in 1877, with an annual subscription of 2s 6d and an annual income of £3 18s 6d. Subsequently Old Tom Morris came up from St Andrews to design an eighteen hole course, extended early this century when the guttie ball went out of use. Further changes took place over the years but Dornoch took its present shape some forty years ago, 6,533 yards, eight out and ten back.

The first eight go along an upper level of dunes, the return being on land closer to the sea and at much the same level.

Like many great courses, the start is not spectacular, quite a short par 4, with the run of the ground favouring your drive. This is followed by a par 3 of about 180 yards to a plateau green, with steep falls at the rear and both right and left. Two deep bunkers guard the front with a mound to encourage your ball towards them. At the 3rd you change level with a downhill drive, followed by a second shot to a plateau green, the ground sharply contoured all around. You are into the heart of Dornoch links. The 4th is another 400 yarder, again with a plateau green, the fairway sloping from left to right with a steep fall away on the right.

The 5th is the first classic hole. It's again played from an elevated tee, with a great mound some 170 yards out to be carried. Go right and you'll be bunkered, left and you'll be into gorse and bent grass. The plateau green is kidney-shaped and the wise man looks for the flag position before driving off. This was a favourite hole of Tom Watson's.

The 6th, 165 yards, has been described as one of the hardest par 3s in the world but it's not length that makes it so. If you miss on the right, you plunge away down a steep slope, making the pitch back a shot requiring nerve, touch and judgement. To the left, thick gorse and bunkers are no more inviting. The 7th is rated the hardest hole on the course at Stroke Index 1 but it's not one of Dornoch's most interesting which the 8th, the furthest you go from the clubhouse, certainly is. The drive is over a precipice and the second shot to this 437-yard hole must traverse a series of humps and bumps and dead ground before reaching the haven of a green set in a dell.

At the 9th you turn for home, and probably into the wind, with the beach all along the left and long grass and gorse to the right at driving distance. Otherwise, however, it's not a difficult par 5. The short 10th again has the beach as a lateral water hazard and so does the 11th, a long and tough par 4. Into the wind it can be a long and arduous journey home, relieved only by the 12th, a par 5, and the 15th, a short par 4. The 14th, 'Foxy', is Dornoch's most famous hole, rated by Harry Vardon 'the most natural hole in golf'. It's the only hole without bunkers and as a long par 4 can be best enjoyed, like the 16th at Deal, when the wind isn't too severely against you. Ideally your drive should be right to left and your long second should swing the opposite way, along a shallow valley and up to a plateau green. If you do manage to hold the narrow, elevated green with your second it really would be a shame to three-putt!

The 16th, played uphill, is rather a slog, coming towards the end of your round, but you may be rewarded with the sight of your long second shot hanging against the sky and then plunging greenwards.

The 17th is a beauty, rewarding your climb with a downhill tee shot amongst the gorse. Your second has to carry a rise, inset with bunkers. The finish is a long par 4, over 450 yards, along the top of a ridge. There are bunkers some 30 yards short of the green, followed by a grassy swale in front of it.

Apart from the quality of the course, with its fine turf, true putting surfaces, and greens that seem to be placed by nature rather than by man, it's simply a beautiful place to be, with the hills of Sutherland, Ross, Inverness-shire, and sometimes even Aberdeenshire, all about the golfer, and, of course, the North Sea also, soothed by the Gulf Stream.

Because of its remoteness, Dornoch is seldom crowded, even in the 'peak' months of the school holidays. The best time to come is early summer, when the yellow gorse is in bloom.

Dornoch has always had its share of famous members, most of whom have lived far off. The great Joyce Wethered and her brother Roger are said to have learned to play from summer golf here and Andrew Carnegie presented one of the trophies, a magnificent one. The famous Ross family were from Dornoch. One, Alex, won the US Open, while Donald became one of the greatest architects in golf's history, much influenced by his early experience of Dornoch.

Let's leave the last words to Tom Watson: 'This is the most fun I have had playing golf in my whole life.'

£ £28, £20 per round

M a handicap certificate

✗ snacks during normal bar hours, lunch and dinner daily except Monday

🚗 aim for the thirteenth-century cathedral in Dornoch centre and follow signs to the course, 1/4 mile away

✉ need to book in advance

STRATHPEFFER SPA

Strathpeffer, Highland
☎ Strathpeffer (0997) 21219

Strathpeffer is way up in the Highlands, beyond Inverness, with Royal Dornoch still some miles away, if that's the main object of your pilgrimage.

Strathpeffer began in 1888 as a nine-hole course, but Old Tom Morris was soon called in from St Andrews to design a second nine. What general directive he may have been given I don't know but the result is a course entirely without sand bunkers. This does not matter as it is a course with plenty of natural hazards, and when the shape of the ground provides hazards in plenty, bunkers aren't really needed. They demand a lot of maintenance which is better devoted to other parts of the course.

At just 4,813 yards, Strathpeffer is the shortest eighteen-hole course in this book. There are no par 5s, the longest hole is 432 yards and there are seven par 3s, although one is rather a monster at 242 yards. The par and standard scratch are both 65 but in close on a hundred years the lowest score recorded is 61, so it's hardly pitch and putt. The heather, broom and gorse can be formidable and several of the fairways are tree-lined.

At the 1st 300 yards, you must negotiate a burn and there's the longest fall from the tee in Scottish golf. At the 2nd there's the kind of hazard no modern architect would dare include in his scheme: a wall just short of the green for you to pitch over. Although the hole is only 257 yards, it's rated as stroke index 3. At the 3rd, a short hole needing a long iron or often a wood, a small loch abundant with trout bars the way.

The 7th is the next tester and is known as 'Rockies'. Although it's only 290 yards, you still need as long a drive as you can manage to shorten your pitch to a plateau green surrounded by all manner of trouble. The 10th is the best of the par 3s. Again you play directly over water, with out of bounds along the right, to a very small green surrounded by heather. The 13th presents a choice for the tee shot: to play short of where the fairway narrows to just 15 yards, some 200 yards from the tee, or go for it, hoping to leave yourself with just a wedge to the green.

From the 10th and 11th holes, the Torridon Hills can be seen to the west, with the Inverness-shire Hills to the south. From the 18th tee you can see over the clubhouse to Dingwall and the Black Isle.

£ £8, £6 per round   M none

X lunch daily except Monday

🚗 ¼ mile north of the village square and signposted

WEST
OF SCOTLAND

MAP 2

KEY TO SYMBOLS

🌳	PARKLAND	☎	TELEPHONE	✕	CATERING PROVIDED
	LINKS	✉	NEED TO BOOK IN ADVANCE	🏠	ACCOMMODATION PROVIDED
	MOORLAND	£	APPROXIMATE COURSE FEE	Ⓛ	RESTRICTIONS ON LADIES AND/OR YOUTHS
	HEATHLAND	M	MEMBERSHIP REQUIREMENTS FOR VISITORS		OTHER SPORTING FACILITIES
	DOWNLAND				
	UPLAND			🚗	DIRECTIONS

AYR BELLEISLE ♣

Downfoot Road, Ayr KA7 4D, Strathclyde
☎ *Alloway (0292) 41258*

In the former county of Ayrshire most golfing holiday-makers will have their sights set on links courses but, especially perhaps if it's been rather too severely windy for a few days, it might be as well to seek out Ayr Belleisle, a municipal parkland course of high quality. It has been used for various tournaments since before the Second World War, including in more recent years the 1971 Ladies' Championship, the 1967 Seniors, and the 1964 Penfold.

The course was designed by James Braid, who together with Harry Colt must be responsible for more of our courses than any other single architect. It features a particularly interesting dogleg left, the 4th, with cross bunkering. It's called 'Braid's Bend'. There is also a right dogleg on the 12th. A burn comes strongly into play at driving range at the 16th and, more formidably, just short of the 17th, which is a medium-iron par 3.

💷 £9	Ⓜ none	🏨 there is a hotel in the grounds
✖ lunch is available at Belleisle Park cafe		🚗 take the A719 south and Belleisle Park is about two miles from the town centre

DUMFRIES AND COUNTY ♣

Nunfield, Edinburgh Road, Dumfries and Galloway DG1 1JX
☎ *Dumfries (0387) 53585*

First laid out by Willie Fernie, a former Open Champion, in 1913, the course was lengthened under the eyes of James Braid several years later. Both did their work with skill and judgement. Although the course occupies less than 100 acres most of the holes have a separate feel about them.

Dumfries is rolling parkland. Because of the fairly mild climate and high rainfall in this part of Scotland, there is a multitude of fine trees, lush fairways and really excellent greens, which have won awards for the greenkeeper.

The first hole would win few prizes. You have to play an iron from the tee and then a little pitch. Perhaps it's there just to get you to the 2nd hole, a really good par 4. Here the second shot is all, a long iron or even a wood through a gulley to a raised green with trouble either side.

From the 4th tee, you can see the River Nith meandering away and open country to the Queensberry Hills. The drive is from an elevated tee and the second played to a plateau green with the bank in front well bunkered. The 5th is another attractive hole, with the river to one side. The green is set well up on a mound with trees to either side, bunkering front – and out of bounds if you're overbold. It's quite difficult to hold the putting surface.

The 7th is the only par 5 at Dumfries, the drive having to pierce a belt of trees, after which everything should be fairly straightforward.

There are few holes as short as 90 yards but Dumfries has one of them, the 14th. There's plenty of bunkering and a towering lime tree to the right. It catches many players between clubs – too far for the sand iron and perhaps too short for a full wedge. It looks too easy and many make a mess of it!

The 18th makes a fine finishing hole, a long par 4, or at least it can play quite long with the drive to rising ground. The green tends to look further away than it really is so beware of overclubbing and putting your second clear through the green and into the members' lounge, an unpopular move.

Practice is quite well provided for: approach area with bunker, putting green and a good-sized practice ground.

£ £12, £15 on Sundays	🚗 take the A701 Dumfries to Edinburgh road from the town centre and look out for the club on the right after about one mile
Ⓜ membership of a golf club	
✗ catering all day	

GLASGOW

Killermont, Bearsden, Glasgow, Strathclyde G61 2TW
☎ (041) 942 2340
Gailes, Strathclyde
☎ Irvine (0294) 311347

Founded in 1787, the Glasgow Golf Club is probably the eighth oldest in the world. It is distinctive in other ways as well: not a few clubs have twenty-seven or thirty-six holes but they are laid out close to each other, over similar land. Not so Glasgow; the two courses are about 35 miles apart and are entirely different in type: Killermont is parkland, and Gailes is a links.

Killermont 🚩

Killermont was the fifth home of the club and was designed by Old Tom Morris in 1904. It is thought to be his last work. The clubhouse, a mansion built around the time of Trafalgar, is worth a visit on its own. It also has a magnificent trophy collection, which can stand comparison with one anywhere. There are silver clubs with silver balls attached and, in particular, a unique cup, presented in 1879 by Sir Charles Tennant to mark his year as captain. The Tennant Cup, prized just about as highly by Scottish golfers as a national championship, is the oldest amateur medal competition in the world and is five years the senior of the Amateur Championship. Its first 36 holes are played over Gailes and the second at Killermont.

The Scottish Seniors' is held every two years at Killermont and two major professional events have come here, the 1949 Daily Mail Tournament and the 1957 Penfold.

The course, however, is not intended to tame tigers. I'm told that the members insist the rough be kept short, and it's only 5,970 yards in length. It begins a little eccentrically with a par 4 only a little over the regulation distance for a 3, followed immediately by the reverse, a 245 yard par 3. Next comes one of the most difficult holes, a well-bunkered 400 yard hole over rising ground.

The 5th, 525 yards, is easily the longest hole, with two changes of direction. As you need to keep your tee shot right and your second left this makes the hole play longer. However, the last three holes on the first nine may provide birdie opportunities. All are short par 4s.

The 10th, however, at 419 yards, is quite a stiff par 4 when the position of the drive is critical, because of trees. This is true again at the 12th, oddly a hole of exactly the same length, with a hog's back green that's difficult to hold, as is the elevated one at the 14th.

£ £25

M introduction by a member is requested but a letter of introduction from your club will very likely be acceptable

Ⓛ there are no lady or junior members but the same terms apply

🍴 snacks daily, lunch daily except Monday

🚌 go north west from the city centre along Maryhill Road to Killermont Bridge. Turn right at traffic lights then right again towards Woodvale Avenue

✉ need to book in advance, no visitors at weekends

Gailes ⛳

This is a much stiffer test than Killermont, sufficiently so to be used as a qualifying course the last three times the Open Championship has been held at either Royal Troon or Turnberry. Other important events to have come here include the Scottish Amateur Championship, the Scottish Open Amateur Strokeplay, the British Youths and the Scottish Professional Championship. The course is thought to have been laid out by

Willie Park Junior in the 1890s and now measures 6,432 yards. Its record is a remarkable 62, returned by that evergreen Scottish amateur, Charlie Green. He was the 1983 *non-playing* Walker Cup captain but in practice was said to be outscoring his team!

Situated on the Firth of Clyde, with views away to the Isle of Arran, Gailes is almost always open in the winter on days when Killermont may be under snow, mainly because of the Gulf Stream.

There are conifers here instead of the oak, beech and chestnut which are such a feature of Killermont, but the main hazard is the abundant heather which lines the fairways, with more occasional gorse.

After a fairly easy start, with a couple of short par 4s, the 428 yard 3rd hole is testing, doglegging through the heather. The 5th, 530 yards, is the longest hole, stroke index 1, with a well-bunkered fairway and green set in a hollow. There follows the first of three short holes and the par 4 8th takes us to the furthest point from the clubhouse. However, though this is a generally out-and-back links lay-out, you aren't likely to feel this for the holes dodge about and the wind comes from every direction, which is very much preferable to a relentless gale.

Both nines are well balanced, at about 3,200 yards with a par 5 each. The most demanding of the three short holes is the 15th, played to a raised green.

€ £22

M a letter of introduction from your club secretary is asked but proof of membership may be accepted

Ⓛ ladies and juniors have to play with a member or obtain prior authority from the secretary

---

✗ snacks daily, lunch daily except Monday and Friday, high teas

🚗 1 mile south of Irvine on Troon road

✉ need to book in advance, no visitors at weekends

KILMARNOCK (BARASSIE)

29 Hillhouse Road, Barassie, Troon, Strathclyde
☎ *Troon (0292) 313920*

This course is used for final qualifying when the Open Championship is at either Troon or Turnberry, and almost 20 years ago, I played my pre-qualifying rounds here before the 1973 Troon Open. The condition of the course was excellent and I wrote at the time: 'I think the course could well be held up as the one where all budding greenkeepers were made to go for a week just to see how eighteen holes could be maintained to perfection by only three men, yes repeat three! Gentle-men, I salute you, the course was absolutely splendid.'

At much the same time, a visitor from London remarked to the secretary: 'I would like to buy this course, this countryside, lock, stock and barrel and transport it to within 70 miles of London. I could charge £500 entrance fee and £200 subscription. I would have a waiting list as long as your arm and everyone would be trying to wangle his pal into membership in front of the other fellows.'

Well, there are many good courses near London – but there are dull, muddy ones too. I'm sure that the visitor's project would be successful – but it would cost him a great deal more than the £2,500 the club paid the Duke of Portland for the links back in 1920!

Barassie was founded in 1887 and golf has been played on the present site for a few years less. The move was made after a farmer grazed Ayrshire cattle over the original land. We golfers used to put up with rabbits and sheep but cattle have never been easily tolerated!

It is a flat seaside course with natural turf. Bunkers are the main hazard, plus heather and whins.

The start is near ideal for avoiding hold-ups in play: two short par 4s, the second of these with a tricky three-level green. A burn comes into play on the 4th, an excellent par 4 of just under 400 yards. You must make up your mind whether or not you're likely to reach it, some 260 yards away, in the playing conditions of the day. You want to be as near it as you dare, because the line into the green is narrow.

The next hole is perhaps the most difficult one on the course, 425 yards with the wind usually against. There's an out of bounds wall all down the right and a burn very much in play for your long second shot, just 30 yards short of the green. Subtle use of the burn has been made on the 6th, 377 yards. It crosses in front of the tee some 100 yards out and then continues up the right edge of the fairway, forcing the intended drive to the left. Be wary about being too bold with your second shot, for that self-same burn is now waiting just through the green for the overhit ball.

The 11th is a classic little par 4 of just over 300 yards. You drive to an island fairway with a profusion of heather and whins if you miss. You'll be wise to use a well-trusted club from the tee and be content with just finding the fairway. Then there is a short approach to play but this will have to be a good one, especially when the flag is at the back: the ground falls away quickly for a shot that's a little too strong.

The 15th is the last and best of three par 3s and asks for your best shot of the round. You must carry it 200 yards or more to a very narrow green, protected on either flank by bunkers and uneven ground.

The close is three par 4s, all around the 350-yard mark. On the first of these a hollow with thick heather cutting into the fairway can be a problem if you drive too far. At the 17th there are sharp falls at the left and back of the green, and at both 17th and 18th the railway is close on the right.

£ £25

M *Visitors: Mondays, Tuesdays, Thursdays and Friday afternoons*

✗ *snacks, lunch and high tea daily*

🚗 *in Troon, head for Barassie Station and clubhouse is then opposite*

LARGS

Irvine Road, Largs, Strathclyde KA30 8EU
☎ *Largs (0475) 673594*

Although Largs is adjacent to the sea, it is a parkland course with trees and brooks rather than sand dunes as its main features.

From the course there are views of the Isles of Cumbrie and Arran and also Bute and the Firth of Clyde. As Largs is in a renowned golfing area, mostly linksland, its merits are often overlooked in favour of its better-known neighbours, but this is unjust. Its fine lay-out was recognized when the British Girls' Championship came here in 1982, the length of a little less than 6,300 yards being nearly ideal for the players.

The most difficult hole is the 15th, a par 4 of near maximum length while the 9th and 11th, both tree-lined and doglegged, are given interest by these features.

The balance of the course is good with both nines being almost the same length, each having a couple of par 3s and one par 5.

🅔 *£20* 🄼 *none*

🚗 *about 1 mile south of Largs on the A78*

✗ *lunch and snacks daily, dinner daily except Monday*

MACHRIHANISH

Campbeltown, Argyll PA28 6PT
☎ *Campbeltown (0586) 81213*

A famous name this but, like Dornoch far to the north-east, less visited than it deserves because of both distance and access. In more leisurely times, when the journey time didn't much matter (how long did it take

Queen Victoria to get to Balmoral I wonder?), Machrihanish was a fashionable place to go for a family and golfing holiday – just as North Berwick was.

Certainly its position, between the Isle of Arran and the Hebrides, with no more land until Long Island, looks remote on the map, yet you can be there in half an hour, and right by the golf course at that, from Glasgow Airport. Of course, many of us would have to get to Glasgow first...

Machrihanish was founded in 1876, when there was not nearly as much golf on the west coast of Scotland as in the east. Getting the club started must have been informal and was certainly very quick, for there was a meeting early in March and members were playing a couple of weeks later – it would have been sooner but for a spell of nasty weather! A few of the founder members went out, perhaps had some discussion about the general route of the ten-hole course and then cut the holes. In no time, the course was ready to play.

That's not nearly as silly as you might think. Machrihanish is ideal golfing linksland, where fine fescues grow more sideways than vertically, and with a good variety of places suitable for putting. Even Jack Nicklaus, today, wouldn't need his normal budget of several million dollars to lay out a course.

However, three years after the foundation, with the golf going along very nicely, the members decided to have an expert in to advise on the layout of an eighteen-hole course. Old Tom Morris arrived from St Andrews and pronounced the ground 'specially designed by the Almighty for playing golf'. Mind you, I've often heard this remark repeated elsewhere, usually with Old Tom quoted as the source. I suspect he *always* said it and surely none of the committees he dealt with throughout the land objected.

Thereafter, the course was little changed for the next thirty years or so until J.H. Taylor was called in in 1914 to revise it for the challenge of better equipment and balls. Taylor's course has remained ever since.

The 1st is one of the most dramatic holes in golf and just about everybody's choice for the best starting hole in Scotland. To the left is the Atlantic; straight ahead the six-mile beach of Machrihanish Bay, with breakers under your nose if it's high tide; and the fairway half right. How much of the beach do you think you can carry? Attempt too much and you're on it or in the Atlantic rollers; go right and there's no chance of getting up in two at this quite long par 4. If you are bold, and play straight towards the flag, the carry is about 200 yards.

At the 2nd your approach shot must carry a rise in front of the green, the beginning of dune country. After the undulations of the 2nd green, the 3rd is very kindly, a bowl which gathers the second shot. Then comes the first par 3 hole, a really short one, little longer than the Postage Stamp at Troon, to a plateau green. The 6th has a fine old-fashioned drive, straight over a ridge with a short pitch to follow. The 7th, a long par 4, reverses the procedure: your second has to soar over a high sandhill.

One visiting American, having played all the famous championship courses of Scotland, declared the first nine at Machrihanish the best he'd played anywhere, as were both fairways and greens.

The homeward nine are rather further from the sea, greener and more inland in character, as so often on links courses. You may still be only a short iron from the beach but those few yards make all the difference.

Nevertheless, there are more fine holes ahead. The 14th could be, depending on the wind, the most difficult hole of all, a long par 4 with a dip in front of the green so you must carry all the way. Two short holes follow in succession, the second of these over 230 yards.

Perhaps there are a few too many blind shots but these are little problem once you know the course. Earlier golfers loved that element of wild surmise as you breast a rise to see what fate has handed out. The moderns, in general, like to see the fairway spread out ahead and the bottom of the flag in sight for the shot to the green.

Three Thomsons of the same family have served the club throughout its life. They were good teachers with simple philosophies about the game. Said Archie: 'Slaw back, keep your ee' on the ball, dinna press, and follow through.' His brother Hector was even crisper, just: 'Hold the club straight out in front of you and sweevel on your henches.' Yes, golf instruction can be more complicated than these simple words.

There are fine views from the clubhouse of Gigha, Jura and Islay with often superb sunsets in summer and autumn.

£ £14	M none
✗ lunch and dinner daily except Monday	

🚗 5 miles west of Campbeltown on B843 after ferry from Arran or a long circuit via the A83 from Inveraray.

PORTPATRICK (DUNSKEY)

Golf Course Road, Portpatrick, Dumfries and Galloway DG9 8TB
☎ Portpatrick (077681) 273

This course is set on the cliffs above the village of Portpatrick, once a major port but now with a population of only about 600. If you are prepared to risk the weather, the best time to come for golf is often from late March to May. When others may be shivering in stern easterlies off the North Sea, you are likely to find the weather far more agreeable in the west of Scotland, enjoying the effect of the Gulf Stream.

This is ideal holiday golf, when most players, especially for 36 holes a day, don't want either too mammoth a trek or too many lost golf balls. But there are plenty of natural hazards on the 5,663-yard course and bunkers have recently been added. A few of the holes are dull, just a way of moving on to more promising country, but there are a number of cunningly devised ones. If you are a short hitter, you'll find steadiness is very helpful. For long hitters there are certainly four chances to drive the green at par 4s, even in still air. But beware. It may not be worth it, especially with a tail wind, because of trouble through the green.

The first hole is a longish par 4, usually into the prevailing wind; whatever the conditions it's difficult to judge distance on the second shot to this 385-yard hole. Now back the way you came and a chance to open your shoulders. It's much the same length but plays a lot shorter. The second shot is blind and it's very easy to run through the green and into the bunkers lurking at the back. Then follows a real par 5. It's 542 yards and might be reachable in two with the wind behind you, but the small green and rocky, gorse-strewn ground just short of it make it unwise to attempt it, except when out for a few holes in the evening. Played as a true 5, you drive to a rising fairway and then hit over a rise and into a hollow. This leaves you a short pitch to the green. Though blind, you'll have seen where the flag is when approaching your ball.

The 4th is the first short hole and is testing, like each of the par 3s. It's played over a gully with clubbing very difficult in anything of a wind, because the tee is partially protected. Many people watch their well-struck iron with admiration only to see it clawed back to fall well short in the gully or soar and then bound onwards into the rough beyond the green.

Both the next two holes, 360-yard par 4s, cause doubt on the second shot. The 5th is to an armchair shape of green with a steep rise just in front of it and out of bounds not far through the back. The next second shot is to a green well below you. You hit, like it, and may well be downcast to see your ball pitch too short or fly the green into rough beyond.

However, so far, you shouldn't have had any real trouble in playing to your handicap. But the 7th, 'Gorsebank', is difficult, a 165-yard hole uphill with lots of humps and hollows and a likely lost ball if you're short. There is a very steep fall-away immediately left of the green and plenty of rough if you go right or through – a strong possibility when the ground is hard.

The next two holes are both drivable for long hitters but most people will require a drive and a nudge in. Because of the shape of the ground however, it's very difficult to get your ball really close to the hole. This is true also at the 13th, perhaps the easiest hole on the course, a very short par 4 at 283 yards. With the wind behind them, and no serious trouble through the green, some players take only a 4 iron. The tee is elevated and hard by the cliffs. Pause and look towards the Mull of Galloway or spread out before you the Cornish-looking Sandeel Bay. It's one of the great views in British golf, even if the hole isn't a good one.

Another apparently easy hole follows close after, the 15th, a par 3 of 101 yards – and an infuriating one requiring both precise judgement and luck. It can be played in a variety of ways in still air, though a high one with a sand iron or a little push with what you fancy are the best alternatives. Keep either a little right of the green. A touch too strong and you'll topple over the back.

As it's blind to boot, it would be difficult for me to make out a case that this is a good hole, but it does move us on to one, the 16th. This gives you a broad fairway to aim at, with a great deal of trouble short, followed by a blind second over a rise to a small green. On your first round, try to get a long one away from the tee and summon the energy to walk up and see what's asked for the second shot.

Although there are only two par 5s on the course, both are grand ones. The finish is the shorter one, just over 500 yards. The tee shot is semi-blind, followed by a thump over a rise. Two straight firm hits with a following wind and you may well be home in two but with the wind against you those same hits will leave you with a medium iron for your third.

There is also a par 3 course which is no pitch-and-putt lay-out, sometimes requiring quite a long and tight line into the green.

£ £15-20, £10-12 per round

M a handicap certificate

✕ snacks, lunch and high tea daily except Monday

🚗 fork right at war memorial in Portpatrick outskirts and follow golf club signs

✉ need to book in advance

PRESTWICK

2 Links Road, Prestwick, Strathclyde KA9 1QG
☎ Prestwick (0292) 77404

Here you are on ground as historic as at St Andrews. Though golf had been played on the links many years earlier, Prestwick Golf Club dates back 'only' to 1851. Nine years later the first Open Championship took place here, with three rounds of its twelve holes played in a day. The length of the course was then 3,799 yards, beginning with a monster hole of 578 yards, certainly a par 6 and perhaps 7 would be more like it. The true par for the course was in the mid-50s. Willie Park was the first champion, with rounds of 55, 59, 60, pushing the Prestwick professional, Old Tom Morris, into second place by a couple of strokes.

These two dominated the championship for the next few years, with 52 being the lowest score recorded. The game's first superstar arrived in 1868, Young Tom Morris. His winning total of 157 that year, at the age of seventeen, broke the previous best by several strokes. The next year he lowered that total by three more and also broke the magic 50 in his last round. In 1870 he reached a peak, winning by twelve strokes with 47 his low round. His three successive victories gave him outright possession of the championship belt. On the 1st hole of the original course he once had a 3, probably needing a wood for his last shot.

Soon after, Prestwick gave up sole rights to the championship, with St Andrews and Musselburgh taking their turn as hosts. It eventually went off the rota altogether in 1925, mainly because of difficulties in coping with the large numbers of spectators.

Just a few yards off the putting green, however, there's a reminder of the beginnings of the championship, a cairn to mark the site of the old 1st tee, with play being to the present 16th green.

The Amateur Championship has been played here on numerous occasions, twice since the war, the most recent being 1987. There have been various changes over the years – it has had 18 holes since 1883 – but you'll still be playing holes where young Tom Morris trod.

Prestwick is a seaside links course, bounded by the railway and the sea shore. The Pow burn is a hazard at several holes. Fairways are often extremly undulating and there are steep sandhills, vast deep bunkers – some sleepered – and stretches of heather, gorse, broom and, nearer the sea, buckthorn.. There are fine views of Arran, the Heads of Ayr and Ailsa Craig from various points of the course.

The 1st, although only 346 yards, is not an easy starting hole with Prestwick Station just over the wall on the right. Just beside the green there's a ruined church and a graveyard. The 3rd is more famous, partly because of the enormous Cardinal bunkers that cross the fairway. It used to be thought that two good hits were needed to clear them but today longer hitters are going for the green on this 482-yard hole, which has the Pow burn all the way along the right, as does the 4th. The 5th, 'Himalayas', is a famous blind par 3 of the 206 yards. You play over the burn, then over a vast sand dune with the green beyond, heavily bunkered. The next few holes are quite stiff par 4s but are much more inland in character and out of dune country.

With the 10th, a 450-yard hole, the course heads straight towards the sea. The 13th, 'Sea Hedrig', 460 yards, is another classic and is very difficult. Play is along a gully. The green slants across the line of play, sloping from front to back, is long and narrow, and is protected by humps and hollows.

The 14th takes you back near the clubhouse and the last four holes loop out and back. Three of these par 4s ought to offer birdie opportunities but the 17th, 391 yards, is demanding and involves a blind second shot. This must clear 'the Alps' and there's a huge bunker just short of the green, with the courtesy of a stairway with eight steps to let you escape with dignity.

The total length of Prestwick is 6,544 yards divided fairly equally with two 5s and three par 3s.

Lunch at Prestwick is a great feature and is served at the table stretching the length of the room with a mass of photographs of figures from the past looking down at you. Take the time, too, to look round the clubhouse, not forgetting the locker rooms, which are quite a labyrinth. There are many items of historical interest in the public rooms.

£ £38, £25 per round

M an introduction from your club

⊠ no visitors Thursday afternoons and weekends

✗ snacks and lunch daily except Monday, dinner by special arrangement only

🚌 from Prestwick Cross, pass the station and railway bridge

RENFREW

Blythswood Estate, Inchinnan Road, Renfew, Strathclyde
☎ *Glasgow (041) 886 6682*

Although the club celebrates its centenary in 1994, this course is under twenty years old, laid out on what was once part of the Earl of Blythswood's estate. It's said the Prince of Wales (later the Duke of Windsor) was a regular visitor in the past and would doubtless have made use of the nine-hole course which once existed.

The holes are tree-lined and at times bordered by the River Clyde. You can see where the *Queen Mary* and *Queen Elizabeth* were built in the heyday of Clydeside shipbuilding.

Played at full stretch from the very back tees, Renfrew is only a touch under 7,000 yards, with unremitting good hitting needed. There are four par 5s, the longest two being 550 and 575 yards, with seven par 4s between 410 and 440 yards. From those tees, there's just one drive and pitch hole of 330 yards and each of the four par 3s requires a long iron or ·something more, even with no wind.

However, as befits a modern course, the opportunity was taken to provide a good range of teeing-off points, so that although the maximum is 6,995 yards, the course can play as little as 5,500 yards, with the regular tees giving a length of 6,600.

Bunkering is American style and there are artificial lakes near the 10th and 12th greens. Although it is a new lay-out, the qualities of Renfrew have already been recognized by a number of championship-level amateur events. These include the Scottish Youths' Strokeplay Championsip, the West of Scotland Strokeplay, the 1982 Scottish Open Amateur Strokeplay and the 1984 Scottish Amateur – quite a roll of honour for a course that has had little time to mature.

Two of the holes of my choice are long par 4s, the 4th and 6th. At the first of these the fairway is tree-lined and your tee shot must be as tight to the left as you dare because the ground runs down to the right to a bunker some 40 yards long. The green is set at an angle to the incoming shot and is heavily bunkered. For your tee shot on the 6th, you must keep well away from the Clyde on your right but also avoid the tall trees on the left. Again, the green is well bunkered.

At only 330 yards, the 12th, from yardage alone, might seem to be the easiest hole, but there are opportunities to come to grief on what the members think the course's most attractive hole. The angled green has trees close by on three sides, and is surrounded by bunkers, and a pond covers the right front.

The 14th is the best of the par 3s, 210 yards and very severe. You must rifle one in to the hogsbacked green which slopes left to right. It's just 10 yards deep and bunkered to the front, rear and sides.

There's a golf range very close to the clubhouse where you can work on what seemed to go wrong during your round or, better still, get the feel of your swing before you go out.

£ £22, £14 per round

M introduction by members only

✗ snacks daily, lunch and dinner daily

🚗 leave M8 on sliproad for Glasgow Airport and bear right for Paisley at roundabout. Turn left for Inchinnan on reaching main road and then right over bridge at traffic lights. Thereafter turn left as though for the Normandy Hotel, and the clubhouse is immediately behind it

ROYAL TROON

Troon, Strathclyde KA10 6EP
☎ Troon (0292) 311555

As far as I know, this magnificent club is the most recent addition to those allowed to use the prefix 'Royal'. The honour used to be showered amongst golf clubs as freely as confetti at a wedding, but that was in days when members of the royal family were more interested in golf than they are today.

The club, however, was founded in 1878, rather recent in Scottish golf history, but golf was much more a pastime in eastern Scotland than the west in earlier days. Today, of course, the coast in the old county of Ayrshire has more fine courses than any comparable stretch in the world.

Troon is quite firmly on the Open Championship rota, where it first appeared in 1923. That year, Arthur Havers won, the last Englishman to do so until Henry Cotton in 1934. Almost more memorable was the fact that Gene Sarazen failed to survive the qualifying rounds and Walter Hagen almost holed a bunker shot to tie on the last hole.

Sarazen featured again, but in very different circumstances, in 1973. This was one of the great sentimental occasions of golf. Playing in his seventies, Sarazen holed in one with a little punched 5 iron shot on the 8th, the 'Postage Stamp' hole. And followed that the next day by missing the green on the same hole and holing out his bunker shot for a two. It's not often you tackle a hole twice and don't use your putter. Besides that little footnote to history, 1973 saw the triumph of one of the greatest swingers of a golf club ever, Tom Weiskopf.

In 1962 Troon saw one of the great championships of modern times. Arnold Palmer was at his best on a course so hard as to be well-nigh unplayable. In one of his practice rounds he had hit a fairway-splitting drive and thought it would be sensible to catch the next plane home when he discovered it had right-angled off into the rough. But he didn't go home and won by the greatest margin of modern times, six ahead of the Australian Kel Nagle, and thirteen better than the next men home.

The championship at Troon in 1982 was a very different affair, perhaps the most confused championship of modern times. With a start unparalleled in almost fifty years, 67, 66, Bobby Clampett seemed to have it all sewn up after two rounds. Of course, as we soon found out, this wasn't so! After two rounds, he could only be caught if he scored badly or others scored phenomenally well. They didn't, but he did, with a finish of 78, 77. Tom Watson was the eventual winner. In 1989 Mark Calcavecchia defeated Greg Norman and Wayne Grady in the four-hole play-off.

Clampett's momentum had first been checked playing the 1st in his third round when he'd thought to play short of the left-hand bunkers with a long iron and ran into them nevertheless. Play down the right and you'll have the best line into the green.

The 2nd, 381 yards, like the 3rd, are of no great length, but it is possible to find the Gyaws burn on the 3rd with your tee shot. The 4th is a stiff par 5, stroke index 4, and the next a par of 3 of nearly 200 yards.

The 6th, stretched to 577 yards, is the longest hole on our Open Championship circuit. After all sorts of problems in his third round, Clampett took 8. Though this kind of score damaged his chances, it also destroyed his confidence, even though he still led the field by five strokes. Thereafter, the shots leaked away, more gradually but it seemed inevitably.

The 8th is Troon's most famous hole. You'll play it at about 120 yards. That can mean a 3 iron into a strong wind or a soft pitching wedge with the wind behind. It's certainly not a difficult hole but hard to hit and hold the green. Otherwise you could well be bunkered and play to and fro from one to another. A German amateur took 15 on the hole in 1950 while Arnold Palmer took 7 in 1973.

At the 11th, the 'Railway', you're playing one of the most famous holes in golf. Playing his first championship Jack Nicklaus took 10 here in 1962 while Max Faulkner compiled an 11 in the same year. Palmer, on the other hand, played it superbly, in par, birdie, birdie, eagle.

In 1982 Watson had made no great move in his final round but cracked in a 3 iron here to about a yard and holed the eagle putt. For you, there'll be no real chance of an eagle as it'll be a par 4, with a tangle of rough left and the railway out of bounds on the right, all the way to the green. Try to get your tee shot along the right-hand side of the fairway.

The 13th, 411 yards, is another difficult hole, which swings right and requires an angled drive in order to give a favourable line in to the plateau green. There are no bunkers and none needed.

You will now be well into Troon's very testing finish. In this section the 15th is the difficult hole for most. The fairway is on a plateau and therefore slightly blind, with three bunkers in the driving area. The green is sunken and it's as well to take at least one more club than you think.

The same policy is needed on the 17th as well, a long par 3 of 210 yards with a plateau green. There are five bunkers in wait for anything short, but there is no serious trouble through the green. The last, 374 yards, again has three bunkers to catch tee shots and the shot to the green is testing with bunkers to the front and both sides of the green. The best policy is to play for the back of the green but good judgement of distance is vital: it's out of bounds through the green.

£ £50	Ⓛ *juniors and ladies are not allowed*
M *written evidence of club membership and handicap*	✗ *snacks and lunch daily*
✉ *visitors on Mondays to Thursdays, only with reservations in advance, to be sure of getting a teeing-off time*	🚗 *the clubhouse is at the south end of Troon*

SOUTHERNESS

Southerness, Dumfries and Galloway DG2 8AZ
☎ *Kirkbean (038788) 677*

This is one of the great 'unknown' courses of the British Isles, mainly because of its rather remote position on the north side of the Solway Firth. However, it's very much worth a diversion if you should happen to be in south-west Scotland. It's fit to host professional tournaments but this may never happen because of the small local population and the lack of amenities.

Southerness is one of the very few links courses to be designed since the Second World War. The owner of the land at that time, Major Richard Oswald, brought in Mackenzie Ross, also responsible for the re-birth of the Turnberry courses at much the same period, to design a course to test modern players. There's no doubt he was successful in this aim. It's difficult enough today but was perhaps too tough when it was opened for play in the summer of 1947. There were formidable carries over rough from almost every tee to narrow fairways flanked by heather and bracken. In anything like a wind, it became almost impossible. In an exhibition fourball in 1952, only one player managed to hole out the course, John Panton, and he was round in 78.

Since those early days, however, the problems have been eased. Carries are fair, if still sometimes nerve-tingling, fairways a little wider and greens larger and watered. The rough, however, is still just as threatening. For most wild shots you'll have to abandon hope of finding that new ball, and even if you're in luck, recovery will probably prove impossible.

The dominant feature of the course is the long par 4s. There are eight of more than 400 yards, and a couple more only just under, which means that Southerness is very much a test of long iron and fairway-wood play. A couple of the par 3s are substantially over 200 yards and the main relief may come at the two par 5s, neither of which is long and both of which can be shortened by the prevailing wind.

The start is tough, three long par 4s into the prevailing wind with out of bounds close along the right. The 2nd can be a bit of a monster, more than 450 yards, and often plays as a par 5.

If the wind's behind you, the par 5 5th hole is certainly reachable in two but your second shot will have to be exactly on line to hold the hog's-back run-up to the plateau green. At the next hole, another of the 400 yarders, a stream comes into play, crossing the fairway about a hundred yards short of the green – intimidating if you didn't get a good drive away.

A stream again comes very much into play on the 11th, where your second shot to the green could well be trapped some 30 yards short. Next you come to the most famous hole on the course. From the tee, looking at the distant flag outlined against the sea, it seems to be a par 4 of impossible length, though the card says it's 'only' 419 and some 40 yards shorter from the yellow markers. Two big fairway bunkers force you to the left (and towards another one) and make the hole quite a sharp left-to-right dogleg, playing longer than the actual yardages unless you can make the carry over the bunkers of around 230 yards – a fairly tall order – or find the narrow stretch of fairway between those bunkers and the heavy right rough. The shot to the green is between mounds and bunkers with a pond very much in play just to the left. Should your drive be well placed and the second shot firm and true, disappointment is hard to bear if you run clear through the green and down to the beach beyond.

The 12th is followed by the two longest par 4s on the course, both more than 450 yards, then a long one-shotter and another long par 4, a dogleg. Anyone who plays this five-hole stretch to his handicap has good reason to feel smug.

The finish is a tricky par 3, and that par 5 where you may get home in two. This wasn't the original layout but was brought in when a clubhouse was built some ten years or so ago. Before that, part of what is now the Paul Jones Hotel was used. John Paul Jones, a sea fighter, was born close to Southerness; he became a hero of the American Revolution and had a well-known dance named after him. He later became a mercenary for Catherine the Great, as Kontradmiral Pavel Ivanovitch Jones – quite a varied career.

Southerness, in 1985, was host to the Scottish Amateur Championship and, in 1990, the British Youths' Championship, while the Kirkcudbrightshire Championship comes every year and the South of Scotland every three years. Although quite a recent course in terms of golfing history, Southerness looks highly traditional and obviously no vast sums have been spent on pushing the landscape hither and thither. Although there is ample use of bunkers, the greens always look very naturally sited. From the medal tees, Southerness plays at 6,548 yards, and over 7,000 yards if the extreme back markers are used.

£ £15-20

M a handicap certificate

✗ snacks, lunch and dinner daily

🚗 16 miles south of Dumfries on the A710

✉ weekend reservations advised

TURNBERRY

Turnberry, Strathclyde KA26 9LT
☎ *Turnberry (0655) 31000*

This hotel and golf course complex is one of the places in golf that I know best as I've returned to it again and again with the BBC to film our pro-celebrity series. Of course, the Ailsa course was also the scene of perhaps the most memorable of all golf's head-to-heads, in the 1977 Open Championship, when Watson and Nicklaus fired pars and birdies at each other for two days with hardly a sign of faltering from either. It was a hard act to follow when the championship returned in 1986 and Greg Norman won his only major in often foul weather.

The story began when Willie Fernie, an Open Champion and professional at Troon from 1887 until 1924, laid out thirteen holes in 1903. By 1906 this was the first hotel and golf complex in the world and an example that has been copied many times since. The Turnberry coastline was designed by the Almighty for the game, as Old Tom Morris might have said.

Fernie's course has long gone, as has the body that made it possible, the Glasgow and South-West Railway, which provided a link between the vast hotel and the nearby town of Girvan. It was very successful in attracting visitors in the years before the Second World War.

The War more or less destroyed Turnberry. It became an RAF Coastal Command training base, and that meant levelling sand dunes, filling in bunkers and making many concrete runways.

After the War Mackenzie Ross was called in to see what could be done, and in due time a Phoenix rose from the ashes, the two courses of Ailsa and Arran.

We hear little of the eighteen holes of Arran but it is a very fine course. Several people playing both in the same conditions find it the more difficult, mainly because it has far more gorse than the Ailsa, so that if you hit just about every tee shot off the fairway you'll probably have a more horrid time. It's well over 6,000 yards and the greens are often difficult targets, but the course is flatter and lacks the drama of Ailsa.

The start at Ailsa is quite flat. Sandy Lyle apparently found the first holes easy enough when he began with a barrage of 3s in a final round of 65, which won him the 1979 European Open. In that round he birdied six of the first seven holes and was able to coast home to a seven stroke victory.

Even so, a good club golfer would be very happy to par each of the three par 4s with which Turnberry begins, the 3rd being easily the longest and a full 475 yards from the championship tees.

At the 4th, a medium-length par 3, you come hard by the shore. Anything hit left will tumble away down a steep slope into rough and perhaps the beach itself. Really it's not a particularly difficult hole but from the tee the green looks a small target, further away than it really is and surrounded by most of the troubles that golf can provide – all quite enough to make many players look up before they've made contact with the ball.

The 5th can be played from at least three different tees, which at maximum length can make it not a particularly long par 5 of about 490 yards, while it can also be a stiff par 4 which doglegs from right to left.

The 6th is a very long par 3, a true all-or-nothing shot to a raised green with formidable bunkering around the green, a steep fall-away to the right, a cavernous bunker to trap anything short on the right and jungle along the left. A long hitter could well be short with a driver into the wind, or find himself using not much more than a 5 iron with it behind him. Whatever the weather, it is a hole that calls for your best efforts. A shot which carries to the heart of the green will long remain in the memory.

The 7th, as a par 4, can be the toughest hole on the course. Your tee shot must carry a burn and should be to the right of the fairway to avoid too severe a second shot. With the fairway rising towards the green, it can be an almost impossible par 4. The 8th also doglegs left along the shoreline, quite a long par 4, where a long iron will probably be needed for the second shot to a two-tier green.

The 9th has what must be the most photographed tee in British golf, set on a rocky promontory with the sea below. It's the tournament tee and visitors play from a few yards further away. Stroll over and look at the tee shot the pros have. The drive is blind, with a stone cairn to tell you where you ought to go. For the second shot you play to the green beyond the lighthouse, with no bunkers.

The 10th and 11th are also played along the shoreline and complete the most memorable stretch of Turnberry. For the rest, you are no longer so close to the sea, but it's still true linksland golf and not at all the pasture that occurs on some links courses when the sea is little more than a 100 yards away.

The 15th, a cruel par 3 of 220 yards from the championship tees, will still probably be a long iron shot for most people from further forward and certainly a wood when the wind's up. The green is small, with a ravine in front and to the right, and bunkered left. In the 1977 Open Championship Tom Watson got in a shrewd blow. With Nicklaus on the green and facing a possible birdie putt, Tom was a little short on the left and in light rough. But he took his putter and holed out from more than 20 yards to draw level – all very unlikely but Tom used to be the best in the business from 20 to 30 yards.

The 16th shouldn't be a particularly difficult hole, not a long par 4, with the run of the ground helping you on the tee shot. The shot to the green is deceptive, however, usually one more club than you think, and you will want to feel confident of carrying the burn which fronts the green. It is rather a fiendish one with sloping banks so that a bad second you hope will stop short will trickle down into it, and a better shot that's almost perfect may drift back. Even so, it's a potential birdie hole but requires good judgement and striking if the flag's set towards the front.

The 17th is also a birdie opportunity, not a long par 5, with an inviting drive from an elevated tee with a second shot through a narrow gully.

Jack Nicklaus needed just a 7 iron for his second shot in the 1977 championship but took a little turf before the ball, came up some 20 yards short and needed three more to get down. That gave Watson a one-stroke lead playing the last, a par of 4 of about 430 yards. Here, Watson hit a good straight tee shot and then put his second almost dead. Meanwhile, Nicklaus had gone for a big drive but ballooned it away to the right and was lucky to be only a foot or so short of unplayable gorse. At this point, Tom must have been mentally rehearsing his victory speech but Nicklaus got his approach onto the green and then holed a putt of improbable length. Watson had to buckle down to it again but his two-footer was always in the middle.

£ £25 if a hotel resident, £40 for visitors	**🏨** the hotel is four star with 126 bedrooms and six suites and there's also a small dormy house
M a handicap certificate is advisable	**🏊** at the hotel swimming, snooker, tennis, pitch and putt course, a solarium and mini-gym
✉ visitors must book in advance, hotel residents have guaranteed times	**🚗** on A77 about 17 miles to the south of Ayr
✗ lunch and snacks daily. Coffee shop, and dinner at the hotel	

WESTERN GAILES

Gailes, Strathclyde KA11 5AE
☎ Irvine (0294) 311 357

This is a classic test amongst that cluster of fine courses along the coast of the old county of Ayrshire. True, it's a little overshadowed by such names as Troon, Turnberry and Prestwick, but hosts qualifying rounds when the Open Championship is held in the area. The Curtis Cup has been played at Western Gailes and the 1984 British Seniors' Open Amateur.

Some years ago the Scottish golf writer, Sam M'Kinlay, said of it: 'Western Gailes occupies a place in the affections of Scottish golfers that cannot be explained solely on the grounds of its undoubted quality, its superb situation, or the creature comforts which it furnishes. True, there are more severe golfing tests; there are courses with longer and more renowned histories. But few have so many of the good things of golf as Western Gailes.'

The club was founded by four Glasgow businessmen in 1897, one of their intentions being to give players whose main golf was on inland courses the chance of membership of a links course for just 10s 6d a year.

You begin by playing due north for a while, the 1st hole a short par 4 with a green set in a natural dell. The 2nd, some 430 yards, is a very testing par 4, one of six over 400 yards in length. The 5th is a fine short par 4 with, as it should be, a very tightly bunkered green. Your pitch will have to be precisely judged.

Some of the most enjoyable holes are played going south amongst the dunes. The 7th is the first short hole, which requires a tee shot through a gap in the sandhills to a green not notably receptive. The 11th, not far short of 450 yards, is difficult, a right-hand dogleg where you'll need to give your best to reach the plateau green with your second shot. It's followed by another par 4 of much the same length, the main difficulty this time being the narrowness of the fairway. Soon after comes a par 5, the 14th, very nearly a monster at 562 yards.

The finish is tough, as it really should be at any golf course – we want a grand finale, not an anti-climax. At the 16th there's a burn to negotiate before the green and at the 17th a ridge which can catch a moderate second shot and leave you with perhaps a mid iron to play for your third to this long par 4.

The course offers some excellent views over to Arran, Ailsa Craig and Jura.

£ £22

M membership of a golf club

✗ snacks and dinner daily, lunch daily except in the heart of winter

🚗 leave A78 about 3 miles north of Troon for Gailes and cross railway to clubhouse

EAST
OF SCOTLAND

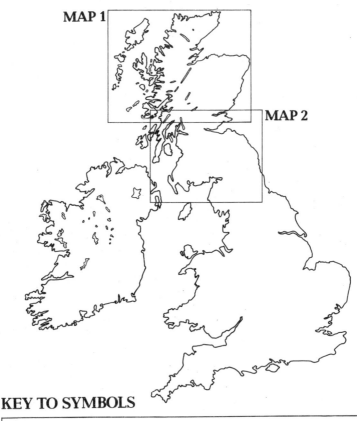

MAP 1

MAP 2

KEY TO SYMBOLS

- PARKLAND
- LINKS
- MOORLAND
- HEATHLAND
- DOWNLAND
- UPLAND

- ☎ TELEPHONE
- ✉ NEED TO BOOK IN ADVANCE
- £ APPROXIMATE COURSE FEE
- M MEMBERSHIP REQUIREMENTS FOR VISITORS

- ✗ CATERING PROVIDED
- ⌂ ACCOMMODATION PROVIDED
- Ⓛ RESTRICTIONS ON LADIES AND/OR YOUTHS
- OTHER SPORTING FACILITIES
- 🚗 DIRECTIONS

ABOYNE

Formaston Park, Aboyne, Grampian
☎ *Aboyne (0339) 886328*

A fairly short course, at little more than 5,300 yards, Aboyne is set in two very different kinds of landscape. Holes 1 to 10 and the 18th run over lush undulating parkland, while the rest are over hilly, quite heathy ground.

For some reason, it's thought a little controversial for a course to end with a par 3. Though why not if they're good ones, as at Parkstone or Lindrick? Aboyne rounds off with a pair, and indeed three of the last four holes take the total for the course up to seven. Cypress Point has the 15th and 16th as consecutive par 3s and even two par 4s in a row of only about 260 yards apiece.

The 2nd and 3rd are two quite long par 4s and are divided by an ancient stone dyke with a hedgerow on top. The holes run parallel to each other in opposite directions, with out of bounds on both if you go over the top.

The 2nd is quite a testing hole. The out of bounds is close at hand and the approach to the green is blind, the entry narrow between two bunkers.

At the 7th watch out for the lateral water hazard, Grant's Lochie, to the right. The next hole is the longest and the only par 5. It is played towards the Loch of Aboyne. This becomes an out-of-bounds threat on the right at the 10th hole, the only par 4 over 400 yards. The members reckon that the 11th is the most difficult hole on the course. Again it runs along the loch, but it's uphill all the way and the elevated sloping green will hold only the very well struck shot. The 12th needs a long and accurate drive to a narrow fairway to shorten the second shot which, again, is uphill.

The most difficult of the par 3s is the 17th. There is a burn crossing in front, bunkering and mature trees close by on the right.

The clubhouse is new and open plan with, from the upper level, panoramic views of much of the course and the Deeside countryside.

£ £10, £14 at weekends

M none

✗ lunch and snacks daily

🚗 going west from Aberdeen on A93 at Aboyne village take the first right, Golf Road

---

BRUNTSFIELD LINKS GOLFING SOCIETY

32 Barnton Avenue, Davidsons Mains, Edinburgh, Lothian EH4 6JH
☎ *Edinburgh (031) 336 2006*

Here it was that competitive golf really began for me: the Boys' Championship of 1946. I remember the thrill of boarding the night train up – I'd never made a journey of anything like this distance before.

How times have changed, yet if 1946 seems a long time ago, it was late in the life of Bruntsfield. The society was founded in 1761, which makes this the fifth oldest golf club in the world. There is a very large membership – 950 – and a new applicant can expect to wait at least ten years until he eventually surfaces at the top of the list. With Dalmahoy I rate it as one of the two best courses in Edinburgh. It does not take lady members but they are allowed to play the course.

The present course was designed by James Braid and is kept in excellent condition throughout the year with improvements having been fairly continuous. Despite the latitude, winter greens are seldom needed.

Despite the name, the course is beautiful parkland, with many fine trees of great variety strategically situated. The society moved to its present home many years ago from linksland, but kept its old title.

The 1st hole is nicely designed. There is an out of bounds on the left but the approach needs to be played from the left half of the fairway to avoid a far more tricky shot. Much the same is true of the 6th, which is much more difficult when played down the right half of the fairway. The 18th makes an excellent finish, the green being very tightly bunkered. None of the holes I've singled out is exceptionally long but they do pose problems. All par 4s of 450 yards must be difficult for the average golfer but that doesn't make them good holes.

There are three spacious practice grounds which include an approaching green and a bunker, and also a putting green.

£ *£20*

M *introduction by a member, or a letter of introduction*

✗ *lunch daily, dinner only during the summer*

🚗 *from Edinburgh centre take Queensferry Road for the Forth Road Bridge. Turn off right for Cramond and Barnton Avenue is 300 yards along on the left*

CARNOUSTIE

Links Parade, Carnoustie, Tayside, Angus
☎ *Carnoustie (0241) 52480*

This is as stern a test as there is in the British Isles, almost cruelly so in a bitter wind. I remember how difficult it was in 1968 for the Open Championship. Gary Player won with a total of 289, the highest winner's score in the period since 1948. I was playing with Billy Casper, a likely winner going into the final round, who finished with a 78, yet even so was 4th. I had a 78 of my own in the second round but still managed to finish 13th.

This was the fourth time the championship had been played at Carnoustie. Tommy Armour won in 1931, the last Scottish-born player to do so, and Henry Cotton had what many would call his finest hour in 1937, when he beat the whole of the American Ryder Cup team. It rained heavily for the 36 holes of the final day and became a deluge as Cotton played his last few holes.

He waited in some suspense – not to see if anyone could catch him but in fear that his last round 71 might have to be replayed because the course was becoming more and more waterlogged. All was well and Cotton had the second of his three championships.

The next championship at Carnoustie has gone down into legend. In 1953 Ben Hogan, beyond doubt the greatest golfer in the world at the time, entered for the first time. He played steadily throughout and invincibly in his final round.

Four championships, and the weather daunting in every one of them – no wonder Carnoustie earned the reputation of being a killer. How different it all was in the last championship to be held here. In 1975 the sun shone throughout and there was a stiff breeze only for the final round. A host of players might have won and in the end it was an unknown who did so... Tom Watson. With his first major championship under the belt, he went on to establish himself as the world's number one. Perhaps this was the end of Opens for Carnoustie too. The event has just grown to be too big but the big amateur events will continue to be held here and the completion of a large hotel may see the Open's return.

Carnoustie is one of the homes of golf. The club was formed as 'recently' as 1842 but golf over its links goes back at least as far as 1560. Former members of Carnoustie have had an enormous influence on the spread of golf both through the British Isles and in the world as a whole. It is thought that more than 300 have become professional golfers and that as many as 200 emigrated to promote the gospel in America.

In general, Carnoustie is a typical links course, although water hazards feature more than you might expect. Jockie's burn comes into play on the 2nd, 3rd, 5th and 6th and the more famous Barry burn on the 1st, 10th, 11th, 17th and 18th. There are also far more trees than is usual and fairways are less billowing. Each hole is individual in character and,

59

because the course is laid out in a square around another one, its organization is very much the opposite of the 'out and back' links pattern. As a result, there are never more than two holes running in the same direction. Providing the wind remains constant throughout your round, it will come at you from every side.

This is the longest course ever used in the Open Championship. From the back tees, it was 7,252 yards in 1953 but more like, 6,800 from the medal tees, long enough in all conscience.

The 1st may get you off to an encouraging start. The fairway is broad and the green, in a hollow, may gather your second shot in friendly fashion.

The 3rd is a drive and pitch hole, and a very good one. Jockie's burn runs directly across the front of the green, which slopes towards it, a threat to anybody who hits irons with much backspin. At the 5th you should drive short of the burn to the angle of the right-hand dogleg. In his final round in 1953 Ben Hogan put his second shot on the edge of a bunker and then chipped in, commenting afterwards that the Lord had been with him!

At the 6th you drive over a burn (it shouldn't come into play) towards two bunkers bang in mid-fairway. You should aim right of these, because there's out of bounds all along the left from tee to green. Beware of Jockie's burn at about three-quarters distance. Almost hidden, it slants into the fairway on the right.

At the 10th the Barry burn really threatens for the first time. It's a par 4 of over 400 yards and, after a reasonable drive, you'll have to carry it with your shot to the green. It's a very difficult hole with anything approaching a stiff breeze against you.

The 12th is none too long a par 5 but, with a ridge protecting the front of the green, it's not easy to get home in two, and there are also plenty of bunkers in the ridge area.

The last three holes may just be the most testing finish of any course in the world. Certainly none of the main contenders in the 1975 championship – Nicklaus, Miller, Cole, Newton and Watson – managed to par them all.

The 16th is a long par 3, over 230 yards, well bunkered both right and left, with a green shape that throws off any ball pitching towards the edges or hit anywhere without enough control. The green itself is fairly small, especially so considering that even power hitters have to resort to the driver even into just a firm breeze. Is it a great hole? I don't think so; we should be wary of thinking that, say, a par 4 of 470 yards, uphill all the way, with chasm or lake to carry to the green, or a monster of a 3, like this hole, are good simply because they can be impossibly difficult. Watson, for instance, never managed to hit the green throughout the 1975 Open!

The 17th 'The Island', is so called because of the tee shot at this long par 4. You're confronted by two twists of the Barry burn. Few people try to carry both with their drive, though Nicklaus did so in the 1968 championship. If, perhaps with a following wind, you succeed, you have only a short pitch left.

Normally, however, nearly everybody aims to carry the first stretch and stay short of the second. Wander right, and you're in the first twist, left and you're in the second. Both Bobby Cole and Jack Newton caught the far bank of the Barry burn's first meander in 1975 at the crisis point and it cost them the championship. From the island of turf between the routes of the two burns, you will then have a long second to play. You either can think in terms of going left, pitching short and running through a gap in the mounds to the green, or flying it all the way to the green over both bumps and bunkers.

The 18th at Carnoustie used to be a par 5 and, of course, is a lot more difficult as a 450-yarder. Again, there's the Barry burn, which you have to carry from the tee, no great distance, and then, in cowardly style, either play short with your second shot or go boldly for the carry as it crosses the fairway just short of the green.

On a still day, Carnoustie shouldn't be an extreme test of your expertise. Once the wind is up, it will be. We saw this most clearly in 1975 when Hale Irwin described the course as a 'sleeping giant'. In the calm, many of the world's top professionals scored very well. In just a firm breeze on the last day, none of the top five finishers could beat 72 and there were plenty of scores in the high 70s and a few in the 80s. There is another course, The Buddon, designed by Alliss/Thomas, which should prove a fine test of golf when it matures and a third, The Burnside.

£ £35

M a handicap certificate on the championship course

✗ snacks, lunch and dinner daily

🚗 leave A92 Dundee to Aberdeen road at Carnoustie sign. Look out for the course sign in High Street

CRIEFF

Perth Road, Crieff, Tayside PH7 3LR
☎ Crieff (0764) 2909

Here is a club which can literally look down on Gleneagles, visible some ten miles away. There are two courses, the Ferntower, 6,402 yards, and the Dornock, 4,772, which is twice round nine holes.

The courses are laid on the slopes below a hill called 'The Knock', and during a Scottish PGA a good many years ago the Ryder Cup player Eric Brown was asked what he thought of the eighteen-hole course. Rather too frankly perhaps, he replied: 'It's a bloody goat track but a very sporty one.'

This was considerably before eleven new holes were added at the end of the 1970s and combined with holes from the earlier lay-out to form the Ferntower, while nine more make up the Dornock. The turf is excellent and there's that Highland air with views over the Strathearn valley and occasionally the Ochil Hills. John Stark's rotunda pro's shop is original and very well-stocked.

There are several good holes.

'The Wee Knock' is a short par 3 of only 124 yards, but being uphill and all carry it plays longer than you think. The green is framed at the rear by trees and it's well bunkered both front and rear. The 12th, 'Gauger's Howe', is a long par 4 of 467 yards, and most people will find it the toughest hole on the course, especially if there's a wind from the east. The green is slightly elevated and attractively set in a copse.

Bushes are a strong feature of the 13th; the hole was carved out of a forest of trees and rhododendrons so you must get a straight one away at the green, 191 yards away. The slopes then make it easy enough to three-putt. The 14th, a short par 4, is a good one of its kind. The 353 yards are played along the edge of a wood with the green guarded by a superb beech tree and bunkers. Position on the tee shot is very important.

A new clubhouse is under construction and it should be operational by the autumn of this year.

£ £12	✕ snacks, lunch and dinner daily
M advisable to bring proof of membership of a golf club	🚗 17½ miles from Perth and just east of Crieff on A85

DALMAHOY

Dalmahoy, Kirknewton, Lothian EH27 8EB
☎ Edinburgh (031) 333 1845

This is one of the premier courses in the Edinburgh area, a country club with the full facilities you would expect, rather than a golf club pure and simple. It can be ideal for a family holiday as apart from golf it offers fishing, clay-pigeon shooting, squash, horse-riding, archery, dry skiing and even polo. It has special significance for me as it was here I met my wife. The clubhouse by itself is well worth a visit. A three-storey Georgian mansion, it was designed for the Earl of Morton in 1735 and is elegant indeed, with fine panelling and family portraits.

There are two courses, the East and West, both providing excellent parkland golf, with the East, which is used for tournaments, being by far and away the longer.

It was designed by James Braid in 1927 and has been used for many events – the Senior Service Wills Open, the Sun Alliance and the Haig Tournament Players' Championship, which was on TV in 1981. Do you remember that dramatic finish? Brian Barnes produced a 62 in his final round, climaxed by driving the green to a matter of inches on the 71st hole. It all resulted in a homeward nine in 28 strokes. Even that was not quite good enough but gave him a tie with Brian Waites. The play-off went to four extra holes before Brian Waites missed a short putt to let Barnes in.

The East begins with an uphill par 5 of no great difficulty but you are then faced by a string of four par 4s, all well over 400 yards. The toughest of these is the last, 461 yards towards Edinburgh Castle on the skyline. Your drive must be up the right half of the fairway for the slope along the left will carry your ball away into trees and rough. What is likely to be a long second shot is also not easy. The green is banked up and has a right-to-left slope.

The 7th is often reckoned the best hole on the course. There is a lake all along the right but this is only in play for a thoroughly bad shot, and even that is likely to be 'saved' by a group of bunkers which will probably keep you out of the water. You do need to be along this side of the fairway, because the ground is very uneven to the left and the narrow green is set at an angle, giving an easier line in from the right. You have to carry a broad gully as well.

The next is an attractive short par 4, only just over 300 yards. With the course being played with the two nines reversed, this is the one Barnes and a few others drove in 1981. A lake is close to the green at the right and can also catch an average length of drive too far right. If you play cautiously too far left, bunkering and tall trees make this line in far more difficult.

The 9th is another shortish par 4, which takes you back to the clubhouse, and you then play an uphill par 5. A feature of this hole, and indeed most drives on Dalmahoy East, is position. Very often, there are slopes to lead your ball into the rough or trees threatening your next shot – and, of course, bunkers.

The West Course is not inferior but it is some 1400 yards shorter. If you are having 36 holes, why not play both?

£ £25 per round for the East and £18 for the West

M a handicap certificate

✕ snacks, lunch and dinner daily

✉ need to book in advance with reservation centre

🏠 clubhouse accommodation is about £93 for bed and breakfast and there are dormy facilities a few pounds cheaper

🎣 fishing, clay-pigeon shooting, squash, horse riding, archery, dry skiing and polo

🚗 7 miles west of Edinburgh on the A71 for Kilmarnock

DOWNFIELD

Turnberry Avenue, Dundee, Tayside DD2 3QP
☎ *Dundee (0382) 825595*

'Downfield is one of the finest inland courses I've played on anywhere in the world. It's a tough, demanding test of golf amidst some of the most picturesque scenery – you have to be very long and straight off the tee to succeed here.' That was the opinion of five-times Open Champion Peter Thomson in 1972, only a few years after the course had been constructed.

It's certainly not an opinion I'd quarrel with. I was most impressed when we filmed the BBC series *Play Golf* there in 1977. This series has been much repeated so the attractions of the course have been appreciated by a very wide audience, which has caused the number of visitors to soar.

Downfield is a modern course, dating back some twenty years in its present form, so it's not surprising that it is long, not much under 7,000 yards. It has been used for several important events including the PGA Matchplay Championship, the World's Seniors' and the Scottish Open.

The start is a tough one: two long par 4s followed by a long 3 hole. Is there then some relief with the par 5 4th hole? Not very much. A narrow ditch crosses the fairway at an angle between 20 and 100 yards short of the green so it's safer to play short of that and hope for a pitch and putt birdie. It is rated as stroke index 1 but the 10th is really more difficult, a par 4 of 440 yards from the back tees. This is the sixth par 4 more than 400 yards so far. The 11th, not a long par 5 at 485 yards, gives long hitters a fair chance of going for the green in two – if they think they can carry the pond and hidden ditch that run across short of it.

Possibly, the second nine is a little less severe than the first as there are a couple of shortish par 4s. However, fairways are wider on the first nine than later. I must point out, of course, that we are talking of the course at full medal length, while visitors will be playing from forward tees. These reduce the length by over 600 yards, so immense hitting powers are not needed to enjoy this superb course. Category 1 players are, however, allowed to use the medal tees if they wish.

The 14th, a par 5, gives a chance of a birdie, particularly for long hitters, but there is the complication of the Gelly burn running along the right-hand side of the fairway, in play until close to the green. The green is tightly guarded and two-tier.

One unusual feature of the club is that, since its foundation in 1933, ladies have been full members. At the time, this was unique in all Scotland and is still rare today.

£ £16   M none   ✗ *lunch, dinner and snacks daily*

⊠ *need to book in advance*

🚗 *take Kingsway By-Pass and branch off on A923. Turn right at the next roundabout and take the first left and first left again*

DUNBAR ⚑

East Links, Dunbar, East Lothian EH42 1LS
☎ *Dunbar (0368) 62317*

Perhaps Dunbar has always been just a little overshadowed by that magnificent stretch of golfing country further up the coast which includes Gullane and Muirfield. Yet golf has been played on Dunbar links at least since the seventeenth century and very likely earlier. There are records of the formation of the Dunbar Golfing Society dating back to 1794 and this may have been the first 'golf club' at Dunbar. The present club traces its history back to 1856 and the original eighteen-hole course came into use in 1880. It is thought that the men of Dunbar were responsible for the spread of the game into north-east England during the 1860s. All this makes Muirfield, though of course not the Honourable Company, a relative newcomer. In fact, the Company considered moving from Leith Links to Dunbar in about 1890 but decided on Muirfield instead.

In 1893 Tom Morris came down from St Andrews and advised on changes which increased the length of the course to just under 5,000 yards, and the introduction of the wound ball caused a further extension in 1912 to nearly 6,000 yards. It is now 6,441.

Dunbar's quality has been recognized by its choice for several championships. I remember playing here in the 1968 Schweppes tournament and the Scottish Boys' Championship is now played every year. In 1923, the first England versus Scotland Boys' International was played there, and also the British Boys' Championship.

The course is in two parts. The 1st to the 3rd and then the 18th are fairly inland in character and are laid out in what was once a deer park. The remainder is typical links, as many as seven holes running hard by the beach with views from most of the course away over the Firth of Forth into Fife and the hills of Angus. To the south are the Lammermuir Hills.

There are virtually no trees. Winter gales lashing in the salt spray have usually put paid to any attempts to get them to grow. There's a certain amount of very prickly gorse.

If there is a gale up, you are fairly sheltered on the first three holes but then emerge into whatever is going. You will have just played the 3rd, a fine short hole with out of bounds left, a green ringed by bunkers with a deep one barring all access to a half-topped shot. The green is both large

65

and undulating so you need to get your shot as close as you can. The 6th is an attractive short par 4, with the Broxburn crossing about 25 yards from the front of the green. You really shouldn't get in it because, after a good drive, you'll only be playing a pitching club for your second shot. There is a burn at much the same distance on the 17th also.

The 9th is the longest hole and for much of the time the highest, and is particularly difficult in a strong easterly. The entrance to the raised green is extremely narrow, as it should be on a par 5.

The 12th is the most difficult hole, 464 yards from the medal tees with the beach hugging the fairway from tee to green. Well, with your drive you can always aim off to avoid trouble but there's no such option for your long second shot if you want to be on in two. It all makes for a most demanding wooden club or long iron second if there's a westerly pushing your ball towards that formidable water hazard, the North Sea.

Watch out for the 16th, called 'Narrows'. Narrow it is, for at this point the course (not just the hole) is only about 25 yards wide. It's a 171-yard par 3 which gives you no 'aiming off' options. You can be out of bounds over the wall to the left or on the beach right. The green is also well bunkered, particularly against those playing cautiously short. It is at its most difficult with a wind from the south-west.

Dunbar has practice bunkers, green and an average-sized practice ground a little too short for wooden club shots.

£ £15 and £25 **M** none	🚗 just to the south of Dunbar on the coast
🍽 lunch and high tea daily but not on Tuesday in winter	

EDZELL   ⛳

Edzell, By Brechin, Tayside
☎ Edzell (03564) 7283

Edzell dates back to the mid-1890s when it was laid out by Bob Simpson from Carnoustie. Apart from some lengthening to its present 6,066 yards from the medal tees, it has changed very little since, and is a delightful place to play golf.

The situation is superb, in the foothills of the Grampians near the little village from which it takes its name, one of the prettiest in Scotland. When the course was founded on land then rented from Lord Dalhousie he laid down the condition that villagers be allowed to play for only 5 shillings a year. However, if they wanted to use the clubhouse, they had to pay the full whack of 1 guinea!

Perhaps the main challenge is at those holes which were probably originally intended as par 5s – the 2nd, 5th, 11th and 13th which are all 420 yards or more. The longest of these, the 2nd, almost 450 yards, is stroke index 1 and quite a proposition so early in your round. However, there are five holes around 330 yards or less to provide birdie opportunities, and the par 5s aren't of monster length.

One of these, the 9th, is a right-hand dogleg which follows the River West Water, a tributary of the North Esk, as does the 8th, 'The River'. The 13th is a difficult long par 4 with a tight drive to be threaded between bunkers, and there's a fine finish consisting of the 17th, a 180-yard hole to a quite small sloping green set above a valley, followed by a par 5 just over 500 yards.

The course is basically heathland, certainly as regards the fine turf, but a major tree-planting programme of pine and spruce about twenty years ago has made it appear more parkland than it once did.

💷 £10	🏨 hotel 75 yards from the club
🅜 proof of golf club membership	🚗 travelling north from Brechin, fork left from A94 onto B966 after about 1 mile. Edzell village is a further 3 miles and the club entrance is at an arch at the south of the village
🍴 snacks, lunch and dinner daily in summer and daily except Tuesday in winter	

ELGIN

Hardhillock, Elgin, Grampian IV30 3SX
☎ Elgin (0343) 542338

Many consider this the finest inland course in the north of Scotland. Maintenance is of a high standard and the fairways and greens are always very neat and trim. It has fine moorland turf, which is perhaps the best surface for golf after linksland, and its other natural features include heathery hollows, gorse-clad knolls and grassy ridges. Pine woods shelter the west of the course and there's plenty of silver birch.

The par 4s are the challenge to the good golfer here. Eight of them measure over 400 yards, with a sequence of three in a row from the 8th to the 10th. The course begins with one of the longest, at 459 yards, named 'John Macpherson' after the first greenkeeper, who served for 45 years. If you've rushed here straight from breakfast, without a few practice shots to get the feel of your swing and the clubhead hitting the ball, it would be better to think in terms of getting on in three.

Indeed, the start is quite tough, for the 2nd is little shorter, while there's trouble in the form of trees, whins and rough to either side of the fairway. However, there are soon to be three par 3s out of four. The most demanding of these is the 6th, 223 yards, played over a grassy pit, where a ball pitching short is thrown away from left to right, away from the narrow entrance.

We now quickly come to the first of that sequence of long 4s. The run of the ground is with us with the drive on the 8th but the two beeches on the left must be avoided. The second shot will probably be long and a ridge slanting across the fairway must be cleared. On the 10th, the saucer-shaped green should be an encouraging target but the ground slopes away on three sides. The 14th, 'The Spectacles', requires a firm drive between two bunkers which must clear the crest to reach level ground. The long second shot to this 462-yard hole must avoid bunkers left and right, short of the green.

If straight, your second shot has to carry or ride through a dip before the plateau green while to the right there's a steep bank and a hollow and bunkers left. Yes, let's settle for a 5!

£ £9   **M** none

✗ snacks daily, lunch and dinner except Tuesday and Thursday

🚗 from the centre of town aim for Rothes and at the edge of town turn for Birnie and look out for the club after a further ½ mile, just a mile in all

---

FALKIRK TRYST

86 Burnhead Road, Stenhousemuir, Larbert, Central
☎ *Larbert (0324) 562415*

This distinctly unusual name for a golf club came about because the original nine-hole course was laid out on ground which had been occupied by the Falkirk Tryst for about a hundred years. This particular tryst or 'meeting place' was nothing to do with lovers' assignations but refers to a rather less romantic cattle market, at one time the most important of its kind in Scotland.

The club was founded in June 1885 by eleven gentlemen, mostly connected with the famous Carron Ironworks. They were soon playing the course – a couple of months later, in fact. The local postman was paid 3 shillings a week for 'keeping the holes clean', presumably on a part-time basis. It cost 2s 6d for membership or 5 shillings for 'honorary membership', which sounds like life to me. Not a bad bargain.

In 1908 the course became eighteen holes and was little changed until the 1950s. The first seven holes are played over quite flat land, with narrow fairways and many bunkers. The 4th, 544 yards, is the longest hole on the course and a true par 5; it has a fairway bunker to be carried on the second shot, for those hoping to get home in two.

The second nine go through a much more interesting landscape. There are far more trees and plenty of gorse and whins. Here the best holes are the 11th, 13th and 14th. The 11th is a short dogleg right par 4 which tempts you to cut the corner. All well and good, but there's gorse a plenty at the angle if you fail. Whatever you do, the pitch to the green will have to be precise for it's surrounded by bunkers. The 13th is a par 5 of about 500 yards and has the unromantic name 'Boneyard', shades of that old cattle market, no doubt. It's rated as stroke index 2, mainly because there's out of bounds and trees all the way along the left and you play safely right equally at your peril because of the thick gorse, which also continues all the way to the green.

At the 14th, there's again out of bounds along the left and also behind the green. However, the fairway's wide but the entrance to the green is narrow.

Finally, you're back to the flat lands, with a splendid par 4 to finish, made by the Capel burn, which crosses the front of the green and then bends round the right-hand side.

Falkirk Tryst has a sandy subsoil, which makes for excellent winter golf, and good turf.

£ £13, £8 per round

✕ lunch and dinner daily

M no credentials required except Wednesdays, when you must have an introduction

🚗 leave M80 on M876 and turn off for Larbert. Turn in Larbert for Stenhousemuir and take second left after railway station along Burnhead Road

---

GLENEAGLES

Gleneagles Hotel Golf Courses, Auchterarder, Tayside PH3 1NF
☎ Auchterarder (0764) 63543

If any golf name is as well known as St Andrews beyond these shores, surely it is Gleneagles, which is a mecca for keen golfers, particularly visiting Americans and Japanese.

There are two courses: the King's and the Queen's. A third, designed by Jack Nicklaus, should be completed in 1992. All enjoy much the same superb situation. The 830 acres or so are on a moorland plateau about 500 feet up, surrounded by the Grampians to the north, the Trossachs westwards and the Ochil Hills in the east and south.

69

The story of the founding of the courses is unusual. Shortly after the turn of the century Donald Matheson, general manager of the Caledonian Railway, was in a train which broke down near Crieff Junction. To fill in time he went for a walk – and came upon Gleneagles. The Glasgow and South Western company was in the process of opening up Turnberry at the time and Matheson felt that here he'd found a site which was equally suited to be a luxury golf hotel complex. Besides the grandeur of the surroundings, which give Gleneagles a strong claim to be the most beautiful inland course in the world, the terrain was highly suited. If purists may claim that linksland is the true ideal for golf, heath and moorland is quite a close second, and Gleneagles has springy turf, a gravel subsoil, which makes for quick drainage, and undulating country with plenty of variety: hillocks, hollows, ridges and ravines.

James Braid (who else?) was brought in for the basic design. In later years it has been said that Braid thought the King's and Queen's courses were his best work. Others say that he thought the terrain so suited to golf that his task had been relatively simple. Braid departed and Matheson supervised the work of construction. The King's and Queen's (then nine holes) opened just after the First World War, with golfers staying in sleeping cars until the hotel was ready a few years later.

The intention was to provide enjoyable holiday golf rather than a course of daunting major championship calibre to test the mighty and dismay the humble and meek. However, Gleneagles has hosted the Curtis Cup, the 1935 Penfold Tournament, the British Ladies' Championship and, in 1921, a Great Britain versus the USA match which was a fore-runner of the Ryder Cup. It has also become familiar through the BBC Pro-Celebrity series which came to Gleneagles in alternate years.

The courses have a few things in common: heather, pine, bracken and fir with many drives from elevated tees to separate fairways. Every hole has a name, something golfers either warm to or hate. Perhaps the best names just 'arrive' and are usually not in the least poetic: 'The Road Hole', 'The Pit', 'The Ravine', 'The Gas Works', and so on. At Gleneagles they were specially invented; here are a few: 'Crookit Cratur', 'Pawkie Howe', 'Sleekit Knowe', 'Dinkie Slap', 'Het Girdle', 'Heich o'Fash', 'Wee Bogle', 'Drum Sichty', 'Lovers' Gait', 'Hinny Mune'. Whether you love them or hate them is totally up to you!

King's

This is the premier course, and can be stretched to more than 6,800 yards. It begins with an encouragingly wide fairway but with a second shot to a plateau green that asks for good judgement of distance. The 2nd gives you a downhill drive to a fairway narrowing in what could be your distance. The 3rd is difficult, with a blind second over a steep face to a kidney-shaped, two-tier green. The 4th can be rather a struggle, uphill all the way and the ground falling away to the left of the green. The first short hole follows, a par 3 where the ground falls away on all sides, the green is slightly domed and bunkers catch the shot falling short. Much easier to play from a forward tee, as our celebrities do.

The 7th, a long par 4, doglegging left, is challenging, with a drive over a ridge, heather left and a pot bunker on the right for those over-conscious of that heather.

The 13th has a name few could argue with, 'Braid's Brawest' (best). Here you drive over a ridge which runs across the fairway at an angle, with very large bunkers in the rise. The second shot also needs a good one, to a plateau green well guarded by bunkering. The 14th is a famous hole, a very short par 4 indeed, at only 260 yards, but even with a good hit there are hillocks and a host of bunkers, starting at about 140 yards, to negotiate.

The last, 'King's Hame', is another exciting drive. Can you carry the ridge? If so, there is a very helpful slope that could well leave you boasting about your 300-yard drive. In the Pro-Celebrity series, Watson, Weiskopf and Norman have all left themselves with just a tiny pitch to the green at this par 5.

Queen's

Many find this shorter course (just under 6,000 yards) even more attractive than the senior partner. Many of the greens are framed or backed by stands or dark firs, which help in club selection.

In all, there are nine doglegs. Loch-an-Eerie is on your right for the last few holes and you have to carry it with your final tee shot, from a very elevated tee with panoramic views before you.

£ *£26 for the King's and Queen's, £12.50 for the 9 hole Wee Course*

M *exclusively for use by hotel guests or golf course members*

✕ *snacks, lunch and dinner daily in either the dormy house or hotel*

🏨 *five-star hotel given 'Hotel de grand luxe' rating by Michelin*

🎾 *tennis, swimming, fishing, shooting, jacuzzi, turkish bath, snooker, squash, a gymnasium, equestrian centre, croquet, bowls, jogging tracks*

🚗 *from the A9 Stirling to Perth road, turn off along A823 and follow signs. The clubhouse is off the main drive to the hotel*

GLENBERVIE

Stirling Road, Larbert, Central FK5 4SJ
☎ *Larbert (0324) 562983*

This club will always be associated with the name Panton. Three times a Ryder Cup player, and born in Pitlochry, John came as professsional just

71

after the war at the age of thirty and was in his late sixties when he retired in 1984, having been appointed an MBE in 1980. Glenbervie is as proud of him as he was of his long association with the club.

His daughter, Cathy, won the British Amateur Championship when a member and went on to become a leading British professional, one of a very select few indeed to qualify to play the American women's tour.

The club dates back to the early 1930s, when it was laid out by James Braid. Of course, in the 1930s, golf courses no longer cost the very few pounds that was the order of the day in the nineteenth century. Even so, Glenbervie cost just £2,500 and took the work of 28 men for a year with little mechanical help for lifting turf, excavating and contriving slopes.

Glenbervie begins with an ideal arrangement to speed the players on their way, a short par 4, followed by a par 5. Here a burn comes into play, as so often at Glenbervie, but only for a fairly extreme error. At the 6th you need a long and straight drive to the top of the hill or a wood will be needed to reach the green. At the 9th woods menace the off-line shot all the way. They are there all along the right but there's also a copse just where you might prefer it not to be, in the driving area left.

The 12th is a cracking driving hole. If you think you can carry a bunker some 200 yards from the tee to the right of the fairway, success will reward you with a much shorter second shot to this fairly long par 4. Otherwise, go left and your second shot will be much longer and menaced by unfriendly territory pushing in towards the green.

The 17th gives another kind of choice I like to see on a par 5. With your second shot, hopefully straight at the flag, can you get both the right carry and length to reach the green or should you just play right of the trees and still leave yourself with plenty to do?

£ £20, £15 per round

✗ snacks, lunches and dinner daily

M unless playing with a member, a letter from your club secretary is required

🚗 on A9 between Falkirk and Stirling

GOLF HOUSE CLUB (ELIE) THE

Elie, Fife KY9 1AS
☎ Elie (0333) 330327

In 1589 nearby Earlsferry was granted a charter which included 'the right of golf'. More frequent references to golf are found from about 1750. In 1812, a famous law suit began which lasted, on and off, for twenty years. The local laird and a tenant farmer were considered to be encroaching on the links, to the extent of ploughing some of it up and quarrying, and other people were bleaching clothes and steeping lint on it. The purpose of the suit was to preserve this 'golphing tract' for the use of local people and establish its boundaries. Golf won.

This is a typical seaside links which many consider the most likeable of its kind in Scotland, in a corner of Fife full of good courses. The turf is particularly good, as are the bunkers, with sand of a very deep colour. There are no trees or heather. An oddity is that there are no par 5s and only two 3s. Five par 4 holes are less than 325 yards. Yet it's by no means as easy as this sounds, partly because the wind is nearly always blowing.

You start with a drive over a mound some 70 yards in front of the tee, with an out-of-bounds wall to the right. The green is huge but you can easily be out of bounds through the back. (An oddity of the 1st is that the tee has a periscope, from HMS *Excalibur*, which enables you to see if the players in front have moved out of range.) The 3rd is a long par 3, considered by Kel Nagle, who won the Seniors' Championship here, one of the best he'd seen.

The 6th takes you close to the sea, with views of the sweep of West Bay to Kincraig Point. You have to play your pitch over old quarry workings. The next hole, away from the sea again, with a following wind, gives most players a chance of driving the green, 263 yards away. The 9th is a very stiff par 4 at 450 yards, with cross bunkers for a weak second shot.

We're back by the sea, and so we remain, playing the next four holes. The 10th, again, is drivable at 269 yards, with a little help too from a downhill run-in to the green. The 11th is a very short par 3 but complicated by the slope of the green, some 20 degrees, throwing your ball towards the sea wall close at hand.

In high summer, on this part of the course, you may find your concentration disturbed by holiday-makers. Rise above it all, for you'll need two of your best hits to get up in two at the 12th, 458 yards, with the beach all along the left. The 13th, called 'Croupie', Scots for either 'cranberry' or 'raven', was judged by James Braid 'the finest hole in all the country'. There's a grassy hollow to clear from the tee and a dip in front of the green, which is narrow and slanting. It pays to be bold with your second shot as, with luck, your ball will come back from the bank towards the pin.

The 16th and 17th are two long par 4s which take us much of the way back to the clubhouse. The 18th is a fine finishing hole. There are bunkers in plenty, out of bounds all along the right and through the green and deep rough to the left. Just short of the green is Elie's version of the St Andrews Valley of Sin.

You should find several birdie opportunities but may ruin your card in that stretch of mainly long par 4s from the 12th to home.

£ £16   M none

✕ snacks and lunch daily

🚗 ten miles south of St Andrews on A917. Along Bank Street in Elie, if going west, take the first right after the post office

---

GULLANE

Gullane, Lothian EH31 2BB
☎ *Gullane (0620) 842255*

As so often in Scotland, you are on historic golfing ground at Gullane (usually pronounced 'Gillan'). As far back as 1650 the weavers of Dirleton used to face their counterparts from Aberlady in an annual match on Gullane Hill, but the first golf club we know of came into existence in the early 1800s. Gullane Golf Club itself has a continuous history since 1882.

At first just three or four holes were played close to St Andrews Church, near the 1st tee on Gullane Number 1. (There are three courses here, called straight-forwardly 1, 2 and 3.) By the mid-nineteenth century there were seven holes with over 1,500 yards in play, and by 1884 a full eighteen holes had evolved. That is really the way Gullane Number 1 came about, though Mackenzie Ross made some changes as late as 1949. The Number 2 course, however, had a designer right from the start, Willie Park, in 1898. He had the temerity to put in a bill for 10 guineas for his handiwork and found that his claim was rejected for quite a time; perhaps it was a little high for days when £5 was nearer the norm!

The club's first greenkeeper was less fortunate. He worked for 58 days a year at 3 shillings a day and made ends meet by tending Luffness as well. No doubt part of the reason why he was able to do this was that sheep and rabbits kept the turf short. Nevertheless, by 1889 it was still thought necessary to make the job full time at 30 shillings a week.

The coming of the railway to Gullane in 1900 increased the popularity of the course. It soon became famous, and indeed one of the first Ladies' Championships, in 1897, was held here, with repeat visits in 1947 and 1978. This how a writer of the time saw the courses:

'Gullane Hill, untouched by the invading ploughshare, has stretches of the most beautiful golfing country in the world. Turf of exceptional closeness and elasticity, natural sand bunkers of endless shape and variety, sierras of benty [stiff reedy grass] dunes and saharas of sand alternating with oases of verdure make the place a golfers' paradise. Here must have been the home of our first golfing parents for nowhere else in the world is the golfing prospect so expansive and enticing. Nowhere does the pursuit of the game seem so inevitable.'

All this remains just as true today. For instance, that turf is still so good that winter rules never apply.

Gullane Number 1
You start by working your way up Gullane Hill from a 1st tee which is really set at the end of the village main street. If you have to wait, why not

pause and look round Archie Baird's golf museum, next to the professional's shop, which Jimmy Hume has stocked exceptionally well. The 2nd hole is a good one, needing a long second into a rather narrow green. Although it doesn't sound like a long par 4 at 378 yards, most people will need a wood for their second.

The 5th is reckoned the hardest hole on the course and is rated as stroke index 1. It's a good driving hole, where you must place your tee shot near the angle of the dogleg to give yourself a good chance of reaching the geen with your next.

By this time, you're on higher ground (the course rises to some 200 feet) and into the wind, which can often be brisk, to say the least. When you reach the 7th tee, you'll experience one of the most exhilarating views that golf has to offer – 40 miles in every direction and taking in Bass Rock, the Cheviots, the skyline of Edinburgh, the Forth Estuary, the hills of Perthshire and most of the Fife coast. Besides the view, your climb up is now also rewarded by a downhill drive on this 400-yard hole to a very well-bunkered fairway.

After a first nine of just under 3,000 yards, you now have a much longer second nine to deal with. The 10th and 11th are both 470 yard 4s but par should be easier to come by at the 12th, a short 5. The 13th is perhaps the best of the four par 3s, with a plateau green set in the sandhills. It's 165 yards and club selection, even for those who know the course in all weathers, is very difficult. The green is heavily bunkered.

The 15th is a real par 5, uphill and 538 yards, with eleven bunkers, and a very sloping green to read once you get there. By now, you are at the top again, and after playing the short 16th you are ready to plunge back down to the village. Here, you've a really elevated tee and very often a following wind. On a really clear day, the green at this 384-yard hole, despite the three cavernous bunkers a little short of it, may look drivable. It has been but a more likely result, if you get a really good one away, will be to find one of those bunkers in the ridge. The last hole is also drivable.

Gullane Number 2

With the 'senior' course being 6,466 yards, Number 2 is the junior partner at 6,219, but it's a fine course for all that, with severe, neatly revetted bunkers. It's easier because it has far more par 4s at 360 yards or less. Even so, both amateur and professional records are lower on Number 1. I suggest you take the time to play both. After all, this course, together with its partner, has been used for final qualifying for the Open Championship, when the event has come to Muirfield – which some Gullane members think of as rather a young upstart.

£ £30 for Number 1 and £15 for Number 2. £10 for a third course, of a little over 5,000 yards

✗ lunch and snacks daily, dinner only by special arrangement for parties

Ⓜ no restrictions on play but at weekends clubhouse facilities only for those who have played Number 1

🚗 leave A1 east along A198. It is 5 miles west of North Berwick

HONOURABLE COMPANY OF EDINBURGH GOLFERS, THE

Muirfield, Gullane, Lothian EH31 2EG
☎ *Gullane (0620) 842123*

What is the best course in the world? At most, no more than about a dozen names could be put forward as serious candidates and, in any event, any poll of golf experts would have Muirfield near the top of the list. Indeed, in a fairly recent poll carried out by an American golf magazine, it came out number one.

Judging a golf course is, of course, very much a matter of taste and opinion. Some people despise parkland golf while others do not care for a links. My own early golf education probably prejudices me a little towards what I think of as the best of both worlds – heathland, preferably with silver birch, gorse and heather a plenty.

Yet Muirfield seems to suit all tastes, mainly because of some distinctive virtues and the absence of vices. It seldom, for instance, becomes a bouncy dust bowl in a dry summer, and has always been thought at least just a little more inland in character than the most typical of links courses. The rough can be very severe, as it was for Nicklaus's championship in 1966, and whatever the state of growth, there's usually the feeling at Muirfield that ahead is a fairway with punishing rough to either side.

Bunkering, unlike at St Andrews, isn't capricious, and almost all are in sight. The punishment for the drive off line and the shot to the green which just misses is clear, whenever you're playing from where you ought to be. The fairways are by no means dead flat but neither are they full of hummocks: if you can hit your tee shot straight, you won't find yourself in mid-fairway with the ball well below or above your feet.

There's another very important factor. Unlike most courses, Muirfield is not over-golfed. Together with a dedicated greens staff, this means Muirfield is always in good condition, with members confining their play mostly to the weekends. They are traditionally dedicated to foursomes play – and that means less wear and tear also. However, any member of a golf club of reasonable ability will be allowed to play during the week – but you must know how to set about it. Just turning up doesn't do.

In Scottish terms, Muirfield is by no means an ancient course. The Company is first recorded playing over Leith Links, a golfing tract used at least since the fifteenth century, and moved to Musselburgh in 1836. In the meantime they had produced the first simple rules of matchplay golf that have come down to us, ten years earlier than the R and A code of 1754, which may well have been based on theirs.

In 1891 the club moved on to Muirfield and Old Tom Morris came down to mark out the golfing ground, with David Plenderleith carrying out the work in detail. Alterations were soon needed but, after contributions from Harry Colt, Tom Simpson and Robert Maxwell, the course has been unchanged in essence since the late 1920s. The members play from the medal tees that champions of those days used, while today's heroes have been pushed back to the full stretch of 6,941 yards. The medal tees give a length of 6,601 yards.

Often the difference between where you would tee up as opposed to the Watsons, Ballesteroses and Nicklauses is just a stride or two. Only the 5th, 6th, 7th, 9th, 11th and the last two holes are substantially longer, while the 9th is an easier par 5 at 510 yards than a 4 of 460 yards.

The moderate club golfer will be surprised to find that Muirfield is really no terror but should remember that he isn't playing it when set up for championship play. Drive tidily, hit the greens and have the right touch for the fast putting surfaces, and you may well beat your club handicap.

The opening hole, however, is a stiff one, a par 4 which championship contenders are delighted to do in par. The rough is severe, the fairway narrow, the green slopes from front to back, and it's 444 yards away.

However, the next two holes are far more comfortable par 4s. In still air they are not much more than a drive and a pitch, but the 2nd green is difficult to read. The 4th is a par 3 of 174 yards with bunkers to catch anything which doesn't quite carry, but if you fail to get your par here, the 5th, just over 500 yards, usually rewards steady hitting, though the green needs a precise approach shot.

The 6th is a dogleg left. Be on the right for the best line in. The par 3 7th, 151 yards, has an exposed, elevated green, often making club selection very difficult.

On to the 8th, arguably Muirfield's most distinctive hole, packed with bunkers all along the right with the 439 yards becoming many more, the further left you go. The shot to the green is over a cross bunker and is semi-blind. In the 1929 Open Championship, noting that the rough was well trampled down, Walter Hagen drove right of all the bunkering and reaped his reward – but today you'd be in buckthorn, planted to prevent this sort of behaviour.

The 9th is another much praised hole. The long driver is faced with a narrow neck of fairway if he's hoping to get a long one away and no chance of reaching the green if he plays more conservatively. There's also a devilish bunker about 40 yards short of the green, more or less in mid-fairway. It catches many good shots and to some people it's the most unfair bunker on the course – but was golf ever meant to be entirely fair?

At this point you have played clockwise round the perimeter of the course and are back at the clubhouse. The second nine is an inner circuit, mostly anti-clockwise. The layout means that you never play more than three holes in a row in the same direction.

The 10th is a very long par 4 of 471 yards. If you can get up in two, the green then rewards you by being the most difficult to read on the course, where short putts lip out if you haven't quite found the line.

However, the second nine is really the easier, continuing with a couple of par 4s of no great length, though the drive at the 11th is the only blind one on the course, and the shot into the 12th must be precisely judged. The 13th is a par 3.

You are now on the stretch where Trevino birdied every hole during his third round of the 1972 championship. Two of them were straightforward; another involved a putt of indecent length; one was a chip in; and at the short 16th he half-thinned a bunker shot, clattered against the flag, and down it plummeted. All in all, it gave Trevino the score which enabled him to beat both Jacklin and Nicklaus on the final day, a 66.

Even so, in the end it all turned on the 17th, a par 5 which Roberto de Vicenzo managed in two blows in 1948. Trevino hooked his tee shot into a bunker, played out and then hit a 3 wood well short of the green into thick rough from where he put his fourth shot through the green, several yards from the hole.

Meanwhile Jacklin, who had teed off on the 17th one stroke in arrears, had driven well and had his second shot some 20 yards short of the front left of the green. He pitched up a little short of the hole. Trevino advanced on his ball and looked along the line almost impatiently. After all, he'd already said: 'I've thrown it away.'

But that Trevino chip ran at the hole and suddenly he noticed that it might go in. It did and a certain 6 and possible 7 went down on the card as a conventional par 5. Alas for British hopes. Tony had to hole his medium-length putt to tie for the lead going into the last. He didn't, and then missed the 3-footer back. 'Ah well,' I remember my fellow commentator Henry Longhurst saying, 'his turn will come again.' Sadly it didn't.

The 18th has also seen its moments of drama, though never anything quite to match this. There was, for instance, that rather unlikely winner, Alf Perry, with right hand far too much under the shaft, thumping home a wood to the last green in 1935. Or Harry Vardon, in 1896, electing to play cautiously short of a cross bunker near the green to make sure of his 5. In 1987 Nick Faldo holed a tough putt that helped clinch his first major.

And there are a couple of finishes that were definitely anti-climaxes. In 1948 Henry Cotton, who had played superbly throughout the week, bunkered his second shot near the green and was then prevented from getting out by a palpable shank. He still got a 5 – but was the crossest winner of modern times.

The most upset was Gary Player in 1959 who, coasting towards a 66 and certain victory, took 6 on the last and broke down in tears, thinking he'd thrown away what might have been his only chance to win a major championship. But the pursuers faltered and he went on to become one of the most effective competitors in tournaments and major championships of the last forty years.

The club's historian describes the clubhouse as lacking 'any architectural distinction' and reflects what the late nineteenth century member who designed it thought was Elizabethan. The interior, however, teems with interest, and is alone worth a visit.

£ £55, £40 per round

✗ lunch daily, except Mondays, when sandwiches are available

M ✉ book in advance with a letter from your club secretary, stating handicap. Visitors on Tuesdays, Thursdays and certain Friday mornings. Fourballs are restricted

ⓛ only on Tuesdays, Thursdays and Fridays

🚗 on the A198 Edinburgh to North Berwick road, turn towards the coast along Duncar Road and follow signs for Greywalls Hotel just to the east of Gullane

LONGNIDDRY 🌳 〰️

Links Road, Longniddry, Lothian EH32 0NL
☎ *Longniddry (0875) 52141*

Here we are in that fine stretch of East Lothian golfing country from North Berwick towards Edinburgh, with Longniddry, laid out by Harry .Colt in 1921, one of the most recent courses. Though near the sea, it isn't basically a links.

There is a strong contrast between the two nines of the course. A feature of the course is that it has no par 5s but many long 4s. The par is only 68 with the standard scratch two strokes higher. The start, with a straightforward but still testing long par 4, is almost a parkland hole, and there are trees in plenty on this part of the course. The 3rd is Longniddry's longest at 465 yards; it is difficult to get home here in two on a hole obviously originally intended to be a par 5.

The 5th is a very interesting short par 4, doglegging left very strongly. Particularly as the tee is elevated to help you on your way, something like a 4 or 5 iron is the club to play, for there are trees either side to punish the inaccurate drive and not much advantage to be gained from a long tee shot. The second demands a pitch to an elevated green with trees and bunkers to be avoided. Another elevated tee shot follows to a par 3, well below, with the green surrounded by bunkers. As usual with this kind of shot, the choice of club is particularly crucial.

This is followed by another long par 4, tree-lined all the way and against the prevailing wind to a well-bunkered green. The 12th is another good par 4, with a fairway narrowing to just 15 yards at one point. The green is elevated, well trapped, and there's a burn behind it if you should happen to be too bold with your approach.

We are now into the open part of the course and prey to the winds. The finish has four long par 4s and one quite short par 3, the 16th, for respite. The 17th is the most difficult, running alongside out-of-bounds gardens and doglegged so that your drive must be well placed to give you a good chance of getting home with your second shot, often into the wind.

Walking at Longniddry is not stiff. Apart from trees and buckthorn, bunkers are the main hazards, while a burn comes into play at the 14th, where it twice splits the fairway. There is very little deep rough but semi-rough is frequent enough, particularly on the later holes.

Longniddry is undoubtedly a course of tournament quality if rather short, at a little over 6,200 yards. It has proved a popular venue for the PGA Seniors' Championship, held here four times between 1970 and 1982. In the 1975 event former Open Champion Kel Nagle set the course record, 64. In 1987 the club hosted the final qualifying rounds for the Open Championship at nearby Muirfield.

The attractive clubhouse was built with stone from Amisfield House in Haddington, after it had been destroyed by fire in the 1920s.

£ *£20, £28 at weekends*	**✕** *lunch and dinner daily except Fridays, when snacks are available*
M *membership of a golf club*	**🚗** *on A198. Turn down Links Road at Longniddry Inn*

LUNDIN LINKS

Golf Road, Lundin Links, Fife KY8 6BA
☎ *Lundin Links (0333) 320202*

In one way this course, part of a stretch of linksland which stretches from Scotscraig to Aberdour and includes St Andrews, resembles Hoylake – you can quite readily be out of bounds on sixteen of the holes. The architect, James Braid (how many courses did this great player design?), also made good use of water hazards, not often a feature of links courses. They come into play on seven holes and guard greens in four instances.

Part of the reason for so many out-of-bounds situations is that the railway line to the east neuk (corner) of Fife used to run through the middle of the course. Though the club now owns the land, it has been kept as out of bounds. Although I think out of bounds areas should generally be beyond the confines of the course, history justifies this one. It's certainly a potent hazard.

Although the course is links in character, there are more trees than you might expect, mainly fir and larch and also whin and broom, covering many areas. The fairways are broad but undulating. This is no 'out and back' links course. Certainly the first four holes take you in the same direction, as do the last four of the journey home, but in between there are almost constant changes.

You start with quite a long par 4, followed by two shorter ones, and then comes one of the most demanding holes. It's a long 4 of 452 yards with out of bounds to think about on the left. A burn fronts the green, set in a dip, which means your second shot must be all carry. However, if you've powered an enormous drive away, you can't play safe by taking a touch too strong a club for your second. If you're too far through the green, you're out of bounds.

The 8th, though not a long par 4, asks for an accurate drive. You could be on the old railway to the right and there are three bunkers left. The green is protected by heavy bunkering and the brook.

The 14th is one of the many called 'Perfection', a par 3 of 175 yards. From the tee you can look east over Largo Bay and on to Kincraig Point. As you'll be at sea level and fully prey to the winds, club selection can be very difficult.

The Home hole, the 18th, provides the stern finish of a long par 4 with out of bounds left, all the way from tee to green. This large green is in front of the clubhouse, with members keen to watch you three-putt.

There is a putting green, a good-sized practice ground and a bunker.

£ £22.50, £15 per round

✗ snacks, lunch and dinner daily

M none

🚗 take the A915 from Kirkcaldy towards Lundin Links. Turn right at the cross roads on the outskirts of the village and then first right

---

MONIFIETH

8 Prince's Street, Monifieth, Tayside
☎ Dundee (0382) 532678

This is a municipal course, always in excellent condition, where the land has been used by golfers for well over 300 years. In 1645, for instance, two men were punished by their church for 'playing the gowff' on a Sunday. Indeed, it was to be centuries before Sunday play in Scotland became fully acceptable.

Monifieth was used in qualifying rounds for the 1968 and 1975 Carnoustie Open Championships and also when St Andrews was the venue in 1970.

At more than 6,600 yards, it certainly doesn't lack length and there are six par 4s of well over 400 yards, four of them on a first nine of over 3,400 yards. However, there is some relief with three quite short par 4s but only two par 5s, both quite long ones.

This is a links course with an east coast position, like Carnoustie. When the wind is from that direction, it can be very bleak. However, the several pine plantations do act as windbreaks as well as separating the parallel fairways.

£ £15, £10 per round

M none

✗ lunch and dinner daily

🚗 the course is 7 miles east of Dundee on the A930, on the railway side of the main street in Monifieth

---

MURCAR

Bridge of Don, Aberdeen, Grampian AB2 8BD
☎ *Aberdeen (0224) 704370*

Murcar was founded in 1909 as a break-away from a club playing over a municipal course. It was possibly unique in having its own light railway for many years. At a cost of one old penny, golfers were conveyed from the tram terminus to the course, about two miles. If they later tarrried too long at the bar there was no 'Murcar buggy' and a long walk home. The service was stopped with the rise of car ownership in the early 1950s.

Murcar is a tremendous natural links course with many sandhills and much gorse. The sandhills rise in ridges from the North Sea beach, giving a terraced effect and views of the sea at nearly every hole. After a start a little away from the sea, the remainder of the first nine hug the seashore with views of Aberdeen Bay to the south and of Cruden Bay and Peterhead to the north. The second nine come back to the clubhouse on a more inland route and on higher ground.

After a start of two fairly short par 4s, the real golf soon begins. At the 3rd the fairway drops away from the tee and there are sandhills round the green. The 5th is good 160 yard par 3, played over a dip and is followed by a long par 4 of 440 yards over undulating ground.

The 7th, 422 yards, has long been recognized as a great par 4. You will need a drive of 180 yards or so to carry the second of two burns, with a large rough hillock to catch any shot hit too far left. The green is on a plateau, with bunkers set into the rising ground to left and right. On first acquaintance take at least a club more than you think and remember it'll be a two-club difference when the flag is to the rear.

The 8th and 9th are shorter par 4s, with the last of these only just over 300 yards but the humps and hollows make them. The 10th takes you to higher ground.

On the second half, the pick of the holes are the 15th and 16th. At the first of these, a par 4 of just under 350 yards, you drive from an elevated tee, commanding views over Aberdeen, and must clear about 100 yards of gorse to reach the fairway below. Your pitch then has to carry up to a plateau green with a stream just short. There's out of bounds right but not quite as close as on the 13th and 14th. The 16th is a short hole of some 160 yards over two bends of the burn to a green protected by bunkers front, right and left.

This 6,200-yard course, which is an immediate neighbour of Royal Aberdeen, is not suitable for beginners.

£ £12

M no restrictions

✉ need to book in advance

✗ snacks daily, lunch and dinner daily except Tuesday

🚗 3 miles north of Aberdeen on Fraserburgh road

NORTH BERWICK

New Clubhouse, Beach Road, North Berwick, Lothian
EH39 4BB
☎ *North Berwick (0620) 2135*

This course seems to go further back into the beginnings of golf even
than St Andrews. Although the club itself only dates from 1832, golf has
been played here for very much longer.

This is also as 'old-fashioned' a course as you are likely to find, full of
such quirks as blind shots, stone walls to confront the drive, long second
shots and even one short pitch. One green has a small but steeply sloped
mini-ravine running through it!

You may not enjoy all of the eccentricities but most people at least like
some of them, and many of the holes are conventional enough. There
are, however, two drawbacks. One is that you could hardly get more of
an out-and-back course than this, which can lead to a very repetitive
beat out against the wind and then to being bowled along by it on the
return journey. The other is that the fairways may well be a mass of
divots by August and September, so I'd recommend you try it earlier in
the year.

In late Victorian and Edwardian times, this was a holiday centre for
the rich and well-connected. People would stay at one of the large hotels
or take a house for weeks at a time. One prime minister, Lord Balfour,
was captain of the club during this period.

You begin with two very sporting holes. The 1st, 'Point Garry', has a
gully between you and the green, 200 yards or so from the tee. Play short
of it – but not too short for you should hope to be playing a high pitch to
the green, which slopes towards the rocky beach. The 2nd is about 100
yards longer, 435 yards, a very good driving hole indeed. The beach is
very close on the right and eats into the fairway. You have to decide how
much of the bend you can carry or go for the safety of the left half of the
fairway, but this will make it much more difficult to get home in two.

At the 3rd, 459 yards, you come across your first wall, which has to be
carried by your second shot. The 4th is an excellent par 3 of some 180
yards, set in a narrow pass with rocky ground just short and left, a hollow
in front and bunkers all around.

Now you enter rather more open ground and a series of holes with a
little less character than the start and finish. The 6th, however, a
160-yarder, features a quarry to fly your ball over and the 7th has the Eil
Burn just in front of the green. The 9th, just under 500 yards, rewards the
bold and accurate drive. The shortest line is a little left, between bunkers
and a wall. With an easterly wind at your back, you should then have a
fair chance of getting home in two.

The 9th tacks across at the far end of the course towards the sea. The
shape of the course from this point on is straight back towards the
clubhouse, very likely with a wind at your back. The 13th sees the start of

North Berwick's intriguing finish and is just under 350 yards. The fairway has a wall running along the left and, another oddity, the green is the other side. As it's long and narrow, your pitch over the wall is easier the further left you are. It's very difficult to judge the strength of an approach played from well right.

The 14th is called 'Perfection'. You drive to a fairway with trouble either side, and the second shot, perhaps a mid-iron, is banged blind over a high ridge set with bunkers. Well, you'll want to be up, but not through the green and onto the shingle.

'The Redan', the 15th, is one of the world's most famous short holes, but this time hardly perfection. The green is set at an angle to the line of shot and is a plateau with a very large and deep bunker under the left-hand side and more to the right. So far so good, but for the first-time visitor, the hole is rather spoilt by a big ridge between tee and green. This hole, 192 yards, has been copied all over the world – usually with the ridge omitted.

At the 16th, you have to clear a ditch a little over 200 yards from the tee and your second is played to a plateau green with the Marine Hotel looking down on you – not one plateau, really, but two, for this is the green with that deep gully cutting across the surface. Best to be on the right one!

The 17th, 'Point Garry In', 422 yards, shares a double green with the 1st so you are again going to have to confront that slippery green tilted towards the beach. The second shot is blind, with a big cross bunker and ridge to carry.

Your troubles ought to be over now, for the last is a short par 4 of 270 yards where you may hope to get on in two with the wind following. However, it's difficult to hold, so you'll probably have to be content with a par.

North Berwick is to be used as a qualifying course for the 1992 Open. The professional is David Huish, who has been a force to be reckoned with in Scottish golf for many years and is a past captain of the PGA. He also led the 1975 Carnoustie championship.

💷 £12	🅜 none	🚗 at North Berwick on the A198, 23 miles east of Edinburgh
🍴 snacks daily, lunch and dinner daily except Thursday		

PEEBLES

Kirkland Street, Peebles, Borders EH45 9DT
☎ *Peebles (0721) 20197*

This is a Braid/Colt design situated in foothills, with occasional views of Peebles and of the River Tweed down the valley. The fairways are broad, mainly devoid of tight lies, and are nicely separated from other holes. So far, not particularly testing, but the course design does have the merit that it isn't enough just to hit the fairway: your tee shots must be well placed to give the right line into the greens, which are well protected from shots from the 'wrong' side.

The first four holes are played over rising ground, starting with a 200-yard par 3, followed by the most testing hole on the course, a long par 4 where you must keep right with your tee shot because of both out of bounds along the left and a mature beech tree on the same side which could block out your shot to the green.

After three fairly short par 4s you come to 'Glensax', a 400-yard hole with a green protected by bunkers and a stream. Look out for birdie chances over the next several holes. The tough finish is rather unlikely to yield one. From the 14th to the last you have a sequence of long par 4s, a long 3 and a 540-yard par 5 to finish. Of these, perhaps the best is the 195-yard 16th, where your tee shot must both avoid trees and clear a stream before reaching the green, which is well guarded.

💷 *£8 per round, £15 at weekends*	🚗 *Peebles is well signposted from either Edinburgh or Glasgow, the course is to the north-west of the town, just off the A72*
Ⓜ *none*	
✗ *daytime snacks and lunch daily*	

PITLOCHRY   ⛳

Pitlochry, Perthshire PH16 5QY
☎ *Pitlochry (0796) 2334*

This is the course where that very good Scottish professional, John Panton, learned to play, one of the best iron players I've ever seen and, as the club rightly say, 'One of the greatest ambassadors Scotland has had'. He was made an honorary member in 1956.

Pitlochry is famed for its magnificent scenery, a must for the golfing traveller, with views in all directions, especially of several miles of the Tummel valley from the higher slopes of the course. The view from the 1st tee should put you in the right mood, with fir trees all around and undulating fairway set with bunkers climbing towards the green almost 400 yards away. There's out of bounds on the right, something you'll find on nine holes in all. The 2nd is another quite long two-shotter but this isn't really typical of the course because there are only four holes in all of around 400 yards, the longest being just 432 – so no par 5s to help you get a shot back.

There are, however, as many as nine holes where you should be playing a pitching club for your second, so at Pitlochry it's accuracy not power that will be tested most. It's also true to say that each of the holes

85

sets different problems and, as this is a hilly course, no two holes are alike.

Such a site very often gives the architect opportunities to produce outstanding par 3s. They are indeed a feature here, with three in all, each very good. The 4th, 166 yards is the first. It is very well protected by bunkers. The 11th is the longest, over 190 yards, and is one of the holes with out of bounds on the right. The best is the 16th, 180 yards or so, played from a high tee with the green well below and guarded by at least six bunkers and another out of bounds at the right.

A stream features on the first two holes and, several feet wide, is the final obstacle when you're playing the 18th.

£ £7   **M** none

✗ from April to October, snacks, lunch and high tea daily except Wednesday, when snacks are available. In winter lunch and snacks only at weekends

🚗 Pitlochry is on the A9. If coming from the south, drive along the main street until you reach the end of the shopping centre and then turn right up Larchwood Road

---

ROYAL ABERDEEN

Balgownie, Bridge of Don, Aberdeen, Grampian
☎ Aberdeen (0224) 702571

This is one of the oldest clubs in the world. As the 'Society of Aberdeen Golfers' it goes back as far as 1780, the present club being founded in 1815. Golf between the rivers Don and Dee goes back much further, but the club moved to its present location at Balgownie in 1888, tired of competing for the use of the original linksland with cricketers, footballers, herring fishermen drying their nets and even turf-cutting to repair the race course.

One of the club's most prized possessions is a ballot box dating back to 1780. When you applied for membership of the society, one black ball was enough to scupper your chances. It remained in use until 1972 with its two holes in the lid, one marked 'NAY' and the other 'YEA'.

The Society also seems to have been responsible for one of the rules of golf. In 1783 it was decided: 'The Party whose ball is missing shall be allowed five minutes to search for it, after coming to the spot where the ball appeared to drop.' Very sensible too, and so it has remained.

The Balgownie course was originally laid out by Robert Simpson from Carnoustie with many changes over the years. I remember it best from an exhibition match I played in 1966 with Eric Brown, Harry Bannerman and my close friend Tony Lema, Open Champion in 1964. At 6,372 yards from the medal tees, it's not a monster, but good driving is essential, with some long carries from the tees, and many bunkers and gorse as the most common hazards. The turf is very good on the rolling fairways, which often twist amongst the dunes, and the greens are usually true and fast. The first nine is the better, and more than 300 yards longer than the second, but that difference will quickly shrink with a wind in your face coming home.

The 1st, just over 400 yards, goes down towards the sea, and at the 2nd, the longest hole on the course, 530 yards, you start by driving over a large sandpit. Carry from the tee is also needed on the next three holes with cross bunkers, gorse and a burn very much in play. The 8th is a very attractive short par 3 of only 147 yards, with the green below the tee, and is more difficult to hit than you might think, perhaps because there are ten bunkers in wait for anything just a touch off line.

At the 9th, you're at maximum distance from the clubhouse for a very testing par 4 of 453 yards, doglegging to the right. Easier if you manage to carry the corner but otherwise good tee shot placement is needed to ease your second to a well-bunkered green.

You start back with a fairly short par 4 of little more than 340 yards but it's quite a teaser, with the tee shot needing to hold the plateau fairway and the pitch to follow over a burn. There are five par 4s around 400 yards as you make your way back towards the clubhouse. One, the 11th, has a green on three levels, and at the 14th both out of bounds and a burn are very much a threat.

The last is a very good final hole, fit to settle a match or wreck a medal card. A drive of good length between bunkers either side of the fairway is the first essential and the second shot to a plateau green may well finish in one of the deep bunkers which surround it. It's very difficult to reach in two shots with a stiff breeze against you.

There's an 18-hole relief course of some 4,000 yards with ten par 3s, and eight short par 4s.

The lounge in the clubhouse has magnificent views over the North Sea.

£ £25

M a letter of introduction from your golf club

✕ lunch and dinner daily

🚗 take the A92 north from Aberdeen along King Street and after crossing the Don take the second turn right at the traffic lights. Next turn right and then bear left along Links Road to the clubhouse

ROYAL BURGESS GOLFING ♣ SOCIETY OF EDINBURGH, THE

181 Whitehouse Rd, Barnton, Edinburgh, Lothian EH4 6BY
☎ *Edinburgh (031) 339 2012*

In 1985 the Royal Burgess celebrated its 250th year of existence as a golf club, which takes us back to 1735, ten years before the '45 Rebellion! This claim makes it the oldest golf club in the world with a continuous history, unless the claims of Blackheath to 1608 are accepted.

Even if the foundation date, which is given in the 1835 *Edinburgh Almanac*, is disputed, there is no doubt at all that the society existed in the eighteenth century. There is a minute dating back to 1773 and a 1776 copy of the society's rules which refers to the year 1773 also, the second oldest sets of rules to come down to us. There is also a written record that in 1774 a boy was appointed to work for the society in various ways which included carrying the captain's clubs for the payment of 6s per quarter.

Another view is that the Royal Burgess may be even older than is claimed. After all, golf had been played on Bruntsfield Links, the original home of the society, since the mid-fifteenth century.

After a move to Musselburgh, the society came to its present home in 1894. The course is parkland in type and was first laid out by Old Tom Morris with James Braid carrying out revisions later. The main hazards are bunkering and trees. At 6,494 yards, there is enough length for this to be a tournament and championship course. It has hosted the Martini and Pringle events and the British Boys' Championship was played as recently as 1985. Six of the par 4s are over 400 yards but there are also three fairly short ones to give hopes of birdies, as also the two par 5s, each only just over 480 yards.

The 4th is an interesting long par 4 of more than 460 yards with a most demanding second shot because of the narrow entrance to the green. The 7th, another long par 4, asks you to carry a fairway bunker to avoid a very long second if you decide to play safely short. The best of the three par 3s is the 13th, where you'll need at least your longest iron to the tightly bunkered green. The dogleg 15th presents you with a challenge on the drive. You must get past a big chestnut on the right to be able to go for the green with your second. So open your shoulders but remember there's an out of bounds all along the right.

The clubhouse is full of historical interest.

£ *£28, £20 per round*   **M** *a letter of introduction from your club*

✗ *snacks daily, lunch daily except Mondays and Saturdays; dinner is arranged for visiting parties of sixteen upwards*

🚗 *take the Queensferry road west towards Forth Bridge and turn north along Whitehouse Road at the Barnton Hotel roundabout. The clubhouse is on the right after about 100 yards*

ST ANDREWS

Links Management Committee of St Andrews,
St Andrews, Fife KY16 9JA
☎ *St Andrews (0334) 75757*

Golf has been played on St Andrews links at least since the fifteenth century and the R and A, properly called 'The Royal and Ancient Golf Club of St Andrews', was founded in 1754. William IV gave his consent to the 'Royal' prefix in 1834.

So very much has been said and written of the long history of the R and A and St Andrews that I don't wish to labour it, but it is worth saying that to come to St Andrews, even if only to look over the fence, is an experience in itself. There is an immediate sense of the past, without even knowing that such early figures in the game as Allan Robertson and the Morrises, father and son, played here. In more recent history, Bobby Jones began his competitive experience here with a 'puzzled dislike' and tore up his card. However, he returned to dominate the 1927 Open Championship from start to finish and in 1930 to begin his Grand Slam of the Open and Amateur Championships of Britain and the United States by taking the event he considered the most difficult to win, our Amateur Championship. Much later, he wrote of the course:

> 'Beginning with the puzzled dislike I had felt for the Old Course when I first played in 1921, by 1930 I had come to love it. I thought that I appreciated its subtleties... Truly, if I had had to select one course on which to play the match of my life, I should have selected the Old Course.'

Let's try to see what it was about the Old Course that might have appealed to the game's greatest player.

The first hole is certainly a puzzler, a flat field with a pitch over the Swilcan burn, but beware, too great a feeling of golf history, with eyes watching from the clubhouse, could lead to a very wayward tee shot out of bounds right on the beach or to one too far left making the approach shot more difficult. Here, though, is the germ of how to play St Andrews from the tee. You can almost always fire it away to the left and not find much trouble. In fact, on this out-and-back links, you may find that you're rewarded for your wildness by landing on another fairway. However, you'll very seldom have a good line into the green from the left. Except for the par 3s, almost every hole gives the best line for the green if you've managed to place your tee shot along the right side of the fairway, close to the rough.

The pitch over the burn on the 1st is another typical St Andrews difficulty. The more 'safely' you play over, the more difficult the downhill putt becomes. One man took the Amateur Championship with three wins on the 1st (played as the 19th) when his opponents knocked their second shots in the burn. Tom Shaw, in the 1970 championship, put his second shot towards the back of the green and then putted back down towards the burn – and into it. It was a mercy that he then holed his chip shot from the other side for a 5, which included the penalty stroke. Much more recently, Ian Baker-Finch in 1984, like Seve Ballesteros in 1976, stole most of the headlines as an unknown, but began his last round disastrously by pitching over and then seeing his ball bite and spin back into the burn.

However, historical disasters apart, you just need to hit a firm drive down the field, pitch cleanly, and not take more than two putts to go on your way in reasonable spirits.

The 2nd is a par 4 of 411 yards. Drive between Cheape's bunker on the left and the right rough. The flag position will vary the ideal second shot and the ridge which runs into the green can dictate line. The 3rd is a potential birdie hole, a drive which avoids bunkers left and right, followed by a second shot clearing the ridge short of the green and, particularly, Cartgate bunker, which comes into the left of the green. At the 4th, 419 yards, there are two humps to avoid, one from the tee shot, and one short of the green.

The 5th has a high plateau green, a huge one, protected by yet another ridge and a swale. The ground falls sharply away down to the green and you'll have to decide for your shot in whether to use the run-up or pitch over it. With the wind helping, it's a birdie opportunity at 514 yards.

The 6th, a par 4, is again guarded by a ridge, and you have to decide whether to play a running approach or pitch full to the green. At the next, more ridges and hummocks are in play and one of the features of St Andrews ought to be becoming evident: the shot to the green is very much affected by the slopes, ridges and bumps which can so easily dismiss any shot not precisely placed. You can have a splendid driving round and hit your shots into the greens very solidly but still not prosper because something more is asked of you.

You are now into the 'Loop', where champions hope to make their score. From the 8th to the 12th, there are the only two par 3s, and three short 4s, each just a little over 300 yards. The 8th is by no means a difficult par 3 and the 9th is possibly the least interesting hole at St Andrews with its flat fairway and a green of no more challenge than a tennis court. Yet it is still historic, for it was here that Tony Jacklin holed his second shot in the first round of the 1970 Open to be out in 29, a miraculous start for a defending champion who had just won the US Open.

The 10th, a short par 4, is often drivable but the ridge in front of the green can thwart a slow-running ball. However, you'll probably be pitching to this green, which slopes from back to front. The 11th is the second and last of the par 3s on the Old Course and a very interesting one, a terror when the greens were hard and glassy. Then, if you were through the back there was a frightening little pitch which would probably dribble all the way into Strath bunker. This is the place where Bobby Jones lost his temper in 1921, after a poor first nine. (Later, he is said to have modelled the 4th at Augusta National on this hole.)

At the 12th you have to cope with invisible fairway bunkers. If you're a long hitter, go straight at the green, but an iron shot along the right side of the fairway gives the best line. Though this hole is only 316 yards, the plateau green has little depth and long hitters can perish in rough country on the left, about 230 yards from the tee.

The St Andrews finish now begins in earnest, after the relatively light relief of the 'Loop'. The 13th is about 400 yards with the Coffin bunkers to avoid in mid-fairway. The green is a big one but in all probability only the top of the flag will be visible, and it tilts from front to rear.

The 14th is one of the great par 5s of world golf – no invitation to a healthy tournament player to give it a whack and wonder which iron he'll be playing for his second. In a left-to-right wind the bravest players tend to go left away from the out-of-bounds wall along the right, yet as close to it as possible so as to make playing the rest of the hole easier, the shot to the green pitching against the slope. A drive left may find the Beardie bunkers and many players, including Seve Ballesteros in 1984, decide to go even further left and onto the 5th fairway. The vast Hell bunker, which catches many a second shot, put paid to Gene Sarazen's chances in the 1933 Open.

The next two holes are difficult par 4s, still with that out of bounds along the right, and both have greens which require precise placement of the second shot. Playing the 16th, in 1978, Jack Nicklaus had faced a burst in which his partner, Simon Owen of New Zealand, had birdied the 9th, 10th, 12th, 14th and 15th and then driven long and straight up this hole, to be a stroke ahead of him. But the lead changed hands again as Owen went through the green for 5, while Nicklaus had a birdie 3.

The 17th has the most demanding drive in golf, and much the same applies to the second shot. Ideally, you manage its 461 yards by driving over the outline of the old railway sheds, finishing as close to the out-of-bounds wall beyond as you dare. From there, the narrow green is as favourable a target as you'll get. In both Open Championships and general play most people go left, which gives a chance of hitting the green, but none at all of holding it. Not so, however, in 1984. Then Tom Watson hit a perfect drive, while Seve Ballesteros, minutes before, had hit to the left. Ballesteros then, with a 6 iron from a flying lie, hit just short and held the green, while Watson, from the perfect position, went through the green, into the road and had little chance of getting down in two. He had over-clubbed.

Played as a par 5, the hole isn't particularly difficult, and I don't know why more championship competitors don't approach it this way: drive left, hit the second shot right, and hope to pitch or run up and single putt. Whichever way you play the Road Hole, however, there's still the Road bunker set into the left of the green. You might pitch or run into it from the left or from the right, but watch the slope, whether with long iron or

91

long putt, as you can find your ball drifts towards it, and then inevitably goes down into it. In 1990, with victory assured, Faldo played for a 5.

There are no problems at the last. You can, it's true, go out of bounds into the town on the right, but you've half the world to aim at along the left. The green is relatively flat, with a slope from rear to front, but there is the Valley of Sin to contend with. This depression just short of the green was, however, far more significant when St Andrews greens were hard and a golfer was thinking in terms of having to play a precisely weighted running approach. Now, at least in still conditions, a high pitch with something between a wedge and 8 iron will normally do and will stop quite quickly.

Many Open Championship competitors rate St Andrews the easiest of the courses on the rota but no one, over four rounds, has come near to making it look silly. Why should this be so? I think for two main reasons. The first is that slopes on the greens can sometimes be subtle, sometimes severe, so birdies are hard to come by and three-putts always a threat. The second reason is the ridges, humps and hollows which so often come into play just short of, or just on the greens, have a great influence on the run of the ball.

The Old Course is just a part of what today can be called a 700-acre golf complex. Everyone wants to play this historic course but there are four other courses to choose from, with the New being well worth playing and far easier to get on.

'New' is only relative. The course was laid out in 1895, and some heretics consider it better than the Old. Again, it's an out-and-back lay-out with some tacking to and fro, measuring 6,604 yards. There are three par 5s, four short holes and four big par 4s.

The Jubilee is so named because it was opened in 1897, the year that Queen Victoria celebrated hers, and has recently been modified to bring it to tournament standard. It's almost 7,000 yards long with four par 5s. The Eden, opened in 1913, is named after the river, and is just under 6,400 yards in length. The most recent addition is the Balgove, a nine-hole course intended for children and beginners.

£ *Old £30, New £13, Eden £10, Jubilee £13, Balgove £2*

M *none*

✕ *lunch and dinner daily in the Links Rooms*

🚗 *the Eden and Balgove is just off the A91 short of the town boundary; the Old is off Golf Place, shortly after entering the town; for the New and Jubilee continue on along West Sands Road*

✉ *starting times may be booked if confirmed eight weeks in advance. Otherwise, there is a balloting system for the Old Course. Give in your names not later than 2.00 pm on the day before you intend to play and the result is published a couple of hours later. Play on the New, Eden and Jubilee is normally by times of arrival on the 1st tee of the respective courses but the Eden may also be booked by telephone on the date prior to the date of play*

TAYMOUTH CASTLE

Kenmore, Tayside PH15 2DE
☎ *Kenmore (08873) 228*

James Braid designed this course in the early 1920s through the deer park of the one-time seat of the Marquis of Breadalbane, a scion of the Campbells. As you'd expect, the general situation is mountainous (Scottish lords liked to lie abed feeling secure from attack!) but this affects your surroundings much more than the terrain you'll be playing over. This is reasonably flat and the fairways are wide and welcoming, with the course being bounded on the west by Loch Tay, and on the north and east by the river. All in all, you won't find many more beautiful places to play golf. The club itself considers itself the most scenic in the British Isles, pointing to its mountain backdrop with a 4,000 foot peak and views of Loch Tay, particularly from the 8th tee.

Most golfers, I know, are more concerned with the state of play than their surroundings, but this is most emphatically a course where you could hope to get away with it if you proclaimed that you were far more interested in where you were than how you were playing, even when six down after ten holes.

However, for stern no-nonsense golfers, on to the playing qualities of the course...

You start with two short par 4s, followed by a par 4 of well over 400 yards, all part of the Braid formula to lead you in gently and then begin making demands on both your skill and your hitting. The 4th, which follows, is a little beauty, a 170-yard par 3 where you carry all the way over a lake – or don't. This one is followed by the longest hole on the course, the only par 5, but there's 543 yards of it. From the medal tee, you've a carry of 220 yards but a perhaps welcome 40 yards less from the blues. The second shot is uphill to a narrowing fairway. The first nine end with three par 4s and 3,143 yards of the 6,066 yards accomplished.

In the second nine, however, there are four par 4s of well over 400 yards and three of these are close to the 450-yard mark. The 15th is one of these, where your drive has to be very well placed to give a fair line in to the heavily bunkered green, while the last, 443 yards, will only yield a par after two good shots.

If you're seeking a family golfing holiday, there are sailing, canoeing, wind surfing, pony-trekking, fishing and hill-walking close at hand.

£ *£16, £20 at weekends*

M *none*

ⓛ *juniors are allowed to play at half fees*

✉ *need to book in advance at weekends*

✕ *snacks, lunch and dinner daily*

🚗 *6 miles west of Aberfeldy on the A827 and clearly signposted*

93

NORTH-WEST ENGLAND

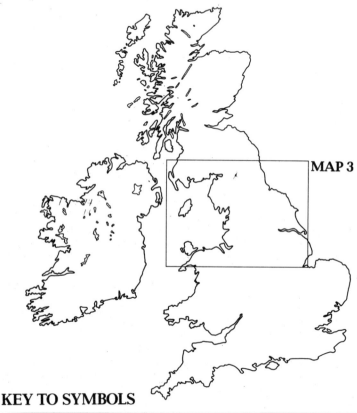

MAP 3

KEY TO SYMBOLS

 PARKLAND

 LINKS

 MOORLAND

 HEATHLAND

 DOWNLAND

☎ TELEPHONE

✉ NEED TO BOOK
IN ADVANCE

£ APPROXIMATE
COURSE FEE

M MEMBERSHIP
REQUIREMENTS
FOR VISITORS

✗ CATERING PROVIDED

🏠 ACCOMMODATION
PROVIDED

Ⓛ RESTRICTIONS ON
LADIES AND/OR
YOUTHS

OTHER SPORTING
FACILITIES

🚗 DIRECTIONS

UPLAND

BRAMPTON

Talkin Tarn, Brampton, Cumbria
☎ *Brampton (06977) 2255*

Some golf courses have the enviable feel of being away from it all even through a fly-over or an industrial estate may be close at hand. Brampton is the real thing, a fell course, without the golfer having a real ascent to tackle, and scenic wonders all the way.

It will stage no championships, because of its position, and may be more than just damp underfoot here and there in the winter months, but the whole feel of the place is marvellous.

The first tough hole is the 3rd which fully justifies its stroke index 2 rating. The Newcastle–Carlisle railway is out of bounds all the way to the green and there is a carry of perhaps 160 yards over clinging rough to reach the fairway. The green is hard by the out of bounds, well bunkered and fairly heavily contoured.

The 4th hole, at over 550 yards, is much the longest. Again, there's a good carry from the elevated tee, while the landing area for the second shot is narrow. Few players will hope to reach this par 5 in two and it's also quite a small elevated target.

The 5th is a severe hole, one of the best on the course. It's usually played into a head wind with bunkering left, a severe drop to the right and a grassy bank to the rear. However, it is easy enough if you're content with a bogey. You'll then have three short 4s on which to relax. Most of the par 4s are indeed by no means long, but all demand a precise shot to the green.

The 11th is an ideal par 5 for club golfers. You could tackle it by knocking a couple of 7 irons along the fairway to get you to the right-angled dogleg, and then play the same club to the green. Or, and it may be rather a big 'or', try to hold a long drive just a little left of centre, to allow you enough space to clear the trees for your second shot. Really, a solidly struck 3 wood and much the same to follow will get you there.

If you've avoided putting your tee shot on the road at the 16th, a classic old-fashioned par 5 is just ahead of you. An immense drive will give you a sight of the green but basically you'll be playing your tee shot to a sweeping rise and then your second over the brow.

This is the beginning of a testing finish. At Brampton you need to make your score earlier and the 18th is the longest par 4 on the course.

Although there are five par 4 holes around the 300-yard mark, architect James Braid succeeded in being testing without resorting to excessive length. Some proof of this can be seen in the course record. Par is 73, standard scratch 71, but neither professional nor amateur has broken 70 in competition. This is mainly because a poor tee shot is often severely punished by heather, whins, trees, rushes, fell grass or a sharp slope.

Talkin Tarn, as the club is often called, after the lake near the 9th and 10th holes, lies at about 400 feet with a hilly backcloth. The new

95

clubhouse looks out on about half-a-dozen holes. Facilities were much improved during 1985.

Some famous names are associated with the club. Syd Scott, second in the 1954 Open Championship, began his golf here at the age of fifteen before moving on to Carlisle and later Roehampton. He won two national championships in the 1950s. A past captain of the R and A, who has also made some impact in political life, Viscount Willie Whitelaw, is vice-president.

There are three practice grounds, which include a practice bunker and green and a putting green.

£ £12	**M** none	🚗 *the village of Brampton is some 8 miles east of Carlisle on the A69 Newcastle-Carlisle road. In Brampton take the B6413 signposted to Castle Carrock for about a mile*
🍴 *snacks, lunch and high tea daily*		
🎱 *snooker*		

CARLISLE 🌳

Aglionby, Carlisle, Cumbria CA4 8AG
☎ *Scotby (0228) 513303*

One of the finest parkland courses in the north of England, Carlisle is laid out in undulating country on a fairly sandy sub-soil which gives fine turf. There are attractive woods all around, mainly beech and pine, and a stream comes into play at several holes. My old friend, Ryder Cup player Syd Scott, was the professional here for a good many years.

The four short holes are all splendidly designed. The 2nd, 183 yards, is backed by a beech wood and guarded by bunkers at front and sides. The 4th, 149 yards, has a long plateau green with the stream at the right, and is well bunkered. The 13th, 147 yards, has a beautiful setting. You play over gorse and uneven ground between an avenue of trees to a two-tier green, well protected by bunkers and trees. At the last of the par 3s, the 17th, you play from an elevated tee with the green well below you, a stream running to the left and bunkers right.

Of the other holes, I particularly like the 11th, where you drive along a plateau, with a dip and lines of trees along the left, your second shot to the green having to be fired through a gap in these. The 15th is a very long par 5 at 563 yards but you ought to get some run off the downslopes. The 16th, a long par 4 of 440 yards, has a tree in mid-fairway and you must find your way through quite a narrow gap between it and an out of bounds.

The course measures 6,278 yards and four holes could be regarded as drive and pitch.

💷 £20	🎱 none	🎱 snooker

🍴 snacks, lunch, high teas and dinner daily	🚗 from the M6 leave at junction 43 along A69 for Newcastle and the course is about ½ mile or so further on the right

FAIRHAVEN

Lytham Hall Park, Ansdell, Lytham St Annes, Lancashire FY8 4JU
☎ *Lytham (0253) 736741*

Used for final qualifying rounds when the Open Championship is at Royal Lytham and St Annes and every other year for that top amateur event, the Lytham Trophy, Fairhaven is very well maintained and occupies a stretch of flat open country, both links and parkland in type. It's one of the courses of which it used to be said there were 365 bunkers, one for every day of the year. Well it seems at least possible that the course was originally planned that way, but the present-day fact of the matter is that there are 125. It's *where* you have bunkers, not how many that really counts.

Fairhaven, at 6,800 yards, is a long course. However, when there is a sandy subsoil, as here, there is usually run on the ball both summer and winter, though there are not a few clay-based inland courses where the ball will bounce and skip forever in a dry summer.

Par 5s should also help, because you really shouldn't need more than a well-struck drive, fairway wood and then a pitch to the green. Very unusually, Fairhaven has six par 5s, none more than a few paces over 500 yards. It was very interesting to me to see that Fairhaven recognizes my kind of thinking. All the par 5s are put into the 'big numbers' of the stroke index and, as I think it should be, the long or testing 3s and 4s occupy the lower index ratings.

Stroke index 1 at Fairhaven is the 4th. There's no doubt in my mind at all that the long second to a tight approach to the green is the most demanding shot to any of the greens. The 10th, rather similarly, asks you to be able to hit an iron or wood over 200 yards to a well-bunkered green, and the 17th, although just 161 yards, is well bunkered and worth its stroke index rating of 10.

Fairhaven is an extremely popular course, where one member, Les Dawson, is said to be one of the comedians who can be just as funny off stage as on, should you happen to be within earshot.

The practice ground is broad but a little short. There are good putting and approaching provisions.

97

💷 *£15*	🎱 *snooker*
🎫 *a handicap certificate*	🚗 *from M55, follow St Annes signs and thereafter for Lytham along Blackpool Road. The clubhouse is signposted*
🍴 *snacks, lunch and dinner daily except Monday*	

HILLSIDE

Hastings Road, Hillside, Southport, Merseyside PR8 2LU
☎ *Southport (0704) 67169*

Although Hillside is overshadowed in fame by its neighbour, Royal Birkdale, it is still a course of championship calibre. As recently as 1982 it saw what was to prove the last approach to golfing greatness by Tony Jacklin when he won the PGA Championship in a play-off with Bernhard Langer.

It had a remarkable finish. Jacklin went into the final round a couple of strokes behind Sam Torrance and Langer, having regained some of his putting confidence with the acquisition of a blade putter. That season the German was apt to twitch on the short putts and let Jacklin in when he four-putted the 16th. Tony took a one-stroke lead into the final hole. All looked over when Langer put his tee shot into a fairway bunker but he played a superb long bunker shot to the green and tied when Tony three-putted. However, on the first play-off hole, Jacklin's putting was hardly tested. He hit the green with his second, his ball coming to rest just a couple of feet from the hole.

Hillside has been the scene of many other events of high status, including the Amateur Championship, the Ladies' British Open, the Home Internationals and the Brabazon Trophy.

Although the club itself dates back to 1911, about half the course was laid out in 1967. The local council wanted part of the original lay-out for housing and by a happy chance this involved some of the poorer holes. Fred Hawtree was called in to design the substitutes, through mainly sandhill terrain. As a result, the first nine out and back to the clubhouse go through fairly flat country while the second are amongst the dunes. Some people consider this stretch the finest in Britain, Jack Nicklaus being among its admirers.

At the 1st you have to contend with the out-of-bounds railway on your left, and at the 4th you meet the first of Hillside's excellent par 3s. This one is almost 200 yards, with trees covering the left-hand side of the green. It's extremely difficult with the wind against you, but at least at the next par 3, the 7th, you would then find it helping from a tee cut into a sand dune.

The first nine end with an excellent dogleg left, where the drive must be long and well placed to give a good line into the green. The 10th, 147 yards, is the shortest of the par 3s. It's very attractive, with a massive sandhill at the rear and a narrow line through pine trees.

From the 11th tee, there's a panoramic view of superb golfing country, which includes Royal Birkdale and the sea. This hole, 508 yards, is an excellent par 5 which bends slightly leftwards through towering sandhills to either side. The 13th, stroke index 2, is a fine par 4 with more sandhills in play, as is the 15th. Here the main test is placement of the drive to the right half of the fairway to avoid an echelon of bunkers on the left.

All good courses ought to end with a grand climax. Hillside certainly does. The 16th, a 200-yarder, has a huge green, perhaps 50 yards from front to back, so pay careful attention to the flag position because your first thought could be three, even four, clubs out! The 17th is the longest hole on the course, a real par 5 of nearly 550 yards. There are bunkers right in your probable driving range to right and left and a big cross bunker further on. Careful choice of club is needed for the shot to the plateau green, because of the dip just short of it.

Statistically, Hillside is a very balanced course. Each nine is almost the same length, a little over 3,400 yards, and each contains a couple of par 3s and 5s while there's not one short par 4 on either half.

🅔 £30	✕ snacks, lunch and dinner daily
🅜 a handicap certificate or a letter of introduction from a club secretary	🚗 leave Southport along Waterloo Road and turn right into Hastings Road before Hillside Station, just after the entrance to Royal Birkdale

MANCHESTER

Hopwood Cottage, Rochdale Road, Middleton, Manchester M24 4LY
☎ Manchester (061) 643 2718

Manchester celebrated its centenary in 1982, which makes it one of the oldest English clubs, and its clubhouse is even older, dating from the early nineteenth century. In fact, there are records of golf in Manchester far earlier, for a Manchester Golf Club played over Kersal Moor, later built over, from 1818.

The club has over 240 acres to play with and this has been used to good effect: no two fairways are adjoining. The ground is undulating moorland in character, with broad fairways and large greens. A brook affects play on the 4th, 13th, 14th and 16th. There are open views in every direction, including sight of the Pennines.

Although the 5th is 'only' a short par 4, it's a good test of driving nerve. There's a carry over deep rough from the tee, with more of the same along the right and out of bounds to the left. If all is well, the shot to the green is straightforward but to the skyline, which can make judgement of distance difficult. The 11th is a slight dogleg left, again with an out of bounds on that side and sloping ground to take you into bunkers.

The 12th, 433 yards, is quite severe, with a ravine falling away to the right of the green, and the 13th, a shortish par 3, is almost a little island with ground falling away all about it.

The last three holes make a good finish. The 16th is a long par 3 played over a valley, while the 17th is quite a long par 4 with bunkering to catch a weak second shot. At the last, there is a good carry to the fairway which slopes away on either side.

Practice facilities are good, with two practice grounds, the smaller being a pitching area with a green and bunker.

£ *£18*

M *proof of golf club membership unless introduced by a member or playing on a society booking*

✕ *lunch daily, dinner daily until 9pm except Thursday, bookings only*

♟ *snooker*

🚗 *leave the M62 at junction 20 along A627(M) for Middleton. Turn left on to the A664 and the clubhouse is on the right after ½ mile*

NORTH MANCHESTER, THE NEW ⚑

Rhodes House, Manchester Old Road, Middleton, Lancashire M24 4FB
☎ *Manchester (061) 643 2941*

This is a very good course indeed, hilly and moorland (like a links at times) and 6,527 yards long with par and standard scratch both being 72. If you can play to your handicap on this course in a wintry easterly, you'll have done much more than just well.

Three lakes are important in the lay-out. Right away at the 1st you have to carry one, and at the 2nd, from the back tees, you must decide how much you dare bite off. Later, others come into play on the 10th and 11th, the 17th, if you're wild, and the last hole.

At the 2nd hole, after carrying the lake, out of bounds is a severe threat on the second shot to this 444-yard hole, just 10 yards through the back, if you go too far, and just 5 yards off the green on the left. An out of bounds, if it's tight, near the green when you're playing a long second shot (perhaps even one not so long) is far more daunting than merely trying not to stray left or right when playing to the fairway. At the 7th, a ravine has been known to annoy even moderate hitters. If you hit your drive more than about 190 yards, down you go. However, you really do need to be as far as you dare to shorten the second shot to a plateau green with a saddle-backed fairway not helping you and the hole 380 yards long.

The 10th is quite a long par 4 of 435 yards, where both lake and fairway bend from right to left. It sets much the same problem as David Thomas's design of the 18th at the Belfry. You can knock it right, quite a short distance safely, and then have not the slightest chance of reaching the green, or go for a longer carry with the attendant dangers.

The course ends with what would be a classic finish to any golf course, a par 3 which will eagerly allow you to ruin your card. It's 172 yards, and while you are thinking about being really sure to carry the lake you may forget about the bunkers right of the green and the trees on the left. What scenes would we witness at the climax of a St Andrews Open Championship, I wonder, if this relatively easy hole were changed so that the Valley of Sin in front of the green was a lake with a ribbon of green beyond, followed by a bottomless pit with the out of bounds many yards nearer on the right and a 'Here be Dragons' sign just to the left?

The club has a fine collection of golfing memorabilia.

£ £16, £14 per round

M membership of a golf club

✕ lunch, dinner and snacks except Tuesday

🚗 leave the M66 at Junction 18 for Middleton and the club is on the left after about ¼ mile

---

PLEASINGTON

Pleasington, Blackburn, Lancashire BB2 5JF
☎ *Blackburn (0254) 201028*

Pleasington is laid out in a rolling deer park, the reason for the club's crest, a stag's head. However, though parkland, it doesn't suffer the common disadvantage, in these days when so many people play winter golf as passionately as in the summer, of becoming soggy underfoot after prolonged rain. This is because the subsoil is red sand, which drains quickly. The sand is also the reason for a springy turf which always gives excellent fairway lies.

There is a great variety of trees, along with heather, gorse and bracken.

Pleasington hosts county events annually, was used for the English

Golf Union's Champion of Champions contest in 1978 and was chosen for the Open Championship regional qualifying in both 1980 and 1984, all proof of its high quality.

Although situated in a heavily industrialized area of the country, Pleasington is tucked away in the countryside, with moorland and hill views in all directions, and occasional views of the wooded gorge of the River Darwen.

There are few problems on the 1st hole, with an open drive and second shot but, at nearly 400 yards into the prevailing westerlies, it's no easy task sometimes to get up in two. The next two are also par 4s, but much shorter. The 4th, however, around 440 yards and doglegged left, is a stiff test. Any attempt to take a short cut will inevitably lead to bunker trouble at the angle, while anything less than a drive of good length means you'll find a bunker astride your line in to the green so it's best to play short of it.

After a sequence of six par 4s, the 7th hole is an attractive par 5. The drive must carry rough and a rise. After 230 yards or so, the ground falls away to the fairway below. This means that long hitters should be able to get up in two while others must make do with the delights of watching their second shots career along towards the open green.

The first nine, as a whole, is quite hilly, but the movement of the ground is more gentle on the second half. The 12th is an attractive par 4, flanked on the right by a wooded ravine and Hoghton Hill beyond. As the green slopes in that direction, you can decide whether to let your ball run in from the left, if you can avoid the bunkers, or carry full to the green, working it from right to left in the air.

The 15th is one of the most difficult holes, though little more than 350 yards. A drive over a dip is followed by a steep slope, so the flag position is likely to be blind. Make a mental note on the 14th tee. The wood and concealed pond on the right can cause problems.

For the remainder of your round, your severest test is likely to come with the second shot to the 17th green. The green is narrow and watched over by trees and bunkers to either side. The 18th is right under the clubhouse windows. Don't be nervous, those watching eyes are probably casual, not critical!

£ £20, £25 at weekends

M proof of golf club membership

✗ lunch daily except Monday, snacks daily, until 7pm, dinner daily except Sunday

🎱 snooker

🚗 either turn off the A677 Preston to Blackburn road for Pleasington village at Billinge End traffic lights or the A 674 Preston to Blackburn road at Feniscowles by the Fielden Arms

ROYAL BIRKDALE

Waterloo Road, Southport, Merseyside PR8 2LX
☎ *Southport (0704) 67920*

Although the club was founded in 1889, Birkdale was one of the last courses to be placed on the Open Championship rota. It achieved this in 1940. The event was cancelled because of the War so the first championship was delayed until 1954. The Australian Peter Thomson then won the first of his five championships, by a stroke from Bobby Locke, Dai Rees and Syd Scott.

But if Birkdale was long in arriving, it's now very firmly established indeed, and is one of the best venues in England and certainly the best of all as regards spectator viewing facilities. It was here that Palmer played what he still thinks the best short burst of golf of his entire career, three under par for the first six holes in the second round on his way to victory in 1961. This may sound nothing much out of the ordinary but it was played in a tremendous gale, when golf would certainly have been cancelled if the rules allowed it. On the present 16th, there's one of the only two plaques on our Open Championship courses; it marks a shot he played from a bad lie in his final round, which made his narrow victory over Dai Rees almost certain.

A few years later came Peter Thomson's finest hour. He had dominated the Open Championship for several years in the 1950s and had then faded from the limelight as Palmer, Player and Nicklaus became the names to reckon with. Thomson's four victories had been achieved when few of the great Americans were in the field and the Australian had been relatively unsuccessful when he had attempted the US Tour.

In 1965, however, his ability at managing a bouncy links in stiff winds showed Thomson at his best. After the first round he was six strokes behind one of his most threatening rivals, the American Tony Lema, but followed that with the best round of the second day, a 68. In the end, Christy O'Connor and Brian Huggett were his closest rivals, with Palmer, Nicklaus and Lema, the holder, far behind.

In 1971, came Lee Trevino's first win, with many unlikely putts holed, and five years later it was Johnny Miller's turn though the man who made even more headlines was Seve Ballesteros, known only at that time to those who followed golf very closely indeed. The Spaniard's little running shot between bunkers to the flag on the last hole when he needed to be down in two to tie for second place with Jack Nicklaus was one we still savour, together with prodigious recovery shots from wild country.

Despite the many difficulties, the field for the 1983 championship produced the lowest scoring ever in the Open. Several players could have won but in the end it was yet another Tom Watson year, sealed with a superb 2 iron shot at the 18th to give him victory by a single stroke.

This championship was also remarkable for a 64 in the first round from Craig Stadler, Denis Durnian's 28 for the first nine holes in his second round, and the 64 of Graham Marsh, who started his final round eight strokes behind leader Tom Watson but looked as if he just might win.

Birkdale is popular with the professionals because it's a 'fair' course. The fairways are relatively flat, so you don't get a drive which has split the fairway catching the side of a hump and bounding away to right or left into bunkers or rough. Stances are usually fairly flat and there are only a few blind shots from the tee or to the green. There is often the exhilaration of playing your tee shot from well above fairway level and then playing to greens clearly defined by sand dunes and willow scrub. The latter is often a source of severe trouble if you overclub. Looking at it all from the panoramic clubhouse windows it all looks, as Lee Trevino once said, 'like the moon'.

The course is laid out in three loops. The first is of nine holes; holes 10 to 14 return you to the clubhouse again before you tackle the last four holes.

From the championship tees Birkdale measures 6,986 yards, 6,703 from the back medal, and a less fierce 6,305 from the forward medal. I'll take the card closest to how the course was designed to be played, the back medal.

You begin with no easy par 4, a 450-yarder whereby you must thread your drive between a mound on the left and out of bounds and a ditch the other side. The next two are also quite long par 4s. A feature of the 2nd is a cross bunker some 30 yards short of the green, so a good drive is needed to lessen its threat for the second shot. At the 3rd the drive should be left, to give a good sight of the green.

These are followed by a par 3 from an elevated tee and the shortest par 4 on the course, 343 yards. This green is surrounded by seven bunkers.

So far, this is all just the same as the championship course, but the 6th is both different and one of Birkdale's most famous holes – a terror. The members play it as a par 5 of 476 yards for for professionals it's a par 5 of 490 yards. Confronting you on the tee is a bunkered ridge, a carry of some 250 yards with a gap of 20 yards or so on the left. Of course, you can play short, but there's then a long blind second shot with masses of rough to clear and greenside bunkers angled to catch a long second shot following a short drive. The hole is played along a narrow valley into the prevailing wind and the frontal slope to the armchair-type green means that you must carry your shot all the way. For players in the Open Championship it's the most difficult hole in the course and many fail to make par.

After a short par 3, the 8th, 414 yards, is another difficult hole, with a ditch most of the way along the right, a narrow fairway in the driving area and a raised green.

The first loop of nine ends with one of the course's eleven doglegs, this one to the right, with a blind drive followed by a plateau green.

At the 10th too long a drive can run out of fairway, the only one that's really undulating. There's plenty of the Birkdale willow scrub on the left if you try to cut across the angle of the dogleg. However, both this and the next hole are relatively short par 4s, but from the elevated 11th tee there's a good carry needed on the drive over rough and scrub into the prevailing wind.

There are two par 3s in the next three holes, both needing long irons from elevated tees. Between them the 13th is a clear birdie opportunity to professionals as a par 5 but a very stiff par 4 of 436 yards from the medal tees, with the green in a setting of sandhills and willow scrub. Nick Price, the South African who had featured so strongly in the 1982 Troon championship, took seven strokes to find the green in his first round in 1983 having sent successive shots into that scrub.

The 15th ranks with the 6th as a great hole. It's a true par 5 of 542 yards into the prevailing wind with bunkers galore – eleven in or along the fairway and a couple of greenside ones. In his very fine opening round in 1983 Tom Watson pushed his second shot well off line, missing all the bunkers, but plunged into willow scrub. Championship contenders are fortunate in having a good spectator following and Watson's ball was found, but not until many others had come to light first.

The 16th, 344 yards, is a dogleg to the right, needing a good carry from the tee with ten bunkers in play on the hole. The 17th is a par 5 where you can try to emulate Bill Rogers' feat in 1983. He holed out from, he said, 228 yards with a 1 iron for an albatross 2, the first recorded in the championship since 1972. On the other hand, Trevino took 7 here in his final round in 1971. His tee shot, which must be placed through dunes to either side, went left, as did Watson's at the same stage in 1983, though Tom got away with it. The green is long and narrow, with a background of willow scrub and dunes.

You may not find the last hole difficult, a par of 476 yards doglegging slightly right, but it's a very severe par 4 of 473 yards for championship contenders, with a long carry over the fairway bunker on the right and out of bounds quite near. However, your pitch to the green is faced by a narrow entrance between three greenside bunkers. The Open returns in 1991 and many hope that it will again host the Ryder Cup.

£ £48, £32 per round	**✕** snacks daily, dinner for visiting parties numbering at least twenty-one
M a handicap certificate	
✉ make a reservation and confirm in writing	🚗 halfway between Southport and Ainsdale on A565

ROYAL LIVERPOOL

Meols Drive, Hoylake, Wirral, Merseyside L47 4AL
☎ *Liverpool (051) 6323101*

Hoylake is historic golfing ground indeed. The club ranks as one of the oldest in England after Royal Blackheath, Royal North Devon, and Wimbledon. Of these, however, only Royal North Devon still continues to play over its original commonland (at Westward Ho!) so Hoylake is the second oldest course set out over its first site.

Of course, there have been many changes over the years since George Morris, a brother of Old Tom, came down from St Andrews to lay out nine holes in 1869. The first was after only two years when a further nine holes was added. The final drastic changes came in the 1920s when Harry Colt remodelled the course. As with so much of Colt's work, that was really that, except for a change made for the 1967 Open Championship which brought in a new 4th hole, with the par 5 3rd being played to its former green.

Hoylake has been closely associated with the Open. The event has been played here ten times and most of them have been memorable. 'This dear flat historic expanse of Hoylake,' as Bernard Darwin wrote, 'blown upon by mighty winds, has been a breeder of mighty champions.'

Some of the most famous 'mighty winds' blew in 1913. At that time only James Braid and Harry Vardon had taken the championship five times. J.H. Taylor, who had first won the title before either of these two, lagged one behind. Taylor got through the two qualifying rounds with nothing at all to spare but found his game when the championship proper began and in pleasant weather lay a stroke behind the leader, Ted Ray, after two rounds. Overnight, what Taylor calls 'a full-throated hurricane' blew up. All the tents and marquees were flattened and as Taylor waited his start time, he saw one of his rivals take 10 on the 1st hole, hardly able to keep his feet.

When Taylor's turn came, he needed three wooden club shots followed by a run-up shot to reach both the 1st and 3rd holes. In the deluge, he was almost immediately soaked to the skin and was able to grip the club only because a supporter had raided the club locker room and 'stolen' some half-a-dozen towels which he stored under his waterproof and produced for J.H. to dry his hands before each shot. Taylor played what he thought the finest round of his career, a 77 with nothing worse than a 5 on his card, and took a three-stroke lead into the last eighteen holes, eventually pulling away from the field to win by eight strokes.

The year 1924 saw the great American Walter Hagen's second championship. After reaching the turn in 41, he had to par his way home to win and did so. Six years later, came Bobby Jones's third win in four entries, when he secured the second leg of his Grand Slam. In the final

Royal Liverpool/N-W ENGLAND

round Jones was cruising to victory when he took five strokes to get down from about 20 yards on the 8th hole and had a stern battle thereafter before winning by two strokes. The next Hoylake champion, Alf Padgham, had to commit a little burglary along the way. On the final day, he had an early tee-off time but had left his clubs in the professional's shop overnight. He found it locked and broke in before going on to win his only championship.

The next Open Championship, in 1947, also coincided with my own first entry. I remember being awed by the splendid condition of the greens but the course was set up at its most difficult, the Irishman Fred Daly playing brilliantly to win.

There are only two more Open Championships in Hoylake's history, both highly memorable. In 1956 the Australian Peter Thomson became, and still is, the only man to win three in a row this century. Next came the 1967 championship when that magnificent striker of the ball, Roberto de Vicenzo, who had been trying to win and often come close since 1948, took the title by two strokes from Jack Nicklaus.

That was Hoylake's last Open. The event had become too big, not for the course, but for all the other facilities that are needed when vast crowds gather: space for the tented village, car parking, accommodation and all the rest. However, there have been changes in these areas in the last twenty years and it's not impossible that the championship will return one day, though the last few holes lack space for spectators.

Besides its Open Championship history, Hoylake has a remarkable number of firsts in other major events. The first Amateur Championship was played here in 1885 and then the first international match of all, between England and Scotland in 1902. In 1921 came the first match between the USA and Great Britain, and four years later the very first English Amateur Championship, won by a Royal Liverpool member, Froes Ellison.

All in all, Hoylake can claim to have hosted more major championships than anywhere else except St Andrews and Prestwick. Amongst its members have been two of the greatest English amateurs, John Ball and Harold Hilton. The medals they won are spendidly displayed in the clubhouse.

Viewed from that large Victorian building, the course itself can look dull because the foreground seems unrelentingly flat. Much of it is indeed just that, contributing to one of the difficulties of playing Hoylake: judgement of distance. Even visitors equipped with yardage charts have been known to waver in their deliberations over choice of club between a 7 iron and a 3 wood.

On the 1st tee you are immediately confronted with a typical Hoylake problem, the internal out of bounds. (It's not too difficult to knock one off the course at seventeen of the holes.) Here, the practice ground is out of bounds and threatens both your drive and second shot to this 428-yard hole. If you should happen to hit your drive into it, you may be comforted by the thought that one Victorian Open Champion, having done just that, said: 'Mon, it's like driving up a spout!' However, there's space to the left and you can play cautiously short with your second shot so that the round doesn't begin too disastrously.

Nothing too disastrous should befall you on the next few holes but

J.H. Taylor thought the 6th, 'The Briars', was 'one of the most difficult in the world of golf'. Played against the wind, he felt the slightest draw put you out of bounds on the left but going more safely right made a 5 at this par 4 very likely. The 7th, 'Dowie', may be the hole that a majority of players would be the most willing to accept as one over par 4 and move on to the next tee. It's 200 yards with what used to be an out-of-bounds bank just to the left of the green, a frightener in a wind from the right.

Another difficult hole is the 12th, about 400 yards, doglegged to the left with heavy bunkering at the angle. The green is difficult to find, narrow and raised. Jones thought the Hoylake finish the most testing in championship golf, about 2,300 yards from the 14th to the 18th. At the 16th, the out-of-bounds practice field comes very much into play at the angle of a right-hand dogleg. Long hitters trying to get home in two at this 533-yard hole have to take the risk of playing over the corner, which is somewhat daunting if there's a stiff breeze from the left. At the 17th, an out-of-bounds road lies very close to the right of the green. However, many have bounced back into play from fence posts, walls or parked cars! The 18th isn't a difficult finishing hole but it's well bunkered.

£ £25

M a handicap certificate or letter of introduction from your home club

✕ snacks daily, lunch weekends only, dinner only for visiting parties of over twenty in number

🚗 from the M6 take the M56 for Birkenhead and then M53, leaving for West Kirby/Hoylake at Junction 2 and follow Hoylake signs along A553 until reaching the clubhouse on right

---

ROYAL LYTHAM AND ST ANNES

Links Gate, Lytham St Annes, Lancashire FY8 3LQ
☎ *St Annes (0253) 724206*

Royal Lytham has been an Open Championship course since 1926, the year when Bobby Jones produced a famous long iron shot from a sandy lie on the 17th in his final round, causing his playing partner, Al Watrous, to three-putt from shock. Jones went on to win his first of three Open Championships. He presented the iron to the club. When the event returned to the course in 1952, the South African Bobby Locke won his third victory in four years. There was an even greater feat in 1958, when the Australian Peter Thomson won his fourth title in five years, after a thirty-six hole play-off with David Thomas.

Five years later Bob Charles won, and is still both the only left-hander and the only New Zealander to have done so. The last four Open Championships at Lytham have all been just as noteworthy. The most popular victories in recent years took place here, Tony Jacklin's in 1969 and Seve Ballesteros' two triumphs in 1979 and 1988. In between, Gary Player mastered difficult conditions to win the first year that the 1.68 ball was compulsory in 1974.

Besides this greatest of all golfing events, Lytham has also seen the Ryder Cup, the Amateur Championship, the Curtis and Vagliano Cups, the Dunlop Masters and many other leading events, both professional and amateur.

Although Royal Lytham is undeniably a links course, water and fertilizer over the years have changed its character quite a lot, making it more like an inland course than it was in Jones's day. The far end is natural linksland, with large sandhills but the course is generally flat and some of the bumps are man-made.

The 1st is a par 3, not generally unusual but unique amongst our Open Championship courses. The green is surrounded by bunkers and a 4 is likely. Peter Oosterhuis began here with a 4 when chasing Gary Player in 1974, against the South African's 2, and that more or less was that.

The next two are par 4s, both well over 400 yards with the railway close along the right. Along the left are bunkers, and the approach to the green is more difficult from this side.

At the 4th there's a carry from the tee over low hills and a tightly bunkered green, but it's the easiest hole so far. After a long iron par 3, there may be birdie chances on the next two holes, both par 5s of 486 and 551 yards. On the 6th a draw is the best shape of tee shot. In his final round in 1979 Seve Ballesteros hit a huge hook some 90 yards off line. Neither he nor his caddie had much idea what club to use next here; the Spaniard eventually sent his ball some 50 yards through the green but got his par easily enough.

The 8th is one of the most interesting holes on the course, a par 4 of 394 yards. It's close by the railway again and the second shot is to a high green. You have to risk going through the back because anything a touch short will fall away into bunkers. There's also a swale short of the green that's invisible as you play your second.

The 9th takes you to the furthest part of the course, where you must carry your tee shot all the way to this 162-yard hole, which is tightly bunkered. The hole is rather spoilt by housing close by, which is quite a feature of golf at Lytham and, with so much development on either side, gives a claustrophobic feel to the course.

It's usually reckoned that a champion must make a good score on the first nine because of the very stern finish at Lytham. The first few holes on the second nine, however, are not too demanding. The 10th is only 334 yards but even so it gave Ballesteros considerable trouble in 1979. In his last round he wasn't on after three strokes and came close to taking 6. The 13th is another short 4, this time 339 yards. Ballesteros used an iron from the tee in his first three rounds but gave his ball a furious lash with the driver, trying to make the green, in his last. His carry this time was almost 300 yards but he caught a mound short and right of the green;

nevertheless he got down in two more, a birdie that made his victory likely.

It is from the 14th that the going gets tough, providing what many people think is the hardest finish on our Open Championship courses, especially when the wind's against, as it usually is.

The 14th is a long par 4 of 445 yards and the 15th 20 yards or so longer. Here you'll need a long drive and even then you'll probably only have sight of the top of the flag. At the 16th, much shorter at 356 yards, you normally try to be along the left of the fairway with your drive over sandhills. It was here that Seve Ballesteros went right in 1979 because, he claims, of the flag position on the last day. He was 60 yards right of the fairway in the BBC car park, from where he hit a sand wedge to 18 to 20 feet and then holed the putt.

The 17th is a 413-yard flat dogleg to the left where Jones made that remarkable shot. Al Watrous commented: 'There goes $100,000.' (He wasn't thinking of the first prize, which would have been about £50, but of the large sums of money that the prestige of winning a championship lead to.) Here, years later, Gary Player missed the green by about 20 yards left, finishing up in very deep rough. He had a frantic scramble to find the ball, and although lots of people had seen exactly where it had burrowed in, as the minutes passed it refused to come to light.

In the end all was well, but Player added a final drama on the 18th by sending his second shot through the green and against the angle of the clubhouse. He must be the only champion to have used a putter left-handed for his last shot to a green! (Except, perhaps, Bob Charles!)

The main problem at the 18th is the diagonal line of bunkers in the left of the fairway. Leopoldo Ruiz, Christy O'Connor and Eric Brown came to grief here in the 1958 championship when a 4 would have given any of them victory or a play-off, while Peter Thomson and David Thomas survived the challenge.

In Jacklin's year he came to this hole needing a par for certain victory over his playing partner Bob Charles. He clinched it with a huge straight drive well beyond all the trouble, becoming the only British player to win the Open between the victories of Max Faulkner in 1951 and Sandy Lyle in 1985.

There is also a nine-hole course which is great fun.

£ £45, £30 per round

M a letter of introduction from your club

🏠 dormy house with eight single rooms and four twin-bedded for gentlemen only; cost £60 per night (half board) plus two rounds of golf

✕ snacks, lunch and dinner daily

🚗 1 mile from the centre of St Annes, away from Blackpool

SILLOTH-ON-SOLWAY ≋⌐

Silloth-on-Solway, Cumbria CA5 4AT
☎ *Silloth (069 73) 31304*

Silloth was a product of what may now seem a strange period when railways laid out golf courses in order to encourage the public to use their trains to get to them. In this case the year was 1892 and the railway company was the North British. It has given its name to the famous Silloth turf and also to a handicapping system devised at the club which gives a pair with a low handicap very few strokes indeed.

The club first came into the public eye through the deeds of Miss Cecil Leitch. She was one of five sisters, Edith, Chris, May and Peg, who were all excellent players and Cecil herself became the greatest woman player of her day. On her first championship appearance at St Andrews in 1908 she reached the semi-finals of the British Ladies' and went on to win the event four times, the French Championship five times and the
. Canadian once. In that event in 1921 she went in to lunch after the first 18 holes of the final fourteen up and then took the first three holes in the afternoon. That 17 and 15 victory is almost certainly a record margin for a major national championship.

It was fitting that when the British Ladies' Championship came to Silloth in 1976 Cecil Leitch was there to present the trophy to Cathy Panton. She died the following year.

Late in life she remembered Silloth golf in the following words:

'Those then were the conditions under which we played our golf, for many years, on an ideal links and with perfect seaside turf on the undulating fairways, and all natural hazards and difficulties – blown sand, bent, heather, whins and that finest tutor of all – a sea breeze which could at times develop into a south-west gale.'

Although Silloth, at 6,343 yards is neither long nor short, it's unusual in that all the par 5s are relatively short (486 yards is the longest) and only one of the par 4s is more than 400 yards and even that, the 7th, is only 408 yards. Moreover, the longest par 3 is only 192 yards.

The 1st hole is quite a testing par 4 of 380 yards, usually into a westerly, but the green, blind, isn't particularly difficult to find with a mid-iron. However, sandhills, heather and gorse are a threat to the drive, as they are on many of the holes. The 3rd and 4th are interesting par 4s. At the 3rd, 357 yards, the drive is from an elevated tee to a fairway with sand and heather to either side, and the second shot to a plateau green with a big drop to the left needs great accuracy. At the 4th there's a carry of some 150 yards over a chasm which is semi-blind. The second is to an island green with drops either side. The 5th, 486 yards, is the first par 5, again with a fair carry to reach the fairway, which is along the seashore. In still air it's not too difficult to reach in two but the fairway is narrow and the beach is out of bounds.

From the 8th tee there are views of the Galloway hills, the Solway Firth and the Lake District. The hole plays through a valley and the green is well bunkered. The 9th, just 127 yards, is perhaps the best of the four par 3s. The tee shot is played from a high tee down to a green guarded by six pot bunkers. It should be easy, but...

The second nine begins with what ought to be a very easy par 4 of only 308 yards, and indeed it's not an enormous hit if you cut across the almost right-angled dogleg to reach the green – but it'll very likely be a lost ball if you fail in the attempt. With an out-of-bounds facing the tee, it's probably best to take a 3 iron, with correct placement in mind, for you'll still have only a pitch left. The green is undulating and normally faster than the rest.

The 13th, 482 yards, isn't a long par 5 but is perhaps the best hole on the course. It's even been called the best hole in the North of England. After the tee shot, you play through quite a narrow gap in heather-covered hills and then along a hog's back fairway to the green, which is high up on a ridge with steep banks falling away either side. If you are thinking in terms of getting up in two, your second shot must be in the centre of the bank leading to the green or your ball will swing away.

Overall, the main problems at Silloth are narrow fairways, long carries if the wind's against on your tee shot, small greens and severe penalties for any shots off-line. The steady rather than spectacular driver should score well.

£ £14	M none	🎱 snooker

✗ snacks daily, lunch and dinner daily except Monday

🏨 two hotels in Silloth provide golf package terms

🚗 leave the M6 for Silloth via the A596 and turn off for Silloth at Wigton

---

SOUTHPORT AND AINSDALE

Bradshaw's Lane, Ainsdale, Southport, Merseyside PR8 3LG
☎ Southport (0704) 78092

S and A, as it's usually called, is more or less in the middle of what most players would agree is the finest stretch of golfing country in England, from Southport to Blundellsands. Hillside and Royal Birkdale are very near neighbours.

The Ryder Cup has twice been played here, in 1933 and 1937, the first of these providing a still famous finish when Syd Easterbrook holed a testing putt to beat Densmore Shute and win the Cup. It is now used for the final qualifying when the Open Championship comes to Royal Birkdale; other important events include the Ladies' British Open, the British Youths' and the old Dunlop Tournament.

The club itself began early this century as a nine-hole course but was redesigned by James Braid in the 1920s. Of course there have been changes over the years, and as recently at 1983 my colleague David Thomas redesigned the 13th green.

S and A is fairly similar to Royal Birkdale in some ways. It shares, for instance, the same flat fairways, except for the 18th, which is full of humps and bumps. Like Birkdale, many fairways wind through the dunes with a few carries to make over them. As at Hillside the railway can affect play.

Like Royal Lytham, you start off with a testing par 3. In the afternoon round of the 1937 Ryder Cup, all four of our foursomes pairings lost the hole, most being bunkered at the left front of the green. Here it's always better to play to be up. Much the same is true of the 3rd. Here you play from a high tee up in a ridge over another to the flat ground beyond. For your second shot you have to find a green set in a hollow. If you're short, a humped-back rise in front of the green will throw your ball off.

The 5th is the hole that usually causes difficulty for most. It's nearly 450 yards and the green has a narrow entrance, being tightly bunkered. At the 6th the safe line for your drive is through the 'gap' which gives the hole its name. However, you can shorten the hole by playing right, cutting off some of the dogleg. This is a tee shot which asks you to decide what you're capable of. At the 7th, not a particularly long par 5 at about 480 yards, you drive between ridges but then play your second over another. This is just one of the 'old-fashioned' carries that are such a feature of S and A. The best of the par 3s is the 13th, not long at just over 150 yards but played between two clumps of trees to a raised green that's rather pear-shaped. This is a hole where you must not over-club when trying to make sure of being up, because there's a pond in wait at the back of the green.

The 16th is S and A's most famous hole, 'Gumbley's', a par 5 of 520 yards. The railway from Liverpool is all along the right. Your tee shot should be placed left and you can then go for the rip-roaring carry over the sandy ridge, faced with formidable sleepers, that gives the hole its name. If you fail, your ball tumbles down into two bunkers at the foot.

The finish is a good one. The 17th is a long par 4, again with the railway along the right, and the last gives you a final choice for your drive. A good one straight over the dunes will leave a relatively easy shot to the green but it's certainly safer to play right of the dunes.

£ £30

✕ snacks, lunch and dinner daily

M a handicap certificate

🚗 3 miles south of Southport on the A565 Liverpool road

WEST LANCASHIRE

Hall Road West, Blundellsands, Liverpool, Merseyside
L23 8S2
☎ *Liverpool (051) 924 1076*

West Lancashire was one of the twenty-four original subscribers in 1886 for the Amateur Championship trophy, which had been won by a member, Alan MacFie, in its first year, 1885, some indication of the age of the club. It was, in fact, founded in 1873 and was a pioneer of golf on the Lancashire coast, followed by Formby, Hesketh and Birkdale.

Naturally, there've been many changes to the course over the years, which in its present form dates back to 1962 when the new clubhouse was opened. This recent course was a completely new design entirely on the seaward side of the railway between Southport and Liverpool, making use of the previous ladies' course and some of the men's holes.

West Lancashire is a links course with most of the fairways separated by sandhills. Although there is one small wood, whins, wild brambles and scrub willow are the main hazards. It has championship status, having been used for the 1981 British Youths' Championship and final qualifying for the Open in 1976 and 1983, when the event was played at Royal Birkdale. Like so many links courses, when the wind is really up and the ground hard and bouncy it can be almost impossible to play, but it has the advantage that winter play on the well-drained fairways is seldom interrupted.

Very much the same length for both nines, the 6,756 yards of West Lancashire are well balanced and there are the conventional numbers of four par 5s and four par 3s, equally distributed between the halves. There are six par 4s of 400 yards and up. The par 3s are especially fine and are set at differing angles to whatever the wind direction may happen to be.

The first four holes run fairly close to the Irish Sea, the pick of them being the 4th, a 412-yard dogleg right. Here you must keep to the right of the out-of-bounds fence but also avoid a large hollow on the right of the fairway. The ideal line is to the left half of the fairway, to ease the approach to the green, a narrow one guarded by bunkers both front and right.

The 7th, a sharp dogleg right of 370 yards, has been holed in one from the forward tees, a feat which was regarded as the longest by the *Guinness Book of Records* for a while. The 12th is the best of the par 3s, 178 yards to an elevated green with willow scrub on the sandhills along the right, with two deep bunkers to fly in the upslope which leads to it.

The 14th is a very demanding par 4 of 440 yards. The drive is blind, over scrub and hollows to a fairway which bends right around a tree-covered hillside. Unless you get a good one away, your second shot usually has to be played over these trees to a table green set into the hillside.

The next, a little shorter at 391 yards, is no less testing, particularly on the tee shot. There are trees and a pond on the right to avoid and the railway presses in from the left, narrowing the target area the further you go. Club selection is decisive on the second shot, for the green slopes quite sharply from back to front.

The last, 'Cuckoo Hill', played from a high tee gives the opportunity for a last look round, and a chance to drive flat out, as the fairway is wide. The carry is quite a long one and there are bunkers and a pond to avoid on the right.

Any courses which have Open Championship venues not too far away tend to be overlooked. West Lancashire shouldn't be.

£ £20

M membership of a golf club and a handicap certificate

✗ snacks daily, lunch and dinner daily except Monday

🎱 snooker

✉ need to book in advance

🚗 from Crosby take Manor Road and follow signs for Waterloo RUFC to traffic island at St Michael's Road. Turn left and then right at next junction along Dowhills Road at St Michael's Church. After 1/4 mile turn left into Hall Road West, over the railway crossing

NORTH-EAST ENGLAND

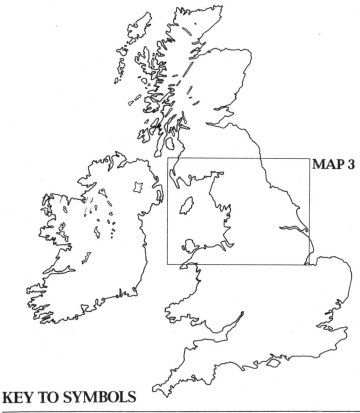

MAP 3

KEY TO SYMBOLS

 PARKLAND

LINKS

MOORLAND

HEATHLAND

DOWNLAND

UPLAND

☎ TELEPHONE

⊠ NEED TO BOOK
IN ADVANCE

£ APPROXIMATE
COURSE FEE

M MEMBERSHIP
REQUIREMENTS
FOR VISITORS

✗ CATERING PROVIDED

🏨 ACCOMMODATION
PROVIDED

Ⓛ RESTRICTIONS ON
LADIES AND/OR
YOUTHS

OTHER SPORTING
FACILITIES

🚗 DIRECTIONS

ALWOODLEY   ⛳

Wigton Lane, Alwoodley, Leeds, West Yorkshire LS17 8SA
☎ *Leeds (0532) 681680*

For about ten years I was just down the road from Alwoodley, while based at Moor Allerton, two courses that are part of a great stretch of golfing country. When, much earlier, I did my National Service, I used to cherish my visits to play here. It's still one of my favourite places, old-fashioned and not a bit the worse for that. In my youth, they used to have a liveried butler.

It's a particularly good choice for a winter visit for the soil is light and sandy and never gets really wet underfoot. Even so, perhaps it looks its best when the gorse is in full bloom, while there's also birch, pine and oak to form a backdrop to the undulating fairways.

The course was originally laid out by Dr Alister Mackenzie, who was the club's first secretary. As an architect he proved to be no amateur, and was later to leave his greatest golfing monument in the Augusta National, home of the US Masters, on which he worked with Bobby Jones and also Cypress Point and Royal Melbourne.

It's certainly a course fit for tournaments, though crowd control would be difficult at times. However, I don't really think the members would really want their club disturbed. This is not as uncommon an attitude as some might think – I can think of several other examples.

However, amateur events are another matter. Alwoodley has played host to Yorkshire championships, the English Ladies in 1967 and the British Ladies in 1971.

The clubhouse, with a verandah for sitting out on warm summer evenings (yes, you southerners, they do have them in Yorkshire), has a particularly fine atmosphere. From there you have open views of the 1st and 18th and parts of the 2nd and 17th. The setting is attractive, the curve of the clubhouse being set into a semi-circular stand of trees with the last green in front.

Inside, it's all very traditional, no doubt helped by the fact that club staff always seem to stay on until retirement. In seventy-seven years they have had just four stewards, one couple accounting for forty-one years. Out of doors the story is much the same – just five greenkeepers and five professionals. The membership used to be rather restricted to the upper echelons of the Yorkshire professions but that's no longer true.

The course begins with a flat opening hole, followed by a short par 4, with a carry of a hundred yards or so over gorse and heather. Such a feature is typical of Alwoodley. There is a rather longer similar carry at the 5th and the drive must be very well placed because the fairway slopes severely right. If you keep out of the rough, there's still a difficult carry over a chain of bunkers to make the green.

The 8th is a famous hole, a long par 5, doglegging left, where you must carry a chain of cross bunkers with your second. However, a tiger can try to skirt Wigton Cover, out of bounds on the left, and may then hope to get home in two. Henry Longhurst used to reckon it one of the finest holes in the country.

The 11th is another particularly good hole, this time a par 3. It has an island green surrounded by bunkers, gorse, trees and rather impenetrable undergrowth. If, with a sigh of relief, you make the green, there are still subtle slopes to contend with.

The 13th is another difficult hole, just under 400 yards but usually into the prevailing wind. There's a chain of bunkers in wait if you let your drive get away to the right and more encircle the green for what is likely to be quite a long second shot. The 15th is another fine par 4 which doglegs right along Wigton Cover. Again, it's likely to play into the wind and there's a large cross bunker to catch a weak second shot.

The 17th is another very testing driving hole, played over a road to a fairway only 25 yards wide at one point. There's a field out of bounds on the left and bunkers for those playing 'safely' right. If you've hit a good one, now may be the time to pause a while to take in some of the magnificent views of Wharfedale.

£ £30	**M** none
✕ snacks daily, lunch and dinner by prior arrangement	

🚗 just off the A61 Leeds to Harrogate road. Turn right at Alwoodley traffic lights 5 miles north of Leeds at the end of the dual carriageway into Wigton Lane. It's 100 yards from the main road

BARNARD CASTLE

Harmire Road, Barnard Castle, County Durham DL12 8QN

☎ Teesdale (0833) 38355

This course is set in most attractive surroundings with views of the hills which overlook upper Teesdale, Swaledale and Weardale. It is fairly undulating and parkland in type, though the turf tends towards moorland – an advantage when this occurs in such a setting.

The most notable features of the course, however, are the meandering streams which come into play at no fewer than twelve of the holes. The course is fairly exposed and strong westerly winds are a frequent test of control.

Barnard Castle is by no means a conventionally balanced course. There are five par 5s, four of these coming on the first nine and the same number of par 3s, four of them on the second half (three indeed on the last four holes). This means, obviously, a big discrepancy in yardage for the two nines. The first is 3,239 yards, par 38, and the inward 2,599, par 33. Does this matter? I think not, except perhaps for the barrage of par 3s at the end.

What counts far more on a golf course is the quality of individual holes and these are varied, with those streams so often a hazard. Three of the par 5s on the first nine, the 2nd, 5th and 9th, play long, because usually the wind is dead against you and this means the 9th in particular, 535 yards, often needs a good deal more than a short pitch to get on in three.

On the second nine, streams strengthen the interest of the 13th, 14th and 17th, the last being the best. Here you can attempt to go left with your drive over a stream while stopping short of a road and out of bounds fence or drive more safely to the right, which will then leave you with that stream very much in play for your second shot instead.

€ £12   **M** none

✕ snacks daily, lunch and dinner daily except Monday

🚗 on the northern boundary of the town on the B6278 for Eggleston

---

BEAMISH PARK   ♣♟

Stanley, County Durham DH9 0RH
☎ Durham (0385) 701133

Golf at Beamish goes back to 1909, but the present course dates from the years after the Second World War when a twelve-hole course was laid out in the deer park of Beamish Hall, once the home of the Shafto family. Henry Cotton was partly responsible for the design.

There have been other changes since. One very unfortunate one was forced on the club. The 1st hole used to be a long par 3 that was a nerve-tingler for the mid-handicap golfer. While players in the low single figures took out a long iron, even a wood, to carry to the green, the less talented were more apt to take out a 5 or 6 iron, the reason being that an out-of-bounds wall hugs both the approach and green on the right. Anything wafted into the air was swept away by the prevailing westerlies. Eventually, the car park to the neighbouring Beamish Open Air Museum had received too many golf balls – 12,000 were collected as evidence of the danger. The County Council asked for changes in the course lay-out; the club resisted. In the end it became apparent that a long-drawn-out legal battle, which might have gone all the way to the

House of Lords, would cost sums that the rates could afford more easily than the club...

So nowadays the 1st hole, a par 5, should make for a comfortable start, though there's a carry over a walled stream if your drive has been feeble, and the green is a narrow target. This stream is again a hazard at the 2nd, a formidable carry if the wind is in your face, and wild shots to the left or right make finding the green nearly impossible. Otherwise, the second shot played to a two-tiered green sliced out of the top of a hillside just asks that you know how to play the shot required on the day.

The 3rd is a long par 3, one of those 3s played over a piece of flat land that is just there to get you to the next tee.

There follows one of the most difficult long 4s in the region. The tee shot is up a very slight rise but is almost always into the prevailing wind. A long drive, which may well be flattered by falling ground after the rise, is essential if you are to get home in two, for your second shot must carry a depression at least 50 feet deep. Land a couple of feet short, and down you'll trundle to the bottom. There are no bunkers on this hole and no need of them.

The 7th is another classic par 4, but is very different. Here the problem is not length with your tee shot, but placement. Your line should be as near the copse of tall trees to your right as you dare. That bit correctly negotiated, you'll have just a short iron to the green. Stray left from the tee, however, and some very tall trees to the left of the green come increasingly into play. If you carry them, your approach from that angle will usually follow the run of the ground into a bunker on the right of the green.

The 12th is played a little downhill with the aid of the prevailing wind, which is as well as it's 475 yards with two ponds along the line of the tee shot. The first will catch a poor drive, the second one that's too ambitious.

The same ponds come into play for anything hit left again on the 14th, a 400-yard par 4 which is uphill all the way into the prevailing wind to an elevated green. Unless the ground is running, you must carry your second shot all the way.

The 15th was Cotton's favourite hole, a frightener at a crisis in a match, or if you've a good strokeplay card. The tee is very elevated and the prospect pleasing but the landing area is extremely narrow, not much more than 20 yards. To the right there are trees and a steep rough bank with more high trees ahead, which make a successful shot to the green very unlikely. There's more space left but, again, two tall trees threaten your second. Even from the ideal part of the fairway, an overhanging bough calls for judgement of whether to go over or under, and you must pitch short and right of the green, or see your ball run away, either into a well-placed bunker or difficult broken ground.

My final choice is the 17th, an excellent par 5, where you'll usually have a little help from the wind. A stream crosses the fairway, which lays down a challenge to long hitters expecting to be able to get home in two. Can I carry it or hope to skip over? A lateral water hazard, immediately followed by out of bounds, runs along the left from tee to green, just a few yards off the fairway. Stray too far right, and a large tree just short of the green, which is always a narrow target, asks for good judgement of both height and length of shot.

£ £11

M a certificate of handicap

✕ snacks and lunch daily, dinner daily except Sunday and Monday

🚗 leave the A1 midway between Durham and Newcastle for Chester-le-Street and follow Stanley signs, turning right for Beamish Museum

---

BISHOP AUCKLAND

High Plains, Durham Road, Bishop Auckland, County Durham DL14 8DL

☎ Bishop Auckland (0388) 602198 or 663648

This very pleasant parkland course with particularly good greens is laid out on land belonging to the Church of England. The Bishop of Durham's Palace can indeed be seen from the course. What may seem an oddity of the club's lease is that the course must be closed on Good Friday and Christmas Day.

After a short and very easy opening par 4 there's the unusual feature of three par 5s in a row. The first is the longest, over 550 yards, but it's slightly downhill. If you get a couple of good woods away, you should have only a short pitch left, but it can be difficult to judge the strength. The next hole, though about 30 yards shorter, plays every bit as long as you return the way you came, uphill this time and often into the wind with a copse to avoid on the right. The last of this trio of par 5s, though again over 520 yards, is the easiest, and if you drive well you have a chance for the green with your second.

The 7th always makes an impact on visitors. It's about 140 yards, from an elevated tee with the green well below. Once, if you missed the green your ball was likely to get lost in deep rough but nowadays you'll probably find a bunker instead. Club selection for a downhill iron shot is always difficult, and there's trouble in the shape of rough and bushes through the back if you're too strong and other problems if you underestimate this distance.

There are two more par 5s on the course, the 9th a sweeping uphill dogleg where you are often left with a difficult pitch over a hump to the green, and the 11th, a birdie opportunity if you avoid the several fairway bunkers.

This is followed by perhaps the two most difficult holes on the course. The 12th is a par 3 of just over 220 yards with out of bounds close on the right all the way from tee to green. If you catch one of the humps near the green you may also squirt away out of bounds. In any case, missing the green will leave you a very difficult little shot to get near the hole. The 13th is quite a long par 4 and gives you an option with your drive: you can

121

shorten the slight dogleg left if you can carry a large tree about 180 yards from the tee or lengthen the hole by playing safely right. This will make for a long second shot, threatened all the way to the green by out of bounds close up on the right. Two more par 4s follow, which require firm hitting, but the course relents at the end with three fairly short par 4s, the last only a little more than par 3 distance.

E *£16, £13 per round*

M *evidence of golf club membership*

X *snacks daily, lunch and dinner daily except Monday*

🚗 *¼ mile outside town on main road for Durham*

BRANCEPETH CASTLE 🏌

Brancepath, Durham, County Durham DH7 8EA
☎ *Durham (0385) 780075*

Brancepeth is one of those golfing gems which are very well known, but only locally. However, it's been recognized as of championship standard for amateur golf, in recent years having hosted the British Ladies' Championship, the English Ladies' and the English Men's County Teams event.

Driving is at a premium. There is often an ideal line to take, and length is usually necessary to make the shot to the green less daunting. An extremely precise shot, better played with a short or medium iron, is demanded at many holes. Ravines affect play at eight holes, sometimes with very fair carry needed, and if you should happen to suffer a fit of topping ... no, it doesn't bear thinking about!

The start is kindly, with a broad fairway and plenty of semi-rough to aim at down the right but trouble in the form of trees and bushes to the left. There follows a slightly downhill pitch which always seems difficult to get close to the hole. At the 2nd, you enter your first ravine, playing a mid to long iron from one side to a shelf-like green cut into the opposite slope. If you miss, you're in tangled rough, and a really poor shot finds the stream at the bottom. Not many players will make a 3 with the aid of a precise little pitch.

Two excellent par 4s come next. At the 3rd hole you must avoid a stand of trees to the right, while there is a hidden bunker the other side, very effective at gathering the ball. As near the trees as you dare is probably the best line. However good your tee shot, you are likely to need a long second shot to this 450-yard hole into the prevailing wind. The 4th plays two or three clubs shorter but the shot into the green is perhaps the most demanding on the course. There's a wide, grassy gully just before the short, steep rise up to the green; the ground falls away sharply to the left, while a tree impedes the line in from a drive too far right.

If your card is tidy so far, Brancepeth now relents, but only a little, with a long par 3 followed by a straightforward but long par 5, well bunkered at each stage of the hole. At the 7th, you play towards the castle and a plateau green, which is heavily bunkered.

The 8th is an excellent driving hole with a carry over a ravine, which slants further away from the tee the further left you go. However, if you decide on the shorter carry to the right, your second shot is much longer and the slopes around the green will probably shrug your ball away.

The 9th is a famous hole, which Bernard Darwin once described as of 'terrifying grandeur'. At 215 yards, most people will be playing a wood over a ravine. The carry is not particularly long to clear this but the penalty for failure is always another ball out of the golf bag. The green itself is a long shelf cut into a hill slope so, once again, if you miss there'll be great difficulty in saving your par. The church and castle are close by.

Having crossed the ravine in one direction, you now go back again for another quite long par 3 of around 190 yards, again from an elevated tee but this time to a well-bunkered plateau green. Thereafter, there are perhaps easier opportunities for scoring well over the last eight holes but some knotty problems too. At the 13th, for instance, your drive must be held to the right as you will almost inevitably be caught by greenside bunkering when coming in from the other side. The 14th is an excellent short par 4 to quite a narrow fairway, while the 16th, only just a par 5, gives you a very fair chance of getting home in two – if you can place your drive so that you are not blocked out by trees. The last hole is a bit of a monster but the tee shot is exhilarating, played from an elevated tee over a ravine to quite a steep upslope. The second shot will be blind unless you have hit a long drive, which is a pity, because for nearly all the time Brancepeth presents its problems fair and square.

Harry Colt designed the course in the 1920s, in what was once Lord Boyne's deer park at Brancepeth Castle. The general character of the course is parkland with more than just a suggestion of moorland, particularly in the spring of the turf. Brancepeth is on the edge of the highly populated Newcastle and Durham region but you'd never know it, and the village is very pretty. The godfather of one of my children, Leonard Crawley, was a member here and a stand of trees at the 16th is named after him. He used to drive to the 'wrong' side of them, in the rough, to shorten the line to the green.

The clubhouse, converted from former coaching houses and stables is very attractive and chintzy inside.

£ £15

M none

✗ lunch daily except Monday, dinner is provided for visiting parties

🚗 5½ miles from Durham off the A690 Crook road. Turn left at the village cross roads and left again at the castle gates.

CLEVELAND

Queen Street, Redcar, Cleveland TS10 1BT
☎ *Redcar (0642) 483693*

Here I'm talking about the only true links in Yorkshire. Yes, I know, the address above says 'Cleveland', but it is one of those counties that have never really caught on. Like cricket, golf has ignored local government re-organisation so Cleveland Golf Club, Yorkshire, it is.

Golf began here as a form of hockey when a few people used to gather at Coatham sandbanks to knock a ball about. Considering the terrain they were playing over, it was, in fact, obviously something closer to golf. Then a certain Captain Williams of the Coast Guard turned up one day with a cleek and a guttie ball.

This was all very much more fun and soon others followed suit. However, the farmer whose land they were playing on began to raise objections. He wasn't anti-golf; he just wanted play to be properly organized and suggested a club should be formed. A meeting of interested parties quickly followed at the Lobster Inn and the first golf club in Yorkshire was duly set up in 1887.

Today the course is a basically flat links with sand dunes, measuring just over 6,700 yards, with six par 4s over 400 yards. I'm pleased to see that these occupy most of the low numbers in the stroke index.

You begin with a par 4 of medium difficulty and then cross over the road to the 2nd tee. This is elevated and gives you a view of the sea and a green 160 yards away, set up on a plateau and surrounded by banks and bunkers. The course is a windy one and the choice of club can vary enormously. The 4th is rated the hardest hole with out of bounds to the left, as on each of the first five holes. There is a two-tier fairway which involves some good carries and the green is well protected by bunkers and undulates.

At the 9th you drive over a path with a fair carry needed to reach the heavily bunkered fairway with a lateral water hazard on the right. At the 10th you head directly for the sea, and for the remainder of your round are heading back towards the clubhouse with the sea on your left. Though this is the shorter nine, it will usually be the windier. The most interesting hole is the 17th, 'Majuba', a par 5 of just over 500 yards. The ground is very undulating for both fairway and the green and sandhills cross it.

£ £12

M *a current handicap certificate*

✗ *snacks daily, lunch and dinner daily but not always on Monday*

▣ *snooker and a leisure centre just to the rear of the club's car park*

🚗 *from A19 take the A174 into Redcar. The course is just to the south-west of the town*

GANTON ⛳

Ganton, Scarborough, North Yorkshire YO12 4PA
☎ *Sherburn (0944) 70329*

Undoubtedly one of the best inland tests in Britain, the course has hosted the Ryder Cup in 1949, the 1981 PGA Championship, when Neil Coles set the professional record of 65, the 1975 Dunlop Masters, the Home Internationals, the Amateur Championship and a host of national and international amateur events.

The course begins fairly quietly, with two shortish par 4s in the first three holes but in between, the 2nd, with a pitch in to a sloping green, is a difficult target after even the best of drives.

The 4th is a fine hole with a gully to be carried in front of the plateau green. The first of only two par 3s on the course follows. It is not long, but the green is well bunkered with a pond to the left and there's gorse to be carried first.

We then come to the stroke index 1 hole, which justifies its rating. A good hit is needed to carry the inner corner of the bunker on the right, which then gives the best line in. Otherwise, you'll probably not get up in two and could well fail to carry a fairway bunker with your second shot.

You continue with a sequence of holes that are testing but not frightening, with a couple of par 5s to ease your journey. Then you come to one of Ganton's oddities, the 14th, a very short 4 indeed, at 283 yards. But there are bunkers all the way and you might do better to play your tee shot for position.

Ganton's famous finish is now upon us. The 15th is well bunkered left but the easier route to the right gives a more difficult second shot. There's also a hollow in front of the green that is apt to bring you up short.

The 16th is the best hole on the course. There's a big cross bunker to carry from the tee – no great distance but you're looking at a 6 if you mishit. If all goes well, the second shot is to a plateau green with a steep slope to carry or run up.

The 17th is my second oddity, and long may it remain, a par 4 of only 251 yards from the medal tees. There's no real problem. It just needs a good very straight hit over the road but there's plenty of gorse to either side, bunkers on the right and, for a shot fairly wildly left, what used to be called the biggest bunker in England – more a grassy hollow now.

At the 18th, you have to carry to a fairway which doglegs left at a right-angle. If your tee shot is too far left, your shot to the green is blocked out by tall trees. If you go right or your tee shot is straight, but too far, you'll probably be in dense rough. Ideally, you need to be as far left as you dare and then have what ought to be an easy enough shot between two stands of trees to the green.

Ganton, droughts or not, is almost always in superb condition. There's been water on tees and fairways for very many years and the greens reward good putting. The subsoil is sandy so this is a good place to visit after very wet weather. If you've done badly, look at R and A secretary Michael Bonallack's card in the clubhouse – he went round in 61 in the final of the English Amateur, despite missing four greens!

You may also come across a fine photograph of Harry Vardon. He first came to fame when the professional here, winning some celebrated challenge matches before the first of his Open Championships in 1896.

The club has its own little community, a place of work for several families living in staff houses. In the clubhouse, remember to sample the famous Ganton cake. Bill Branch was the professional here and during his tenure his wife started the first section in a pro's shop catering for ladies' golf fashion wear – you could get a double-knit cashmere for about £3 10s.

£ £30, £35 at weekends	✗ *snacks and lunch daily, dinner only for large visiting parties*
M *a handicap certificate*	🚗 *on the A64 10 miles west of Scarborough look out for the signpost in Ganton village*

HALLAMSHIRE, THE ⛳

The Club House, Sandygate, Sheffield, South Yorkshire
S10 4LA
☎ *Sheffield (0742) 302153*

Here is a club with a lot to answer for! It introduced the Alliss family to the game of golf. My father was brought up a mile or so away and began to caddie here before the First World War. Of course, it wasn't long before he hit his first golf ball and was soon well and truly hooked.

The course can be windy for it's set in an elevated position, nearly 1,000 feet up, west of Sheffield, with fine views over moorland towards the Peak District and the Rivelin valley. A rocky escarpment borders its northern boundary.

There's fine moorland turf underfoot and much heather and gorse as hazards. Rather like at Brancepeth, a deep gully adds interest to many of the holes.

You will have done well indeed if you get off to a good start for the early holes are tough ones. The severe first hole is a par 4 of just about maximum length, and it is followed by quite a long par 3 and then two more holes over 400 yards. There's some respite at the 5th, quite a short par 5 and rated at 15 in the stroke index. The club has the right indexing policy. The par 5s are not in the low numbers nor are long par 3s automatically rated amongst the last strokes received.

The 6th is an excellent par 3, nearly 200 yards, with a carry over a dip and trees to the green. The remainder of the first nine won't make great demands on your hitting powers but the gully is a threat to your tee shot on the 8th, asking you to carry about 180 yards. It also crosses the 10th and 11th fairways, requiring a fairly short carry of some 130 yards at the latter. Again there's a good carry required at the 13th and then you have three par 5s in the closing holes, which might help you improve your handicap position. One, however, the 15th, is long, 550 yards. The 17th, a short par 3 of little more than 130 yards, can make the nerves tighten. You play it from a high tee over a quarry filled with gorse.

£ £25, £30 at weekends	**♟** snooker
M proof of golf club membership	**🚍** take A57 from Sheffield centre towards Crosspool and fork left into Sandygate Road after a couple of miles. The clubhouse will be on your right after a further mile
✗ snacks daily, lunch daily except Tuesday, dinner by prior arrangement except Tuesday and Sunday	

HORNSEA   🌲 ⚑

Rolston Road, Hornsea, Humberside HU18 1XG
☎ *Hornsea (0964) 532020*

Some parts of the course come within quarter of a mile of the sea but Hornsea is really parkland and heath in type. A strong feature is the par 4s. There are two monsters over 470 yards and another of 450, which are, in fact, thrown at the golfer one after another – the 14th, 15th and 16th.

The course has four other par 4s around the 400 yard mark, one of which is 450. There's no doubt then that good long iron play and use of fairway woods is the key to playing Hornsea well, especially as the course is fairly exposed to the wind.

However, by way of relief, there are also five short par 4s. One of these is the 11th, where the green is protected by a pond. It all means that you should find yourself playing every club in the bag.

Hornsea has been used for county matches and in 1985 hosted the Yorkshire Ladies' Championship. It plays to a par of 71 with the same standard scratch; its record, which is held by that fine Yorkshire Walker Cup player Michael Kelley, is 68. Playing it to your handicap is very difficult.

There is a long, if narrow, practice ground, an approach green and a putting green.

£ £15	**♦** snooker
M proof of golf club membership	**🚗** from A165 take B1244 to Hornsea and follow signs for Hornsea Pottery. The entrance is a few hundred yards past it
✗ snacks, lunch and dinner daily except Monday	

ILKLEY

Myddleton, Ilkley, West Yorkshire LS29 OBE
☎ Ilkley (0943) 600214

Ilkley is a pretty parkland course in Wharfedale with the river a strong feature. Nearby is the lovely stone-built Yorkshire town of Ilkley, which incidentally has several fine restaurants. The Box Tree, in particular, has been in all the food guides for perhaps as long as twenty years.

The course is laid out along the north bank of the Wharfe on fairly level ground with wooded slopes around and a rise to Ilkley Moor. At each of the first seven holes, the river is very much in play, on the left.

The 1st, at more than 400 yards, is a fairly testing start, on grounds of length alone, and presents you with a choice. To get home in two, it is a far easier second shot if you hold your drive quite near the river bank. Go right and you lengthen the hole, may well be trapped by bunkers and also have a more difficult second to play as the green is well guarded against an approach from that side.

Just after this green, the river splits in two and you play a short hole to the island that has been formed. It's no great carry but you can easily find water to either side of the green. For the 3rd, you play another par 3 of just over 200 yards the full length of the narrow island. If this hole were on a very famous course it would be even more widely known that it is, on a par, perhaps, with the famous 18th at Killarney, which most threatens a wayward shot to the right. You must be straight with your long iron or wood.

You are not quite done with the island yet. The 4th is a par 5 played 'back to the mainland' which offers you that classic choice of deciding how much of the river you dare bite off, for it runs across diagonally. For the second shot you again have the choice of hugging the river bank or playing more safely out to the right where, as at the 1st, bunkers are in wait and an approach shot more difficult from that side.

The 5th is another 200-yard par 3 along the river bank but the punch-bowl green eases the shot, though the entrance is narrow, between bunkers. The river remains in play at the 6th but not as tight, so this par 5 of less than 500 yards is probably the easiest hole so far.

The 7th is a difficult par 4, quite long at 420 yards and slightly uphill.

There is also a bank swinging across which helps to form the plateau green, a well bunkered one.

In one way, Ilkley is a little like the traditional links 'out-and-back' pattern. The 7th green is the farthest point from the clubhouse and you now make your way back towards it, usually not so close to the Wharfe and jinking backwards and forwards at times. You should find the 8th easy after the earlier tests. It's not a long par 4, with downhill drive. You complete the first nine with a good two-shotter, the rising green set amongst tall fir trees.

After a short par 4, you play a long one of some 440 yards, again to a green in the pines. The 14th is another long par 4, one of the many on our older courses designed as a 5. You drive out of an avenue of trees and over a bank, trying not to go too far right, as a copse of trees may either trap your drive or block out the second shot. A shot to the left gives an open approach to the green.

The 15th is the last of five par 3s and asks you to pitch to a narrow shelf with only a 10-yard wide entry, bunkers in wait. The course finishes with three par 4s, all of fairly demanding length on meadow turf that gives little run on the ball.

One good judge has called Ilkley 'the most fascinating and the best' of all the river courses he had seen. The condition of the greens is particularly good.

£ £20	🎱 snooker
M a handicap certificate	🚗 along the A65 from Leeds turn right at the traffic lights in the centre of Ilkley, cross the river and take first left and left again
✗ snacks daily, lunch and dinner daily except Friday	

MOOR ALLERTON

Coal Road, Wike, Leeds, West Yorkshire LS17 9NH
☎ Leeds (0532) 661154

I once said that Moor Allerton is a golfing experience larger than life, and the passing of the years hasn't made me change that opinion. This is the only course in the UK designed by the most famous golf architect of the last forty years or so, Robert Trent Jones. It bears many of his familiar trade marks: large bunkers, sometimes in fantastic shapes, and roller-coaster greens that can produce too many borrows for all except the most experienced players. However, if your shot in was hit without full control of the ball, the chances are you won't be on the green anyway but will have drifted away into one of those elegant bunkers.

Certainly the contours of the greens, and the protective bunkers, are a main feature of Moor Allerton's twenty-seven holes, but there is also sheer length, seven lakes and the occasional stream to cope with. However, if to par several holes is quite a major achievement, there shouldn't be much difficulty in recording a one over. Probably the main difficulty for the handicap player who is a medium-length hitter is not the carries from the tee but the shots to the green, with perhaps a ravine or lake to contend with.

This is quite a recent course. The original Moor Allerton was laid out in 1923 alongside Moortown Golf Club but housing development and rights of way across the course made the club look elsewhere in the late 1960s. It bought some 230 acres of the Harewood Estate and constructed the three loops of nine holes and a splendid modern clubhouse.

The start is demanding, a long par 4. The drive is downhill but there's rising ground to the green and a stream perhaps forty yards short. The 3rd can be quite a teaser, a short par 4 where it's all too easy to run out of fairway. Best to play something like a 4 iron unless the wind's against you. You'll still have just a pitch left to the elevated green. Next, you play a short par 3 from an elevated tee to a green well below – very difficult to judge until you know the hole reasonably well. Then comes a par 5 where it's very possible to get home in two after a good drive. But there's a lake right in front of the green, and a malicious greenkeeper may have set the pin only just over. You can't just blaze away in wild hope because there's plenty of trouble through the back. Perhaps best to play it with a drive, mid-iron and the most precise little pitch you can manage. The 8th, another par 5, is a monster at 550 yards. The tee shot is blind with an out-of-bounds road along the right and it often plays into the wind. I once played it with Johnny Mathis, who blazed three out of bounds, tried out his vocal chords and said: 'Thank God I can still sing even if I can't play golf!' The first half ends with a testing par 4 with the tee shot to a rising fairway, and it's difficult to find the green with your second shot, which will probably be quite a long one.

On the second nine, one of the key holes to look out for is again a par 5, the 14th, a very difficult driving hole. Along the left there's first a lateral water hazard, followed by a lake with the flow of the ground being right to left so anything going that way in the slightest will probably find water, particularly in running conditions. However, you can't go cautiously right because that way you may find bushes and be blocked out by trees. You have to decide whether it's worth risking what you hope will be a long and very straight drive through the gap, between water left and undergrowth right, or to play short of the worst of the trouble with an iron. Of course, after a shortish tee shot more water is more likely to come into play for your second and third shots, though the hole is not particularly long at just over 500 yards. No problems at all, however, if you manage a couple of firm straight 3 woods and a pitch.

If you have found water, however, the 15th, a par 3, has a small lake eating into the green on the right-hand side and this will hardly be a welcome sight!

The finish is a good one. The 17th is a swirling dogleg with a gully in front of the green, and then the 18th requires a good drive, if the second shot over a pond to an elevated green is not to look rather fearsome.

On holes 19 to 27, the Jones trade marks are less in evidence and there's less water to contend with. This section is my favourite amongst the three nines, just over the fence from where I lived in Blackmoor Farm for about ten years, first as professional and then adviser to the club. The 27th makes a fitting climax, with a drive from an elevated tee at the mercy of prevailing winds and then a long second needed to make the shot over a gorse-covered ravine to the green as easy as possible. Seve Ballesteros has been on in two at this 572-yard hole (from the back tees) but few others have.

In years to come, this course may feature more on the tournament circuit, especially as fairways improve with the years, and has hosted the Leeds Cup, our oldest professional event, and the 1982 Car Care Plan International.

£ £25

M a society or club handicap

✗ snacks daily, lunch daily except Friday, dinner daily except Friday and Monday

🎱 snooker, squash, tennis, sauna, driving range, crown bowling

🚗 from Leeds, take the A61 to Harrogate and turn right into Wigton Lane about 1 mile past the intersection with the A6120 ring road. From Wetherby, take A58 to Leeds and turn right for Scarcroft at the New Inn along Syke Lane, taking the second right after Scarcroft Golf Club. It's 5 miles from Leeds, 6 from Wetherby and 9 from Harrogate

---

MOORTOWN

Harrogate Road, Leeds, West Yorkshire LS17 7DB
☎ Leeds (0532) 681682

This is one of a group of courses in a small area a very few miles to the north of Leeds which has no clear superior anywhere in the country for its size: Moortown itself, Sand Moor (just across the road), Alwoodley, Moor Allerton, Scarcroft and Headingley.

As anyone would guess from the name, this is a moorland course, peaty, with much heather and gorse and framed by a silver birch wood. Like its near neighbour, Alwoodley, it was laid out by Dr Alister Mackenzie.

It was here that the first Ryder Cup on British soil was played after the USA had taken the inaugural fixture at Worcester, Massachusetts, by 9½ to 2½. After the first day at Moortown, it looked a little like a repeat story, with the USA taking the foursomes by 2 to 1. For the second day, one point seemed to be already in the bag. Walter Hagen had arranged to play the British captain, George Duncan, and said: 'Well boys, that's one point for us.' Of the first two matches out, I'm not sure which finished first but it couldn't have been deep into the afternoon before Charles Whitcombe had won his, first off, by 8 and 6, while Hagen was eclipsed by 10 and 8. After that, it was nip and tuck, and the final result was USA: 5; Great Britain: 7.

One of golf's odder happenings also took place at Moortown. Playing the last hole, in the Brabazon, Nigel Denham landed his second shot at the back of a bunker and from there it bounded on through the open smoke room door. Out of bounds, of course? Not so at that time. He was able to lob his ball through the window and nearly got the putt.

Many other important events have been held at Moortown, both professional and amateur.

A feature of Moortown, unusual at the time it was laid out, is that every fairway can be seen from the tee and there are no blind holes. As the course is more than 7,000 yards, you might expect a number of long par 4s and that, indeed, is what you get – ten over 420 yards but only three par 5s. After one of these to start off with, you are in at the deep end with the 2nd, 457 yards, with trees to the right and heather left. Your tee shot should be over a group of hummocks and short of a meandering stream. You'll most likely need a wood to get home with your second shot. Another par 4 of much the same length follows, with a cross bunker to carry from the tee then another long shot. There follows an excellent short hole of 170 yards or so. If you are off line, you can expect to find trees on the left and heather and rough the other side. The green is well bunkered and a stream curls across the front, some 20 yards short. The 10th, known as 'Gibraltar', because it is built on a rock, is another short hole of the same length. A huge bunker lies in wait for a shot missing to the left, with more on the right, reinforced by heather and scrub, and a sloping green.

At the 11th, trees are less in evidence and moorland begins. The 12th is a long par 5 at 559 yards. When George Duncan played it against Hagen he was dormy nine and had just a short pitch for his third shot. He lifted his head and thinned it along the ground – stone dead. Thanks for the game Walter! On another occasion, Archie Compston holed a brassie shot for a 2, for many years the only time this had been done.

The 14th starts you on your way back to the clubhouse, with an out-of-bounds wall and a ditch to the left and heather the other side. Soon you are back in more enclosed country with a sequence of stiff holes to finish with.

£ £25

M a handicap certificate

X lunch daily except Monday, dinner daily except Sunday

P snooker

🚗 about 5½ miles north of Leeds on the A61 Harrogate road, on the left if going north

NORTHUMBERLAND, THE ⟨⟩

High Gosforth Park, Gosforth, Newcastle-upon-Tyne, Tyne and Wear NE3 5HT

☎ *Newcastle-upon-Tyne (091) 2362009*

Two great minds worked together on the design of this course, Harry Colt, primarily, and James Braid. Once their course had been completed after the First World War the main changes since have been to put in new tees to lengthen some of the holes.

Golf was certainly played in the Newcastle area as far back as 1646, when Charles I is recorded as playing on the Town Moor while a prisoner. However, this was mainly knocking a ball about a field, and it was for much the same reason that the Northumberland club was founded in 1898, on land more suitable. Very unusually, this was a racecourse and the first, primitive, course was mainly outside the track, whereas today it is mainly the land encircled by the racing that is used.

The quality of Colt and Braid's course was recognized in 1929 when the English Amateur Championship was held here, followed in 1938 by the *Daily Mail*. More recently, I remember competing in the 1966 Senior Service tournament. However, the most prestigious event to come to 'the Park', as it's known locally, was the 1972 Dunlop Masters.

The course begins with quite an inviting downhill tee shot which should leave you with a short pitch to the green, angled well right. The 2nd is a difficult par 4 of 432 yards with a stream and out of bounds down one side. This is followed by quite an easy par 5 which yielded several eagles and many birdies in the Masters. Then comes another par 5, rather more difficult, both of them running inside the curve of the racetrack. The 5th is a very difficult par 3 where no one recorded a 2 during the 1972 Masters although it's no monster at 186 yards.

I particularly like the 6th, quite a long par 4, where the drive has to be well placed and quite long to give a reasonable chance of getting home in two, for the hole doglegs right around a stand of trees.

The 13th, when it was a par 4, was a terror. You had to hit a really long drive, carrying the racecourse en route, to give any real chance of reaching the green, protected by trees on the right and the racecourse to the left. It's a narrow target and there's also a rise up to the green. Many members had never got home in two or ever thought to. However, it's rather easier as a par 5 but not one you'd look to birdie – only two did it in the Masters, though it's only 481 yards.

The 14th is a pleasant shortish par 3, again over the racecourse and with many trees and bushes clustered about the green.

The pick of the closing holes are the 16th, with a fairly long carry over the racecourse rails to the fairway, followed by a long second shot to a well-bunkered green, and the 18th, a scenic hole, with the green very close to the clubhouse. The drive is again over the rails (remember, if you get a low clean hit away, you can catch one flush and your ball will fizz back over your head, causing first alarm and then despondency). The second is uphill along the sweeping fairway to the large well-bunkered green.

The 6,640 yards of this course are basically heathy in character but there are also a large number of trees affecting play and many small oak bushes and heather. The club considers itself – and is thought of – as having the premier course in the area, particularly as many others are by no means of tournament length.

The 1912 clubhouse speaks of another age in the best sense.

£ *£20*

M *a handicap certificate and letter of introduction from your club secretary*

✗ *snacks and lunches daily except Monday, dinner for visiting parties but otherwise for members only*

🚗 *leave Newcastle along the old A1 through Gosforth and 2 miles after look for a slip road over a flyover just past Wheeler's Garage. The entrance to High Gosforth Park comes shortly after*

SEATON CAREW

Tees Road, Seaton Carew, Hartlepool, Cleveland TS25 1DE
☎ *Hartlepool (0429) 266249*

Despite the very early beginnings at Blackheath in about 1608, the golf invasion of England from Scotland really dates from the 1860s, when such clubs as Royal North Devon at Westward Ho!, Royal Liverpool at Hoylake and Alnmouth were founded. Seaton Carew dates from 1874 when a certain Dr Duncan McCuaig from St Andrews set up his practice in the area and noticed that the linksland known as 'the Snook' was similar to the Old Course where he'd twice won the Gold Medal. He began to play with friends. Others soon joined in.

By 1882 there were fourteen holes and the name 'The Durham and Yorkshire Golf Club' was chosen, an indication of how little golf was to be found in these two counties at the time. It was later dropped, as the numbers of golf clubs increased.

By 1891 the course was upgraded to eighteen holes and quite interestingly had the length of a typical course for guttie days – 4,712 yards. The shortest hole was 159 yards and the longest just 356 yards, long enough to be thought of as a bogey (par) 5.

The first professional was Tom Park of the famous Musselburgh family which won seven Open Championships in all. He was succeeded by an almost legendary golfer, James Kay, who stayed from 1886 until his death in 1924. He has gone down in golfing folklore as the man who helped Harry Vardon to his first Open Championship at Muirfield in 1896. Vardon was playing the last needing a 4 to win. After a good drive, he was considering whether to go for the green with his next shot, with a dangerous bunker between him and the flag. Kay pointed at the ground a little short of the bunker. Vardon took the hint, got his 5 to tie with J.H. Taylor and went on to win the play-off.

Kay was a very good player in his own right and performed well in challenge and exhibition matches, against Vardon and James Braid for instance – a type of golf which has sadly become so little a part of the scene today.

The course remained basically unchanged from about 1925. The club, however, brought more land into play near the sea in the 1970s and took the course length up from about 6,600 yards to nearly 6,900 from the very back tees.

Seaton Carew is a championship course today, used for the English Girls' Championship, the British Ladies' Strokeplay, the Brabazon Trophy and the 1978 and 1986 Boys' Championship. For some years, the Seaton Salver for scratch amateurs has attracted a high-class entry.

The course is truly links with a drive-and-pitch hole to start off with, followed by a long par 5 of over 550 yards. The 3rd is a good par 3, calling for a mid- to long iron over a rough dip to a green on the same level as the tee. The new holes which come around the end of the second half are good ones and were designed by Frank Pennink. The finish of three par 4s is a very testing one and many people would settle for three 5s and walk in.

The 16th is a long par 4, played from an elevated tee and is doglegged. The 17th is a famous hole, christened 'the Snag'. You drive over dunes, whins and gorse to what looks like a very narrow stretch of fairway but it's the second shot that really makes the hole. Your shot must be placed very precisely if it's not to veer away into bunkers. Nothing less than a near-perfect shot will do, to this pear-shaped green with subtle undulations.

The last is less difficult but a straight drive is a must, with out of bounds on the right and rough to the left. If you get a satisfactory tee shot away, judgement of distance is still not easy for the shot to the green.

The ranks of captains' photographs in the clubhouse, dating back to 1874, are evidence of the traditions of the club.

£ *£18, £22 at weekends*	♟ *snooker*
M *membership of a golf club*	🚗 *on A178 just south of Seaton Carew, about 3 miles from Hartlepool*
✗ *snacks, lunch and dinner daily*	

SELBY

Brayton Barff, Brayton, Selby, North Yorkshire YO8 9LD
☎ *Gateforth (0757 82) 622*

Here we're at a mecca for local golfers when autumn and winter rains set in for days on end and on many Yorkshire courses golf is a matter of splashing round. Selby is hardly ever wet and only snow actually closes the course. Even this soon goes because of salt in the subsoil.

The reason for its winter suitability is simple: Selby is laid out on a sandy ridge. The views around can stretch for perhaps 40 miles and because of the height there's usually at least a slight breeze. The ground undulates gently and there is much gorse and broom and many trees. The club was formed in 1907 with nine holes; a second loop (both starting and ending at the clubhouse) was added in 1930.

Selby isn't one of the famous names in British golf; it's simply a very pleasant place to be. The balance is good with five par 3s and three 5s, and there are at least four quite short 4s where you can hope to pitch close for your birdie. The most severe test comes, as nearly always, on the long par 4s. Selby has four around the 450-yard mark and the three most difficult come on the first nine.

On the 3rd you have to be specially wary of the out of bounds on the right because the tilt of the fairway helps your ball that way. At the 5th, besides sheer length, the problem comes with the second shot: the largest bunker on the course is set squarely in mid-fairway, the distance of a short pitch from the green. Although this is rated Selby's most difficult hole, the 7th is just as testing, with bunkers strung out along the right and the green well guarded.

£ £20, £17 per round

M a handicap certificate

✖ snacks, lunch and dinner daily except Monday

🎱 snooker

🚗 from the M62 take the A19 for Selby and on the outskirts of the town turn for Gateforth. Turn left into Mill Lane and the clubhouse is on right after about 1 mile. From Leeds along A63 turn right into Doncaster Road at traffic lights on outskirts with sign for Gateforth. Turn right into Mill Lane

---

WOODSOME HALL

Fenay Bridge, Huddersfield, West Yorkshire HD8 0LQ
☎ *Huddersfield (0484) 602971*

To anyone contemplating a golfing holiday in the area, Woodsome Hall really is a must, an undiscovered gem which seems known only to those who live fairly locally. The clubhouse alone is worth the visit, one of the most interesting and beautiful anywhere.

The site has been occupied from at least as far back as 1236, and the present mansion mainly dates from Elizabethan times. A great hall, 30 feet square, rises two storeys and has a working clock that was installed in 1652. The ladies' locker room is embellished with a plaster frieze depicting a merman and mermaids.

In some ways the golf course itself owes just as much to Lancelot 'Capability' Brown as the golf designer who laid it out in the early 1920s, for he was responsible for shaping the parkland through which the Woodsome Hall course runs. He also designed the magnificent terrace, basing his design on Haddon Hall.

If this course and clubhouse was anywhere in the London area, entrance, membership and green fees would be astronomical, but as it's in Yorkshire they're very reasonable. You don't often get the chance to tee off from ancestral lawns, and the names of some of the holes echo the history of the estate: 'Tythe Barn', 'Dower House', 'Butts' – and others.

The first drive needs to be straight, with trees to the left and bunkers right. The 2nd hole is also around 400 yards, straightness again demanded. If you find the middle of the fairway, you'll be in the right frame of mind to appreciate the good view of the old stone manor and its backcloth of trees.

The 3rd is one of the finest holes, a 200-yarder where you must carry to the green over bunkers and plenty of ups and downs. Both the 8th and 9th are especially attractive. The first of these is 450 yards with a drive over a pond to start with. The longest hitters must be sure they don't go too far and reach the stream which crosses the fairway. Oak trees force the hole to play as a dogleg and the green is well set in an angle of the woods.

The 9th takes you back to the clubhouse and is played round a hillside, at 518 yards the longest hole and one of only two par 5s. The green is close by the clubhouse and is surrounded by rhododendrons and huge beech trees.

On the second nine, the par 3 13th, laid out in the middle of a wood, is particularly good. The 16th is also interesting. Its 499 yards are all downhill, so many players have a chance of getting home with two good shots. The course ends with two fairly short par 4s of 333 and 343 yards. The first of these has a green sloping fairly sharply left to right. It has been holed in one.

You finish with a dogleg formed by trees and bunkers to a green just beyond a crest in front of the clubhouse.

£ £18	snooker
M membership of a golf club	about 6 miles south east of Huddersfield on the Sheffield to Penistone road (A629)
X snacks, lunch and dinner daily except Monday	

THE
MIDLANDS

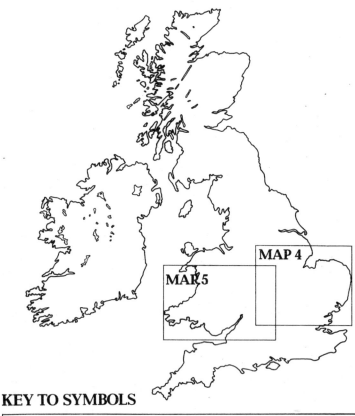

MAP 4

MAP 5

KEY TO SYMBOLS

🌳	PARKLAND	☎	TELEPHONE	✗	CATERING PROVIDED
🚩	LINKS	✉	NEED TO BOOK IN ADVANCE	🏨	ACCOMMODATION PROVIDED
🌿	MOORLAND	£	APPROXIMATE COURSE FEE	Ⓛ	RESTRICTIONS ON LADIES AND/OR YOUTHS
🌾	HEATHLAND	Ⓜ	MEMBERSHIP REQUIREMENTS FOR VISITORS		
🏞	DOWNLAND			🏹	OTHER SPORTING FACILITIES
🗻	UPLAND			🚗	DIRECTIONS

BEAU DESERT

Hazel Slade, Hednesford, Cannock, Staffs. WS12 5PJ
☎ *Hednesford (0543) 422626*

A very attractive course indeed, Beau Desert is basically moorland in type. Set on Cannock Chase, it is surrounded by Forestry Commission fir trees, and heather is one of the main hazards and delights.

The course begins in fine style with a short par 4 of less than 300 yards but you are immediately asked to make a good carry with your tee shot over a large pit. The 5th also needs another of the same but this time the hole is a long par 4, rated as stroke index 1. As a whole, you'll probably find scoring comes more easily on the first nine, only 2,870 yards, with only two holes, that 5th and the 440-yard 2nd, demanding any real length of shot.

The second nine begins with a short hole of 150 yards; it's rather all or nothing because your tee shot has to clear a ravine. From here on, all the par 4s are quite testing in length and one of the course's two par 5s is a long one. This is the 15th, 555 yards. The length of this nine is 3,415 with the par being only two strokes more than the 34 of the first.

Beau Desert has hosted the Staffordshire Open and has been used as a Midlands qualifying course for the Open Championship.

💷 *£25*	🚗 *take the A460 for Rugeley from Cannock through Hednesford and turn right along Rawnsley Road, followed by the first left*
Ⓜ *membership of a golf club*	
✗ *snacks, lunch and dinner daily*	

BELFRY, THE

Lichfield Road, Wishaw, North Warwickshire B76 9PR
☎ *Curdworth (0675) 470301*

There is no golf club here. Instead, there's a 120-bedroom hotel which is also a conference and leisure centre with two eighteen-hole golf courses, the Brabazon and the Derby.

The first of these has been made famous by television. The Hennessy Cognac Cup came here in 1978 and the English Golf Classic from 1979 to 1983, followed by the Lawrence Batley Classic in 1984. More recently, of course, there has been the Ryder Cup. Those who criticized the choice of this rather American-style course on the grounds of condition and because it would suit the 'enemy' were proved wrong. The course was built to give Europeans experience of target golf, with shots to be played over water and the team appeared to solve the problems better than the Americans did, leading to the first victory since Lindrick in 1957 and an end to American dominance of the event. In 1989 the Ryder Cup came to a thrilling climax when many players found the water on the last.

Opened in 1977, the Brabazon was designed by David Thomas and built by Alliss/Thomas Construction. It had its problems early on, especially as the 1976 drought had killed off thousands of young trees. But very good progress was made during the 1980s.

After a gentle start, the 4th, against the breeze is a very good par 5 and the 5th has a difficult drive. Perhaps the 6th is the most dramatic hole of all. The drive is to a fairway 30 yards wide between two lakes, and the green itself lies just 10 feet from the water's edge. Both shots test the nerves. The 7th, another unusual hole, has been nicknamed 'the stockade'. It caused quite a lot of controversy when the course was opened because the green was faced with split trunks, which have since been removed, and is surrounded by sand. This is really David's version of the traditional use of railway sleepers to support bunkers, such as at Prestwick and Brancaster. The 8th is a magnificent par 4.

The 9th is another dramatic hole, another 4 just under 400 yards, where you should keep to the centre or right and pitch over water to an elevated tiered green, cut in by the lake .

The 10th was made famous by Severiano Ballesteros, the year after the course was opened. Playing in the Hennessy in 1978 he faded a drive about 310 yards to the heart of the green and over trees. Greg Norman later repeated the feat, and there are two plaques to commemorate their deeds on the tee. Normally, however, the hole is played as just about a right-angled dogleg with an iron from the tee. Your second shot should not be too strong for, although you'll clear the protecting stream, you'll then be bunkered or caught up in a grassy bank. I believe that the tee should be moved forwards for tournaments so that 90 per cent of the field think they've a chance of reaching the green, rather than just half a dozen. This is done for the Ryder Cup. It would also save wear on the fairway.

Some people say the 18th is the best finishing hole in Great Britain, but this is not so because too many players settle for approaching it as a 5 hole. It measures 455 yards and the ideal drive over water should bite off as much as you dare in order to shorten the second shot which, again, is over water to a monster three-tiered green.

A final feature is the par 5s – three between 540 and 569 yards.

The Derby is a shorter and less testing examination of your golf and lakes are not a feature. Brooks do come into play on the 2nd and 16th, however. Good progress has been made to upgrade the course.

The Belfry has good practice facilities, which include a twenty-bay driving range. Overall, the facilities rival those at Gleneagles or the Old Course Golf and Country Club at St Andrews.

🅔 *£55, £45 per round for the Brabazon, £20 for the Derby*

Ⓜ *proof of a handicap of no worse than 28 is required for playing the Brabazon, no restriction for the Derby*

✕ *snacks, lunch and dinner daily*

🏊 *squash, tennis, swimming, snooker, Turkish baths, sauna, jacuzzi and a 'trimnasium' at the hotel*

�car *leave the M6 at Junction 4 for Lichfield along A446, looking for the entrance right after about ten minutes*

BUXTON AND HIGH PEAK ⛳

Townend, Waterswallows Road, Fairfield, Buxton, Derbyshire SK17 1LJ
☎ *Buxton (0298) 23453*

With a superb setting among the limestone hills of the Peak District, only some 10 miles from Kinder Scout or the nestling villages of the Hope Valley, this is a moorland course with undulating fairways, of about 6,000 yards. The rough can be very punishing, and quarries are a feature. Founded in 1887, Buxton is the oldest club in Derbyshire and one of the most testing in the north Midlands.

The club's most famous son is Harry Bennett, an England international shortly after the Second World War who twice reached the final of the English Amateur Championship.

The course begins with quite a long par 4 of about 420 yards, where you have to take the right line from the tee if you're to have much chance of attacking the green. The 4th is a dramatic hole and a real challenge to the long hitter; the fairway is crossed by an old quarry which can only be cleared by a good drive. Shorter hitters must play short and think of the hole as a par 5.

Much the same is true of the 11th, a par 4 of just about maximum length at 473 yards. A quarry again comes into play on this dogleg with out of bounds along the right.

The clubhouse must be amongst the oldest in England.

🅔 *£18*

Ⓜ *evidence of golf club membership or introduction by a member*

✕ *snacks daily, lunch and dinner daily*

🚗 *leave Buxton by the A6 for Manchester and bear right at Links Garage with the clubhouse about 500 yards further on the right*

DELAMERE FOREST

Station Road, Delamere, Northwich, Cheshire CW8 2JE
☎ *Sandiway (0606) 882807*

Quite a lot of golf clubs think of planting trees as good in itself, and those that arrive as a gift of nature are usually welcomed. Not at Delamere Forest. The club abhors, for instance, the planting of parallel lines of trees to separate fairways and removes trees that may affect the playing quality of holes. This is also true as regards trees which may eventually affect natural windflow.

This is quite a controversial position and I'll do no more than point out that so many clubs *do* plant trees with little thought to the natural appearance of the terrain in years to come. Trees should always be planted in clumps where they'll be both aesthetically appealing and contribute to the playing quality of the course.

Delamere is not a particularly heavily wooded course. It only lies on the edge of the 100 square mile forest from which it takes its name. The course is laid out on heathland, with a wood of several acres in the middle forming a natural out-of-bounds area. There are also a number of small copses, with gorse and heather in profusion, and a small lake. The Pennines are sometimes visible to the east and there are local hills in view but the main feature is the seclusion provided by the forest.

Delamere is laid out in two loops of nine, both starting near the clubhouse. The first nine has six holes of more than 400 yards but less than 445. Two of these holes are rated as par 5s.

It is a splendid course for golfers who think winter play every bit as important as high season and hate teeing off from a mat or putting on winter 'greens' that are seldom worthy of the name. Play is from grassed tees to normal greens throughout the year.

The 6th is a very interesting short par 3. The green is kidney-shaped and guarded on the left by a long bunker with the approaches and green itself sloping towards it. However, if you play away from this hazard, there are three bunkers to the right in wait.

The 10th, played from just outside the windows of the men's bar, requires a long and straight drive to carry the breast of a hill. The player who is short will find his ball running away left or right. The 15th is a fine short par 4 at just over 300 yards. It's a right-angled dogleg, following Delamere Forest, with out of bounds to the left and also through the green.

The 18th makes a fine finishing hole, a long par 4 played from a high tee with a gambler's drive. How much of the out of bounds do you dare try to carry? The bolder you are, if successful, the more likely you are to manage the narrow gap for the second shot between reeds one side and the wood the other. However, you haven't won the hole once you are on in two. The green is one of the most difficult on the course to read.

There are two practice grounds and a practice bunker.

🄴 *£15, £20 at weekends*

🄼 *none*

✗ *snacks daily; lunch and dinner daily except on Friday, if ordered in advance*

🚗 *Turn off the A556 along B5156 Tarporley to Frodsham road for 1 mile. Turn right just before Delamere Station and the clubhouse is after 500 yards*

EDGBASTON

Church Road, Edgbaston, Birmingham B15 3TB
☎ *Birmingham (021) 454 1736*

It's hard to realize that the centre of Birmingham is just a mile or so away for the Georgian clubhouse is the only building in sight. The course is in beautiful undulating parkland, made more picturesque by a large lake. On the far side of this there's a nature reserve with a great variety of bird life.

The club was founded in 1909 and the course design was by Harry Colt, of whom it can truly be said that he never produced a poor golf course. Edgbaston is fairly short, mainly because there is just one par 5. Most of the 4s are of very fair length, especially the 10th, which is the most difficult of the holes. At 467 yards, two good hits are needed and there are cross bunkers to clear with the second shot, awkwardly placed some 20 yards short of the green.

Of the four short holes, pride of place goes to the 7th. The raised plateau green is cut into a beech wood and is difficult both to hit and to stay on.

The 12th is very attractive, running all along the lake. Water also comes much into play on the 13th for the tee shot. The player has to decide how much he can carry to give a short line into the green.

The club hosted the British Girls' Open Championship in 1979 and has been used for Warwickshire amateur and professional championships.

The clubs has two small practice areas and a putting green.

🄴 *£22*   🄼 *none*

✗ *lunch daily in both members' and visitors' dining rooms, but with a limited menu on Monday*

🎱 *snooker*

🚗 *from Five Ways, in central Birmingham, take Calthorpe Road for a mile through two sets of traffic lights. The clubhouse is then on the right just past Edgbaston Old Church*

HAWKSTONE PARK HOTEL 🌳

Weston-under-Redcastle, Shrewsbury, Shropshire SY4 5UY
☎ *Lee Brockhurst (093 924) 611*

Hawkstone is associated with one of the leading names of modern British golf. Sandy Lyle, Open Champion in 1985, was touring professional here throughout his early career.

Although the main course only dates back some fifty years, the history of the hotel and park is very much longer. There is a thirteenth-century castle in the grounds, built during the reign of Henry III, with a well more than 200 feet deep, said to have taken seven years to complete. Part of the main tower is hewn from solid rock. Within the parkland there are a variety of antiquities and follies, mostly the work of Sir Richard Hill in the late eighteenth century. Richard Hill was also responsible for Hawk Lake, which forms the boundary of one side of the main Hawkstone course and is 2 miles long.

Yet this is not one of the many hotels or country clubs that until recent times was a country mansion. Hawkstone was opened as an inn as far back as 1790 and quickly came to be considered one of the most spacious and elegant ones in Britain.

Water and sandstone cliffs are a distinctive natural feature of the two courses here, the premier Hawkstone and the more recent Weston, constructed in the 1970s. The latter was intended both as a relief course and also to provide less strenuous work for society outings. However, though it measures only some 5,300 yards, there are six par 4s over 400 yards, which is a fair enough ration, with three less than 300 yards to make the going easier.

As their names 'Cascade' and 'Reservoir' show, two of the par 3s feature water. The 9th is a long par 4 of 430 yards, rather more than just a dogleg as its name 'Swan's Neck' suggests.

The Hawkstone begins with a par 4 and the first more severe test comes at the 2nd, a par 4 rated as a stroke index 3. The 8th is an interesting par 5, doglegged and with a difficult, narrow approach shot needed while the next par 5, the 10th, is remarkable for its beauty. The 16th is very much a fun hole. Only 255 yards, it's just over the par 3 limit and gives you a good opportunity of getting home with your tee shot, which is blind to a gathering basin green. The last hole, quite a long par 4, demands a firm drive if you're going to reach the green with your second shot.

£ *£26, £31 at weekends on Hawkstone; £19, £23 at weekends on Weston*

M *a handicap certificate for Hawkstone*

✗ *snacks, lunch and dinner daily*

🏊 *swimming, croquet, a games room, lawn tennis, a sauna and solarium, snooker, trimnasium*

🚗 *14 miles north of Shrewsbury in Weston village, just off the A49 Shrewsbury to Whitchurch road*

✉ *parties of 12 or more need to book in advance*

🏨 *59 bedrooms all with private bathroom*

KING'S NORTON

Brockhill Lane, Weatheroak, Birmingham, West Midlands B48 7ED
☎ *(0564) 826706*

King's Norton has twenty-seven holes running through 250 acres of undulating parkland. The River Cole flows through the course and can come into play on about a third of the holes.

The course is laid out in three loops of nine – the Red, Blue and Yellow. These give different starting points and are all around the 3,300 yard mark. Each of the three possible combinations for competition has a standard scratch of 72 and each nine holes a par of 36.

The club was first formed in 1892 and the Malvern professional summoned to lay out a course was paid 35 shillings for his pains, rather below the going rate even for those days!

By the 1960s, however, the club was increasingly concerned at being surrounded by high-rise flats and housing estates, and there was also a threat that it might be subject to a compulsory purchase order. The land was sold to Birmingham City Council, Weatheroak Hall was bought and Fred Hawtree engaged as course architect. He also designed a twelve-hole par 3 course on which a short-course professional championship has been held.

The course quickly attracted professional tournaments. The 1973 and 1974 Wills Opens were held at King's Norton, Texan Charles Coody and Neil Coles being the winners. Two years later Brian Barnes won the Sun Alliance PGA Matchplay.

Blue

The 3rd is an excellent par 3 of 218 yards where there is no alternative to carrying your tee shot all the way, with club selection difficult in anything of a wind because the tee is fairly sheltered. A large oak tree has to be carried some 30 yards short of the green by any shot coming in from the right and the green is particularly well bunkered to the left. Anything not quite good enough will fall away on slopes at the left rear of the green.

The 6th is a testing long doglegged par 4 of 430 yards with out of bounds all along the inside of the angle. To get your par, you really have to risk carrying some of that out of bounds or you'll have little chance from a safe tee shot of getting up in two. The River Cole crosses the fairway but is well short of the green. It comes into play only for a poor second shot.

The 7th, a 175-yarder, has water across the green entrance and there are falls in the ground around the green as well as a large bunker at the front and side left.

Red

The 7th is quite a short par 4 at 360 yards but rather a terror. There's out of bounds all along the left and the River Cole runs along just right of the best line from the tee, forming a pool starting at about 170 yards. You can play over to the right but then have to play your second across the river, perhaps a pool just to the right of the green, and bunkers at the wrong angle to hold the green – and with out of bounds not far through. It's definitely a problem hole. The answer is to hit a straight tee shot.

The 8th, a 176-yard par 3, is again full of problems. The river runs diagonally across the hole with a pool close to the tee and another no more than six yards to the right of the green with a ball landing on the green tending to run in that direction. Perhaps that's as well because out of bounds is equally close on the left.

Yellow

The 4th is a 209-yard par 3 to a green sloping from back left to front right, which means that most putts have considerable borrow. The 414-yard 6th has bunkers right and left in the driving area and then a cross bunker, followed by a hollow, to negotiate before your second can get to the green. On the 7th, a par 3 of 174 yards, the main problem is stopping your ball on a green which slopes from front to back with a steep bank beyond. The hole is also tightly bunkered. Before you get there, however, there's a water hazard to be cleared as well as tall trees.

£ £20

M visitors on weekdays only, except Bank holidays, Christmas week and Easter Tuesday. Proof of club membership and handicap certificate required

---

✕ snacks daily, lunch and dinner daily except Monday

♦ snooker and table tennis

🚗 situated about 8 miles south of the centre of Birmingham, the club is best found from junction 3 of the M42, turn towards Birmingham and follow signs to Weatheroak

---

LEICESTERSHIRE, THE

Evington Lane, Leicester, Leicestershire LE5 6DJ
☎ (0533) 738825

This course has been lengthened over the years to over 6,300 yards to give a par of 68 and a standard scratch of 70. Nevertheless, the South African Harold Henning, who gave such a fine performance in the 1983 Open Championship at Royal Birkdale, once managed to breeze round in 63!

It is a pleasantly undulating parkland course with a brook twisting through it that influences play on several holes, especially the 5th, 6th, 7th and 11th.

The 5th is a long par 4 where you must carry that stream with your drive and then face a long second uphill to a well-guarded green. The 9th has a copse to the right that you can allow to influence your drive too much, followed by cross bunkers that can then intimidate you for the second shot to another well-guarded and rather narrow green. The main problem at the 11th is that you will be faced with a hanging lie for your second shot unless your drive has been a very long one. As the second shot is over a stream, the tricky lie becomes much more difficult. At the 15th, positioning of the drive is crucial and you must hold it up left to get good sight of green and flag. This shot is downhill, which makes distance difficult to estimate, and the green is easily run through.

£ £22

M a club membership card

✗ snacks daily, lunch daily except Monday, dinner by arrangement with the steward

---

🚗 from south, along A6, leave Leicester Building Society HQ on your left and right at second traffic lights into New Street and Stoughton Road and left into Gartree Road until roundabout. Here take right turn into Stoughton Drive and then right at traffic lights. From the north keep on ring road, leaving it with General Hospital on your left into Wakerley Road and turn left at traffic lights at top of hill

---

LITTLE ASTON

Streetly, Sutton Coldfield, West Midlands B74 3AN
☎ Birmingham (021) 353 2942

Little Aston is one of the finest inland tests in Britain. It is mostly parkland, but with a short stretch of moorland golf after the first nine holes, and has some of the best turf to be found on an inland course. It has been used for many major events including several Dunlop Masters, the English Amateur Championship, the Brabazon Trophy and the English Open Amateur Strokeplay Championship. When you're playing here, there's no indication that you are not many miles from the centre of Birmingham. The course is one of the surprisingly few laid out by Harry Vardon, in a former deer park in 1908, but he left behind too many severe carries from the tees for the members' liking and Harry Colt was called in to make the necessary changes.

You begin with a not too stressful par 4 but this is followed by an uphill two-shotter of well over 400 yards. Relief comes on the 4th, not much more than 300 yards, which is drivable with help from the wind. None of the remaining holes on the first nine are easy but it is on this stretch that you need to score for the second half is the longer by some 350 yards.

The 10th is a good par 4 of about 440 yards, with two bends in the fairway. Placement of the drive is all-important. The 12th, a par 5, has a pond, which was added close to the left-hand side of the green, and is very much a threat to those trying to get up in two. The 14th, a short par 4 of some 320 yards, has a well-placed large cross bunker that I'm sure catches out many players trying to carry it from the tee.

The show hole, however, is the 17th. It is some 360 yards and has a tight driving line followed by a well-bunkered plateau green with some severe slopes and a lake away to the left. The last is a slightly longer par 4 and again cross bunkers come into play, this time for the second shot, often with wood as it's uphill.

Don't miss the putting green, a gem.

£ £30

M a handicap certificate and a written application

✗ lunch by prior arrangement, but not at all on Monday

🚗 off the A454 about 9 miles north of Birmingham, ½ mile from Streetly

---

NOTTS (Hollinwell)　　　🏌

Derby Road, Kirkby-in-Ashfield, Nottinghamshire NG17 7QR
☎ *Mansfield (0623) 753225*

Designed by Willie Park Junior and later revised by John Henry Taylor, Hollinwell is one of the best inland courses in Britain and has been listed amongst the top twenty-five courses in these islands and the top 100 in the world.

Opened in 1900, it is heather in type and meanders through a natural valley where there's also plenty of silver birch, oak and gorse. In recent years, we've heard a very great deal about the club professional, Brian Waites, who in 1983 became the oldest British player ever to make his debut in the Ryder Cup team.

Tournament golf comes to Hollinwell quite often. I recall playing there in the 1957 Dunlop Masters, won by Eric Brown, who set a new course record of 64 while doing so. The first John Player Classic came here in 1970, and the Brabazon Trophy has come twice. The first of these, in 1975, produced a very fine finish between Sandy Lyle and Geoff Marks which enables me to describe the last three holes. On the 16th tee Lyle had a two-stroke lead and then pitched dead for his birdie at this 350-yard hole with Marks some 10 yards or so away – but he holed it. The 17th is a short par 5 of some 480 yards and Sandy duly put his second shot on the green. Marks did likewise and then holed from the length of a cricket pitch for his eagle, against Lyle's birdie. One stroke in it, with the 18th a testing 450-yard finishing hole. Both men were just a touch short in two. Marks then sent his third shot too boldly at the hole, went 3 yards past and missed the return. It was Sandy Lyle's first important victory.

Hollinwell begins with a fairly comfortable par 4, followed by what Henry Longhurst described as: 'a great hole. Drive to the right or you cannot see the flag, drive too much right and you are out of reach of the green.' Behind the green on this hole there's a rock known as Robin Hood's Chair, a reminder that the course lies within the bounds of Sherwood Forest. The next offers hopes of a birdie, being a slightly downhill par 5. This is also the case with the 6th. Although it's the longest hole on the course, at some 530 yards, the ground helps your ball to run once you're over the first crest.

The 8th is the most picturesque hole. It also gives the course its name, which comes from the 'Holy Well'. From the very back tees your drive must carry the length of the lake, a distance of about 180 yards, and also find a narrow gap through trees. If you accomplish a good tee shot, you'll then have a clear shot at the green from the angle of the dogleg, perhaps a birdie opportunity. Look for more on the next few holes as there will be fewer later.

The 12th plays very differently according to wind direction but is always tricky and is well over 400 yards. The drive must clear a valley and also stay on the mound beyond. If you go too far, your ball tumbles away into another valley. True, you'll be nearer the green but you will have a completely blind shot and one that's particularly difficult to judge.

The 13th has often been called a great par 3 but it's a little too long for my money, more a 3½ but a very satisfying place to get a 3. Before the finish I've already described, there come a couple of long par 4s. No real problems from the tees but the greens are a very small target to hit with a long iron and even a wood; both are excellent holes.

Notts has a driving range and a practice ground.

£ *£30*

M *membership of a golf club and current handicap certificate*

✗ *snacks, lunch and dinner daily*

🚗 *leave M1 at Junction 27 and head along A608 and A611 for Mansfield and look out for the course on the right after about 3 miles*

ROSS-ON-WYE ♣

Two Park, Gorsley, Ross-on-Wye, Herefordshire and
Worcestershire HR7 7UT
☎ *Gorsley (098982) 267*

Ross-on-Wye is a course of 6,491 yards cutting through forests of oak,
silver birch and pine. Such origins mean that most of the fairways have a
private feel and are also fairly narrow, almost as if the course architect,
C.K. Cotton, didn't wish to lay too many trees low. Similarly, the greens
are on the small side but have very good putting surfaces. The English
Seniors' came here in 1983. No one in the present form of the course has
bettered 69, the record held by Gordon Brand Junior, while the best
amateur score is also 69, made as recently as 1988.

The best opportunities for scoring well will probably come on the
short par 4s. You begin with one of these, 313 yards, while the 3rd is only
284 yards. Sandwiched in between, however, is something rather more
formidable, the 455-yard 2nd. This illustrates one of the contrasts of
Ross-on-Wye – there are half-a-dozen short 4s and five two-shotters of
more than 400 yards, four coming on the second nine.

On the longer first nine, much of the yardage comes from a sequence
of three par 5s in the space of four holes, the 5th, 6th and 8th. These are
followed by a difficult par 3 of 218 yards, with the green close by the
practice putting green, which is out of bounds.

The second half begins with a long par 4 of 448 yards of which Peter
Townsend, now professional at Portmarnock, once said you needed a
rifle to play the tee shot. It is followed by another hole with a demanding
tee shot, a par 4 which doglegs right with an oak tree in the centre of the
fairway at the angle, with out of bounds to the right.

Of the remaining holes, both the 14th and 17th require two good hits
to get home, with the latter also being uphill.

Although the club itself was founded in 1903, this is a modern course,
designed in the 1960s; it is one of the very best inland courses to have
come into being in the last forty years.

💷 *£21*

Ⓜ *membership of a golf club*

✗ *snacks daily, lunch and dinner
daily except Monday*

🚗 *just off the M50, north of
Junction 3 in the Kempley direction*

🎱 *snooker*

SANDWELL PARK ⅋

Birmingham Road, West Bromwich B71 4JJ
☎ *Birmingham (021) 553 4637*

This oasis just 4 miles from the centre of Birmingham was founded in 1895 on land which formed part of the Earl of Dartmouth's Sandwell Hall estate. The members raised £120 to construct the course, but the quite large traditional clubhouse cost £1,058 16s 6d a few years later!

The course as a whole is a good test of driving with good short holes. It has views of Cannock Chase some 20 miles away and the tree-covered Barr Beacon. It is basically moorland in type with trees in plenty, mostly oak and silver birch and some fine varieties of beech and pine with patches of gorse to catch a wayward drive.

The 4th at 198 yards, with the green defended by five deep bunkers and trees to the back and right, is a good test of a long-iron shot. The 5th is a par 5 with plenty of hazards. The tee shot is played along a heavily wooded area with a tight exit and bunkers lying in wait. If you get past this, look out for the water hazard in front of the green. The 16th, a difficult par 3, is played from an elevated tee through trees to a green surrounded by more woodland and bunkered left and right.

The 17th is another fine hole. Again there is a narrow exit through trees for the tee shot, which needs to carry perhaps 120 yards and a valley eating into the fairway on the angle of the dogleg. The 18th green finds us just where we should be: right under the clubhouse windows.

£ £25	🎱 snooker
M golf club membership	🚗 leave the M5 at Junction 1 for Birmingham and the entrance is just 100 yards or so away on the left
✗ lunch and dinner daily except Monday	

SHERWOOD FOREST ⅃

Eakring Road, Mansfield, Nottingham NG18 3EW
☎ *Mansfield (0623) 23327*

One of the best courses in the Midlands, Sherwood Forest begins fairly comfortably with three par 4s which are by no means long and then a par 3 which takes you back to the clubhouse.

Sterner stuff is to come, although the course doesn't really show its teeth until the second nine. Few people would expect to make up lost ground here. The total course length is 6,709 yards.

On the last five holes of the first nine, there are two par 5s where professionals and good amateurs will be looking to be on in two. The most testing hole of the first half is the 6th, 433 yards. The fairway is wide but in driving distance there are two large bunkers and copses either side of the fairway, and the green, partly hidden by a fold in the ground, makes the second shot a problem.

The 10th is a good par 3 of 191 yards over heather to a long green with plenty of slopes. This is the beginning of a sequence of holes which really test long-iron and wooden club play, while the tee shots usually have to carry over heather to the fairways beyond.

The 11th is 464 yards but you are usually helped by the prevailing wind and the slope of the ground running in your favour, but not by the green, which is well bunkered and very small for so long a hole. The 12th is stroke index 1, 432 yards and doglegged to the left. The well-guarded green is downhill which makes club selection difficult if you aren't merely giving it all you've got. At the next hole the drive is very tight, to a narrow fairway with trees on both sides and out of bounds close by on the right. Once again, the fairly small green at this 447-yard hole is difficult to hit.

The 14th is the third of consecutive doglegs left. This time, the fairway slopes right to left towards a very well-placed bunker at the angle of the dogleg. The small green is well bunkered just short and in front on both sides, and you'll probably be playing a long iron for your second at this 428 yard hole.

Undoubtedly this stretch from 10th to the 14th is the toughest but there's still plenty to do over the closing holes.

£ £25 per round, £30 at weekends

M club membership certificate

✕ snacks, lunch and dinner daily

🚗 from Mansfield market place take A617 and turn left into Carter Lane and then right into Eakring Road. Look out for clubhouse left after about 2 miles

---

WILMSLOW

Great Warford, Mobberley, Knutsford, Cheshire WA16 7AY
☎ Mobberley (056587) 2148

Situated on the edge of the Manchester stockbroker belt, this course is just 18 miles from the city centre, and, founded in 1889, is amongst the earliest English clubs.

The first course was played with roped-off greens (to keep the cows at bay), and because of damage to the hedges an odd local rule was created: 'Any ball played into a hedge must be taken out and teed behind the hazard with a loss of two strokes.' However, you were allowed to play out of a dead hedge and I dare say this caused a few heated arguments in those far-off days.

Years later, a new hazard appeared – crows. It all began on the 15th. A few used to perch in a tree at average driving distance and swoop down to snatch up golf balls. Encouraged by their success, they told their chums and soon there was trouble on most of the closing holes.

A partial solution for a fourball was for the player with the honour to put down an old ball (these were disdained as the crows preferred a quality product) and then set off to stand guard over the other tee shots. If this wasn't done, two out of four new balls might disappear.

Shooting was tried, with little success, and then table-tennis balls filled with mustard were scattered over two fairways. In just a couple of hours about half of them were deposited outside the pro's shop, undoubtedly a crow comment that all this just wasn't golf.

Eventually, the crows departed but they're commemorated by the club's emblem: a single crow picking up a golf ball.

Wilmslow is demanding but not monstrously long at just over 6,500 yards from the medal tees, with good greens throughout the year. They still putted well during the 1983 Martini International when the drying qualities of the course were tested to the utmost in a deluge.

The 1st is one of the best holes on the course, a 366-yard par 4 with a valley to be carried with your tee shot and a spinney very much in play on the right at about 200 yards. It doglegs to the left all the way from tee to green, around a wood. A long par 4 of 444 yards follows, stroke index 1. Quite long par 4s are a feature of Wilmslow; there are six altogether of 400 yards and up but this is the longest.

Valleys and streams often come into play, for instance at the 144-yard 9th where the Mobberley Brook wanders across the front of the green, which is also tightly bunkered. It's in play again at the 14th, one of the finest par 3s in the region, but it's fairly well short of the green so that only a poorly struck tee shot will find it. The main hazard here is that the green is almost entirely encircled by a wood and anything wide of it is likely to mean either an unplayable lie or a lost ball. The 184 yards can certainly feel long when the prevailing wind is stiff.

The 16th, 400 yards, is the most picturesque hole on the course, a dogleg to the right with the second shot played through the woods. It's well bunkered at the angle of the dogleg with a pond shortly after, very much in play for either long tee shots or mishit seconds. The 17th is another attractive and difficult par 3 of 170 yards. From the tee you again play over the brook to a tightly bunkered green with woods close by.

The last hole is another good one, a par 5 of 477 yards, shortened to 433 yards for the Martini to make it a demanding par 4. Your tee shot must cope with the ground sloping from right to left down to woods and a lateral water hazard, and then you play down a valley to a plateau green with a steep slope on the right and, more significant, a stream only 8 yards to the left of the green.

£ £20　　　**M** none

✕ snacks daily, lunch and dinner daily except Monday

🚗 leave M6 at Junction 18 for Holmes Chapel and at Chelford roundabout follow signs for Alderley Edge, turning for Great Warford about 2 miles short. Leave M56 at Junction 6 for Wilmslow and follow signs for Mobberley

WOLLATON PARK

Wollaton Park, Wollaton, Nottingham NG8 1BT
☎ Nottingham (0602) 787585

A great feature of this parkland course is Wollaton Hall, which lies immediately to one side. It dates from Elizabethan times, and there's a story that the wall round the park, which is seven miles long, took seven men and seven apprentices seven years to build. Well, perhaps.

You approach the club down the splendid lime tree avenue which was the approach to the hall. Trees continue to be a great feature of the course throughout, as are the deer you may well chance upon.

The 1st tee is set amongst trees and that avenue of limes is out of bounds to the right, but it's otherwise a reasonably comfortable opening hole. You'll soon reach the 3rd, where a good carry from the tee is needed to begin a long par 4 of nearly 450 yards. Stroke index 1 follows at the 5th, where the trouble is mainly along the right.

The 8th is very attractive, with the green set close by the gardens of the hall. It's slightly higher than the tee and is very well bunkered, a feature of the work of Tom Williamson.

I particularly like the 14th, an uphill par 4 which plays longer than its 423 yards partly because there's a bank in front of the green which must be carried. The 15th is the best of the four par 5s. With the ground sloping away right, you may be tempted to go left and be trapped by bunkers on that side. There is a dogleg right about a hundred yards from the green.

The clubhouse is most attractive with eaves sweeping low, in Frank Lloyd Wright manner.

£ £18.50　　　**M** none

✕ snacks daily, lunch and dinner daily except Sunday and Monday

🎱 snooker

🚗 leave the M1 at Junction 25 along the A52. The course is about 2 miles from the city centre along Middleton Boulevard

WORCESTERSHIRE, THE

Wood Farm, Malvern Wells, Worcestershire WR14 4PP
☎ *Malvern (06845) 64428*

Dating from 1880, this was the first club to be founded in the Midlands and for quite some time was the first course you would have reached in a journey from Westward Ho! Its first premises were a converted slaughterhouse and for well over forty years play took place on common land.

Golf on common land has always produced problems. There tend to be rather too many sheep, cows, geese and even people. With increasing car ownership in the 1920s, the problems became acute, resulting in 1927 in the move to the present site. Part of the course was ploughed up in the Second World War and an emergency hospital was built on another part, so that the Worcestershire became, and remained for some years, a nine-hole course.

Today, however, the senior Midlands club has the full eighteen holes, stretching to 6,425 yards over gently undulating land at the foothills of the Malvern Hills. These are always a background to the west and from higher parts of the course you can see across the Vale of Evesham to the Cotswolds. Streams influence play on six holes and there are also three ponds.

After quite a short par 4 to set you on your way, the 2nd, 353 yards, is one of the most teasing holes. There's a lateral ditch at driving range on the left and the raised green is no easy target, some 40 feet above the fairway. The 4th at only 479 yards is not a long par 5 but it begins with a blind drive and out of bounds close on the left. The second shot is also blind, if your drive is a short one, and there's trouble near the green on both sides.

The 10th is stroke index 1 and 441 yards, with a ditch angling across the fairway to avoid on the tee shot. The hole slopes uphill, and into the wind it is highly difficult to get home in two strokes. My final choice is the 14th, another long par 4 with out of bounds from tee to green on the left and a stream crossing the fairway about 90 yards short of the green. This is the last of four par 4s over 400 yards but there are a few others where you can hope to be on with a drive and a pitch. Sir Edward Elgar, who was a member, once did rather better than this, holing his second shot for a 2; it is his only golfing feat to crop up in the club's records.

💷 *£16, £20 at weekends*	🎱 *snooker*
🅼 *membership of a golf club*	🚗 *from the A449 Malvern to Ledbury road turn off along B4209 for about 200 yards*
✕ *snacks daily, lunch and dinner daily except Monday*	

EAST ANGLIA

KEY TO SYMBOLS

🌳	PARKLAND	☎	TELEPHONE	✗	CATERING PROVIDED
	LINKS	✉	NEED TO BOOK IN ADVANCE	🏠	ACCOMMODATION PROVIDED
	MOORLAND	£	APPROXIMATE COURSE FEE	Ⓛ	RESTRICTIONS ON LADIES AND/OR YOUTHS
	HEATHLAND	M	MEMBERSHIP REQUIREMENTS FOR VISITORS		OTHER SPORTING FACILITIES
	DOWNLAND				
	UPLAND			🚗	DIRECTIONS

ALDEBURGH ⬤

Aldeburgh, Suffolk IP15 5PQ
☎ *Aldeburgh (0728) 452890*

Could this be the hardest place in Britain to play your handicap? The amateur course record, for example, is just three under par, and the professional, held by John Panton, equals the par 68 (professional tournaments are, however, very rare here). Standard scratch is 71. There are no fewer than nine holes of more than 400 yards and seven of these are over 420. Not one, however, gives the relief of being a par 5, though in bogey competitions four are rated as 5s. There's just one short par 4, 324 yards.

Aldeburgh dates from 1884, which makes it very early for England. In those days of the hard guttie a course of 4,700 yards was laid out about a mile from the sea; it was basically heathland in character with fine springy turf and sandy soil. Visiting it in the 1920s, the great golf writer Bernard Darwin said: 'In texture, it is very like one of the best of Surrey courses.' Much later, it is said that in old age Darwin hit his last golf shots here one summer evening. He went out with just a 4 iron and played three balls to the 9th green. The last finished inches from the hole. Said Darwin: 'Now I can retire gracefully from this unspeakable game.' In 1907, J.H. Taylor came up with Willie Park Junior, both Open Champions, to upgrade the course, following the arrival of the wound ball, and it has changed relatively little since. One of Taylor's notions was the bunkers should not be 'shallow like spittoons', so some of Aldeburgh's are deep indeed.

The 4th, a short par 3, features a sleepered bunker in front and along part of the right-hand side, with a kidney-shaped green beyond. It's followed by a very testing run of three holes each over 400 yards. The last of these has a famous view from the tee westwards to the River Alde, 'Little Japan' and Iken Church.

On the second nine, some of the fairways become almost links in character, with very pronounced folds. The 14th is particularly well thought of. You drive between two great trees with a ridge to cross before doglegging to the plateau green. In 1952, the late Ryder Cup player Harry Weetman, a very long hitter, ignored the dogleg and reached the green in one.

In the early seventies a nine-hole course was opened, intended mainly for beginners and without bunkers.

💷 *£22.50, £27.50 at weekends*

✗ *lunch is available daily with prior notice, snacks daily except Sundays*

🚗 *from the south, turn off the A12 for Aldeburgh and turn off along A1094 ½ mile beyond Farnham for 50 yards or so*

HUNSTANTON ◢

Golf Course Road, Old Hunstanton, Norfolk PE36 6JQ
☎ *Hunstanton (0485) 532811*

Hunstanton is a championship course and has hosted more than a dozen of them including the English Amateur Championship, the English Open Amateur Strokeplay and the British Ladies', and the Schweppes PGA. The old club brochure used to claim the course was 'the finest test of golf between the Humber and the Thames'.

It's a links course running between the sea and the River Hun, following the basic out-and-back pattern. However, only once do as many as three consecutive holes run in the same direction and half a dozen are played directly towards the Hun or the sea so that there are fairly constant shifts of wind direction.

Perhaps the most remarkable of all hole-in-one feats took place here. In 1974 R.J. Taylor holed out with a 1 iron on the 188-yard 16th. The next day, in a different wind, he did it again with a 6 iron. But that's not all. When he reached the 16th tee for the third time he is said to have been offered odds of a million to one against continuing his sequence. Out came the 6 iron again – and down went the ball. All this on one of the best par 3s in Britain. The tee shot is all carry with the narrow green set up up on a ridge with bunkers to either side. As we've seen from Taylor's club selection, it's exposed and therefore needs anything between a shortish iron and a whack with a driver.

The start is fairly undemanding, a short par 4, though there's a sandhill with a bunker set in the face to be carried from the tee; it does not need a long hit, however, but it may make you think for your first tee shot of the day. In fact, the first few holes are not particularly exciting. Many people consider that the course really begins at the 6th, a short par 4 and a very good one. The fairway is widely inviting but your pitch is to a high plateau with plenty of trouble around – bunkers and a deep grassy hollow. The 7th is a good short hole of 160 yards, played from one plateau to another with an uninviting gully between. Two par 5s complete the first nine, played in reverse directions, with views of sea, marshes and countryside from the 9th tee.

The 11th is a tiger hole, a long par 4. There are no bunkers and no need of them, as it's played into the prevailing wind and has the beach along the right-hand side. You hit through a narrow valley, with less room the nearer you get to the green, and usually with heavy rough on either side.

The 13th, 387 yards, is most unusual. You have a blind drive over a sandy ridge to quite a short stretch of fairway. You then have an elevated shot over a series of humps and hollows to the green. It's best to overclub, if anything.

If some people would call this one old-fashioned, they're likely to feel the same about the 14th, a blind long one-shotter of nearly 220 yards with bunkers set in the upslope before the green. The 15th is quite a short par 5, played along a 'secret valley' and protected by sandhills from winds on the right.

The finish is a good examination. After the short 16th comes a long par 4 of some 440 yards. The fairway falls away to the right and there's a very large bunker to catch a poorly hit drive. A ridge runs along the left into which, eventually, the shelf-like green is set. Better to settle for getting on in three, for it's a very difficult target for a wood or long iron.

The last is another attractive hole, along a valley with a carrying second shot needed to the plateau green.

The course is some 6,600 yards, more or less evenly balanced between the two nines, and it's difficult to play to your handicap.

Hunstanton dates back to 1891 as a short nine-hole course, extended a few years later to the full eighteen. Later still, James Braid was called in to advise on changes.

Most of the present course can be credited to James Sherlock, a contemporary of Vardon, Taylor and Braid. He won the *News of the World* Matchplay Championship in 1910, beating Harry Vardon in the final, and also played against the Americans in a fore-runner to the Ryder Cup in 1921. He lived to the age of 91, as all good golfers should.

£ £22

M membership of a golf club and a handicap certificate

✕ snacks, lunch and dinner daily except Monday. Dinner must be booked in advance

🚗 from King's Lynn, turn left after Caley Hall Hotel or right if from Sheringham

---

LINCOLN (Torksey) 🏌

Torksey, Lincolnshire LN1 2EG
☎ *Torksey (042 771) 721*

Torksey, as it is most often known, is an inland course set on a sandy subsoil, which makes for near-ideal golfing terrain. As J.H. Taylor, five times Open Champion, reported in 1903: 'It is the kind of ground that one usually identifies with the best of seaside courses. The subsoil is productive of the very finest kind of turf that can be wished for. Once the course is got into decent playing order it will practically keep itself.'

Taylor laid out nine holes and Torksey was later redesigned and extended to 6,438 yards. It undulates quite gently and there is a good feeling of the separateness of holes, many fairways being lined with Scots pine and silver birch. Driving areas are quite generous but the course is heavily bunkered and some fairways are rather links in character, with uneven stances and lies to contend with. Greens are true and, at best, quite fast.

You should try to make your score on the first seven holes, which include a par 5 and four par 4s of no very great length. Mark James did this when he set the course record of 65, which is five under par. He reached that position after the first seven holes, and managed to maintain it to the end.

After this start, there is a sequence of four fairly long two-shot holes, the 8th, rated as stroke index 1, being the most difficult. Trees either side and a sloping fairway provide some difficulties for the drive and bunkering makes the second none too easy. The 9th is also over 420 yards and the green has a narrow entrance, which makes placing your drive well most important.

After the sequence of long 4s, you may tend to relax at the 14th. It looks easy enough but your drive must be straight. The 15th was recently extended to a par 5, though with the right shape of drive you may have a chance of getting home in two. It's a dogleg left and you must bend your drive round the angle with trouble both sides of the fairway. You'll still have a long iron at least to the green, which is well bunkered. The 16th is a good shorter par 4. With out of bounds along the left, many people play too far right where their tee shot comes to grief in a well-positioned bunker. If all is well so far, you still have a Scots pine guarding the front right and a water hazard at the back.

The 17th is the best par 3 of only three. At 186 yards it's by no means short and asks you to carry a small lake while being mindful of out of bounds on the left and the bunkers.

£ £18

M membership of a golf club

✕ lunch daily, dinner daily except Tuesday, when snacks substitute

---

🚗 on the A156 Lincoln to Gainsborough road or the A1133 Newark to Gainsborough road

---

LUFFENHAM HEATH   ⎍

Ketton, Stamford, Lincolnshire PE9 3UU
☎ *Stamford (0780) 720205*

As the name implies, this course, one of the many splendid ones laid out by James Braid early this century is on heathland. Most of the fairways plunge straight through scrub but there are doglegs as well. In general they are quite gently angled.

Trees are a good feature – elm, ash, birch, pine, dogwood, oak, cherry and hawthorn, though they don't come strongly into play often, unless you're well off line. There is a great deal of gorse, heather and low bushes, which are more of a threat. The fairways are undulating and the course plays well in winter months.

Golf courses really do help to preserve bird, insect and plant life. Luffenham is in a conservation area and the club is very willing to help in what ways it can, just as Royal Birkdale and Royal St George's do. The club has identified some quite unusual plants: common centaury, bryony, tor grass, agrimony, pignut, cleavers, lady's bedstraw, purging flax and three-nerved sandwort.

The course is close to the River Chater and there are fine views, particularly from the 4th, 10th and 17th tees and also the 7th green.

The 6th hole is an excellent test, particularly from the back tee. This is set back into woodland some 150 yards and elevated. The drive to safety is very narrow. The 13th, a left-hand dogleg, gives similar problems for the tee shot. There are trees all the way from tee to green along the left and they continue along the right until you reach the corner of the dogleg.

The 17th is a testing and fairly long par 3. You must carry all the way to the green which is heavily bunkered and also protected by banks and heather across the front.

£ *£25*

M *a club handicap certificate*

✕ *snacks daily, meals by prior arrangement*

🚗 *6 miles south east of Stamford through Ketton on A6121 or leave A47 along A6121 for Stamford and look out for clubhouse right after about 4 miles*

PETERBOROUGH MILTON 🌳

Milton Ferry, Peterborough, Cambridgeshire PE6 7AG
☎ *Peterborough (0733) 380489*

This is one of James Braid's later courses, being opened in 1938. It is parkland type and fairly flat. Its features include old trees, water hazards and Milton Hall, the home of the Fitzwilliam family since 1502. Most of the holes are doglegged, though often only slightly.

Peterborough provides what is an ideal start in a straightforward par 5 as it helps reduce hold-ups on the 1st tee. The first real challenge comes at the 4th, a strategic par 4 and stroke index 2. With out of bounds along the left, the player is penalized if he plays too far right for safety. His mid-iron then has to clear trees about 100 yards short of the green. The narrow green is also an easier target when played from left of centre of the fairway.

The 7th, another slight dogleg left, offers a wide fairway, but the second shot must be well struck to have enough backspin to hold the hog's-back green. The 10th is stroke index 1, with a good drive right of centre giving the best approach route. The second shot has to get past a blind, deep valley short of the green. Few people like playing a little pitch from down there.

The 15th uses the natural hazard of trees well. The fairway doglegs right around large oak trees, and then you usually have to clear a chestnut tree some 45 yards short of the green. Shots over trees are not included in the design of a golf hole all that often. More often the golfer plays such a shot when he's off line, but it can be a fair and interesting feature.

Peterborough Milton is a stiff test, all in all. The course record of 66 is held by Joe Higgins.

The practice facilities are good with a large main ground, putting green, practice bunker and pitching green.

£ £20

M a handicap certificate or introduction by a member

✗ lunch and dinner daily except Monday

🚗 some 2 miles west of Peterborough on the A47

ROYAL CROMER

145 Overstrand Road, Cromer, Norfolk NR27 0JH
☎ *Cromer (0263) 512884*

Situated right on the cliff edge, this is quite a hilly course where you'll experience plenty of variety of lie – uphill, downhill and sideways. Although there are relatively few trees, some of the course is parkland in type with several lushly grassed fairways. Elsewhere, links fescues occur. Gorse and fern are the main natural hazard.

The club has a long history, its centenary coming up in 1988. A few years after its foundation James Braid was brought in to design the present course, though there have, of course, been changes over the years, including recent alterations which brought the length to more than 6,500 yards. Some of the changes have been brought about by erosion. For instance, there was a very early ladies' course which toppled over the edge of the cliff, and the original 17th hole was an early casualty. In recent years two new holes have had to be constructed, the 2nd and 3rd. The main cause of parts of the cliff edge slipping away is not the sea, but constant buffeting by the wind.

The most exhilarating holes, as you'd expect, are those closest to the cliff edge, and the wind is likely to be a major factor in the playing of the course. It is a fair test because it comes at you from all points of the compass as the course lay-out changes direction.

You begin with a long dogleg right with a large depression short of the right-hand green. At the 4th look out for fine views from the very elevated tee and also the rather tight out of bounds on the right which runs virtually the whole way.

The 7th might be considered old-fashioned because of its blind drive. The second shot is very attractive, to an elevated green at the end of a small valley.

'The Lighthouse', the 14th, is Cromer's most famous hole. The drive is difficult, to a small plateau on a fairway wandering above tee level with the sea near at hand on the right and heavy gorse with no mercy the other side. The green, however, is large and set close to the lighthouse but it takes a good shot with wood or your longest iron to reach it.

💷 £20	🍴 lunch and dinner daily
Ⓜ membership of a golf club	🚗 1 mile east of Cromer on main coast road for Overstand. Aim for the lighthouse and Lighthouse Road to locate the clubhouse

ROYAL WEST NORFOLK

Brancaster, King's Lynn, Norfolk PE31 8AX
☎ Brancaster (0485) 210223

At Brancaster, as the course is usually known, you'll be impressed first of all by the feel of remoteness. As Bernard Darwin wrote three quarters of a century ago:

'I should imagine that Brancaster, before golf was introduced there, must have been one of the quietest and most rural spots to be found in England. Even now it is wonderfully peaceful, and has a distinct charm and character of its own. We get out at Hunstanton Station and drive a considerable number of miles along a nice, flat, dull east country road till we get to the tranquil little village, with a church and some pleasant trees. In front of the village is a stretch of grey-green marsh, and beyond the marsh is a range of sandhills, and that is where the golf is.

And very fine golf indeed, on a treeless links course with sand dunes to the south and marram grass to the north. Dominating the place are the tidal marshes which have to be driven at the 8th. Indeed a combination of high tide and high wind can lead to flooding, and the access road from the village is often under water for up to three hours during high water. To be on the safe side, leave your car in the village and proceed on foot.

Brancaster was laid out in 1891, it is said on the suggestion of the Prince of Wales (later Edward VII), while he was out shooting over the land. The club has had its 'Royal' title right from the start and indeed there have been four royal captains, the Duke of Kent being the most recent of these in 1981, succeeding that fine golf writer, the late Pat Ward Thomas.

Over the years the course has changed very little, although the sea destroyed a couple of holes many years ago. This means that to some eyes it is old-fashioned, with some blind shots and huge wooden railway sleepers shoring up bunkers and revetting greens. It must have been formidable in the days of the shorter guttie ball.

The 1st is a long dogleg 4, the first test being to keep your nerve on the tee when faced with the chasm. At the 3rd one of those sleepered bunkers comes fully into play for the first time. This is a 400-yard hole with a big cross bunker about 50 yards short of the green, following an angled drive to avoid the marshes. If the drive is good you shouldn't have much problem but it'll catch any second shot not well struck.

The 4th is another of Brancaster's famous holes, only about 120 yards from an elevated tee to a green raised up and fronted by bunkers and more of those sleepers. It's particularly difficult to hold with anything less than a perfectly struck pitch.

The next few holes are played close to the marshes, which cut the 8th into three. You drive over one arm on this hole, biting off as much as you dare and hopefully arrive on what is really an island fairway. After a successful drive, the green could be in range over the second inlet.

The 9th takes you to the far end of the course, with another drive over marshland and another huge boarded bunker to be carried by your second shot to a green set in the dunes.

Undoubtedly, the first nine are the more formidable, especially with the wind against you, and at 3,300 yards are 400 yards longer than the second nine. However, there is usually a wind at Brancaster and you may have to battle your way home through it, nearer to the sea as well. The 11th and 12th are amongst the dunes with the celebrated 14th the next great golf hole. This is a long par 4 of 430 yards with a depression and short rough to carry some 50 yards short of the green, which is set close by the beach. It is followed by a formidable longish par 3, if the wind is up, with a cavernous bunker on the direct line between tee and green, a little less threatening than it looks because there is dead ground afterwards. The actual carry is not quite what it looks. Brancaster ends on a typical note. The last hole, 380 yards, has a green protected by a sleepered bunker at the front and another to the rear; the latter is easy to get into for the greens are often unkind to any shot less than truly struck.

Like its near neighbour at Hunstanton, here you will find some of the fastest greens in Britain. Being true, they are a very fair test, however.

£ £25

M *prior arrangement with the secretary*

✕ snacks and lunch daily with the
clubhouse closing at 5pm in the
winter and 8pm in the summer

🚗 take the beach road from
Brancaster village, about 1½ miles

ROYAL WORLINGTON AND
NEWMARKET

Worlington, Bury St Edmunds, Suffolk
☎ Mildenhall (0638) 712216

Royal Worlington, as the course is most often called, is the home of
Cambridge University golf.

Often courses are founded with only nine holes but then it is felt
essential to add another nine to achieve the magic figure of eighteen.
Yet how often the original nine are very much better than the later,
simply because a good stretch of golfing country had been found for
them. What followed all too often had to be cobbled together, perhaps
over a couple of flat fields, very likely on a different subsoil, and with
bunkering and planting trees as the only way of creating interest.

In its nearly one hundred years, there must have been opportunities to
extend Royal Worlington but the temptation was resisted, and it
remains only nine holes. The course is set on sandy soil which ensures
fast greens, superb winter drainage and excellent fairways, but round
about the land is far more likely to be clay, even marshy.

The result is what Bernard Darwin called 'the sacred nine' and
Herbert Warren Wind, the American golf writer, 'far and away the best
nine hole course in the world'. Indeed there have been some to argue
that this is the best nine-hole stretch anywhere.

Two of my close friends have been great enthusiasts of the course.
Henry Longhurst, who captained Cambridge in the early thirties, used
to come roaring down here in a 3-litre Bentley, and Leonard Crawley,
godfather to one of my children, settled down here. He once had a 64
over the course at the age of sixty-two. The record for just nine holes is an
amazing 28, set many years ago. It could stand for ever!

You start with a par 5 of no great difficulty, though it's possible to be
out of bounds all along the right. Then comes a long par 3 of some 220
yards that's every bit as difficult as the 16th at Carnoustie. The green is
shaped a little like a bowler hat. Anything that isn't very well struck will
leak away to either side and the shot back is very difficult. Leonard
Crawley used to say that the 3rd was one of the best two-shotters in the
country, yet it's by no means long. The drive is over a cross bunker to a
hog's-back fairway with a pond and trees to the right, but there is worse
left, as the slope will take you into a ditch. Another ditch winds across the

165

front of the green with bunkers guarding the left.

The 4th is a 500-yard par 5 with an undulating fairway, and a dyke to avoid on the right, where your second shot may wander. But the key is the pitch to the very small green which slopes away from the player.

The 5th is another famous short hole, 157 yards to a narrow green which has a bit of a saucer at the front and is convex at the rear, where the flag is usually set. Your ball may be thrown off right down to a stream or left into the grassy 'Mug's Hole'. However, as this par 3 is so much shorter than the 2nd, you will only be using a mid-iron.

The 6th is a very long two-shotter, while the 7th is a medium-iron 165 yards to a green guarded on both sides by bunkers and a gully in front.

The last is only 299 yards, much shorter if you go for the green, risk the out of bounds and carry some tall trees. If you make the carry, the green is still the most contoured one on the course, so three putts are likely. However, here, as always at Worlington, good putting is rewarded. When you see your ball running true at the hole, it will hold its line and not twitch away as it dies.

£ £20	**✕** snacks and lunch daily
M a handicap certificate, but no visitors at weekends or on bank holidays unless with a member	**🚗** bypass Newmarket along A45 and then take the A11 for Norwich and turn for Worlington after about 4 miles

SHERINGHAM

Weybourne Road, Sheringham, Norfolk NR26 8HG
☎ *Sheringham (0263) 823488*

Sheringham will always be associated with the name of Joyce Wethered. In 1920 at the age of nineteen she came here to compete in the English Ladies' Championship. Her idea was not so much to try to win as to keep a friend company. However, round succeeded round and eventually she reached the final where she faced Cecil Leitch, thought to be by far the best British player. However, Joyce Wethered won, and was an overnight sensation. She went on to become what both Bobby Jones and Henry Cotton considered to be the best player ever, man or woman.

Sheringham is a downland course set on cliffs and with a lot of gorse. The holes vary strongly in type. The first two are in open country; they are followed by five along the cliff edge, with exhilarating views of sea and beach. Then come seven holes carved through the gorse and finally four over very undulating ground.

There is the almost ideal start to get a crowded field away, a short par 4 with a long 5 to follow. The 1st is a tricky little hole. Only 335 yards, it swings quite sharply left with bunkers and a grassy pit to trap a greedy drive. The green is shelf-like and surrounded by various kinds of trouble.

The 3rd, 424 yards, brings the cliffs into play, but not too threateningly as the best line for the second shot is to play away from them. The 5th is a very fine hole. You drive from a high tee set on the shoulder of a hill and down to a plateau fairway. The second shot is thrilling: over a dip to a shelf green with the cliff edge on the right.

The 6th is the first par 3 and 217 yards. It's played from a high tee, into the prevailing wind, to the green in the valley below, with a grassy hollow left and a bunker creeping into the green on the right – and cliffs close by.

The 10th, 440 yards, is the longest par 4 but you may well have the wind at your back, needed because it's gently uphill all the way. The narrow fairway slopes right. The 12th is another very good par 4, which doglegs round the foot of a well-bunkered, gorse-covered slope. The best line is only a little left because greenside bunkers make a second shot from that side unlikely to succeed.

There are some shorter par 4s to follow. The 16th, 349 yards, is the pick of them. With your tee shot you have to carry a large sand quarry, followed by cross bunkers. You then pitch up to a green at the top of a rise, with the ground falling away sharply to the left. Bunkers near the green favour a tee shot that has been placed down the right, close to the out-of-bounds fence.

The 17th is the scene of a famous Joyce Wethered story. She made sure of her championship by laying a long putt dead on a green close by the railway while a train came puffing by. When asked afterwards how she had kept her concentration amidst the hubbub she asked: 'What train?' Well, it's not the point of my story, but apparently it was the 4.20...

The green has since been moved and is now a plateau on a ridge. If you've avoided the railway from the tee and hit a good one, the finish of this 405-yard hole demands a brave second shot over diagonal bunkers, carrying the steep rise up to the green.

The 18th is the last of seven long par 4s, perhaps the main feature of the course. A drive close to the out-of-bounds railway is again rewarded with a far more open second shot. The 423 yards complete 6,464 yards of downland golf of a very high standard.

£ £23 or £28	✕ lunch and dinner daily
M a handicap certificate	🚗 the clubhouse is about 5 minutes walk from either the town centre or the station. By car, take the A149 west towards Weybourne for about ½ mile
ℚ juniors must be accompanied by an adult	

THETFORD

Brandon Road, Thetford, Norfolk IP24 3NE
☎ *Thetford (0842) 752258*

Thetford Golf Club is situated in the Brecklands, an area of sandy soil, and was once far more heathland in type and more abounding with rabbits than it is today. It has large areas of heather, gorse and broom but belts of trees – birch, oak and pine – now separate one hole from another and have become strategic features governing the right line for the tee shot on many holes.

Thetford was founded in 1912 and its architectural pedigree includes the names of C.H. Mayo, James Braid and Mackenzie Ross; later changes have mainly been to lengthen holes to keep pace with the improvements in golf equipment. It now measures 6,879 yards. It is excellent for winter play and has some fairway watering for dry weather.

You begin with the challenge of quite a long par 3 of 195 yards, over a valley to a terraced green. Heather is a feature here, and at many later holes. The 5th is a particularly good par 4, with the tee shot played over a wide valley with trees, bunkers and an old chalk pit very much in play. The undulating green is just over the brow of a hill, and falls away to the left.

Because a by-pass was recently built for Thetford, the course lost five holes, 7 to 11. New holes were constructed and opened in May 1989. They are long and testing, adding almost 400 yards to the course.

The 9th, at 421 yards, is slightly uphill and played into the prevailing wind. It is stroke index 1. The 10th is a par 5 of 546 yards and is banana-shaped – it does much more than dogleg: The drive has to be carefully placed if there is to be any chance of attacking the flag. The 13th, 522 yards, was the longest hole on the course and begins with a testing drive through the trees. Beware also of a bunker which eats into the fairway about 100 yards short of the green on the left. The silver birch trees at the back of the green make it a well-defined target.

The 15th rewards placement of the tee shot. The drive to this 375-yard hole should be held up to the right because there are trees along the left until you reach the green, and they tend to block out any tee shot along the left side of the fairway. This is followed by quite a daunting par 3, even though it's only 157 yards with bunkers just about all the way from tee to green and all around it as well. It frightens the life out of players who lack confidence in their sand irons!

The course ends with a very testing par 4 of 467 yards, a dogleg to the right, where a 4 will very often win the hole. A bunker to the right of the fairway some 250 yards from the tee discourages any attempt to shorten the hole and the green is set just over the brow of the hill in front of the clubhouse. Always aim a little right of the flag.

One of the great English all-round sportsmen, the cricketer J.W.H.T. Douglas, used to be a member and a trophy commemorates him.

£ £25

Ⓜ a handicap certificate

✗ snacks daily, lunch and dinner are available

🚗 leave A11 at roundabout on by-pass, take B1107 for Brandon; the clubhouse is off this road to the left

THORNDON PARK 🌲

Ingrave, Brentwood, Essex CM13 3RH
☎ Brentwood (0277) 810345

This is one of many courses laid out in ancient deer parks, in this case a very spacious one so there's good separation between each hole. A lot of the fairways wander through woodland, and the greens often have the sense of total seclusion. Thorndon Park has been used for the PGA Close Championship, an event which ran for a good few years.

After a quiet start, the tee shot at the 389-yard 3rd hole makes some demands on the nerve for it has to be played over the end of a lake.

A water hazard comes into play on the next hole also. Here a stream runs left to right diagonally across the fairway to just short of the green. If you drive left you can be in it but that side gives the best line into the green. The 7th is another good hole, a 392-yard dogleg right with a ravine across the front of the green.

Quite stiff par 4s are really the main feature of the course. Only the 6th could be described as a drive and pitch. The 8th, 422 yards and stroke index 1, needs two good hits.

The 13th is an excellent par 4 of 396 yards which bends around a wood. You can hope for some run on your tee shot but the second is uphill and hopefully over a line of bunkers set in the ridge short of the green. It's stroke index 2.

The 15th is the best of the four par 3s, 183 yards with a ravine running diagonally from the left of the tee to short of the green on the right. There are also bunkers to either side and in front. The round ends with two stiff par 4s of around 400 yards.

£ £35, £25 per round

Ⓜ membership of a golf club

✗ snacks daily to 6pm, lunch and dinner daily except Monday

🚗 2 miles south of Brentwood on the A128. From the M25 leave along the A127 for Basildon and Southend and turn left on to the A128

WOODBRIDGE

Bromeswell Heath, Woodbridge, Suffolk IP12 2PF
☎ *Woodbridge (03943) 2038*

Although not as widely known as Brancaster, Worlington and Hunstanton, this is one of the very best courses in East Anglia.

It's laid out on a sandy heathland plateau with an abundance of gorse, heather, scrub and woodland. There's not one bad hole and there are a number of very good ones.

The first course came into play in 1893 with nine holes; a couple of years later there were eighteen, sited to avoid a rifle range which had been 'interfering with play'!

One feature that may help you to score reasonably well is that there are several par 4s either short or medium in length, although there are also half a dozen more testing ones. Both varieties set the golfer a good spread of problems.

The course begins with two quite short 4s of 346 and 329 yards, with the second given interest by a stream which comes in from the left and flows into a pond a little short of the right front of the green.

The 4th is another short par 4 of 330 yards and the tee shot should be to the left centre of the fairway. Go too far right, however, and you will probably find a particularly formidable bunker. The green is ringed by five bunkers. Two longer par 4s follow, doglegging in opposite directions with the 6th, 401 yards, being well bunkered to catch either an off-line drive or a second shot not quite well enough hit.

Perhaps the most difficult hole is the 10th, 431 yards, uphill all the way to a long and narrow green right at the top of the slope. The best golfing stretch, however, is from the 14th to the 17th.

The 14th is a right-hand dogleg of 425 yards, played over a dip from a high tee, where you need to get as far up the slope as you can. There are bunkers to trap either a poor drive or second shot. The green itself is well trapped to catch anything short. The 17th, 400 yards, is a sharply angled dogleg to the right with bunkers in the corner which encourage a drive rather too far left, where there's an out of bounds. The last is an interesting finishing hole. If the match is still in the balance, players may try to bite off some of the right-angled dogleg – and perish.

If the main course should happen to be crowded, there's a short course of 2,243 yards, with several interesting holes.

💷 *£25, £10 for the short*	🚗 *leave the A12 at roundabout for Melton and thereafter the B1084 for Orford. After crossing the River Deben, bear left at next roundabout and club is then about 300 yards on the right*
Ⓜ *a handicap certificate*	
✕ *snacks and lunch daily, dinners can be booked by visiting parties*	

THE
WEST COUNTRY

KEY TO SYMBOLS

MAP 7

🌳 PARKLAND	☎ TELEPHONE	✗ CATERING PROVIDED
🏴 LINKS	✉ NEED TO BOOK IN ADVANCE	🏨 ACCOMMODATION PROVIDED
🏔 MOORLAND	£ APPROXIMATE COURSE FEE	Ⓛ RESTRICTIONS ON LADIES AND/OR YOUTHS
🏞 HEATHLAND	M MEMBERSHIP REQUIREMENTS FOR VISITORS	OTHER SPORTING FACILITIES
DOWNLAND		
UPLAND		🚗 DIRECTIONS

BRISTOL AND CLIFTON

Failand, Bristol BS8 3TH
☎ *Long Ashton (0272) 393117*

This is a parkland course, running through undulating and heavily wooded country, yet with not many trees on the course itself. The club celebrates its centenary in 1991. Only eight years after its foundation a new clubhouse was necessary, such had been the rise in membership. This building may well be unique in that the design is based on a typical Malayan planter's bungalow.

The start is by no means comfortable. You're right in at a fairly deep end with two good hits needed to reach the 1st green. A short 4 comes next, but the green is tricky and then comes a very long par 4, though the green is not sternly guarded. It also plays into the prevailing wind.

The 7th is one of those very short par 3s that can be so exasperating. You really ought to be able to lob that wedge, or whatever club you fancy, onto the green but... It's around 120 yards long and Peter Oosterhuis, who holds the course record with a 64, once said he thought it the best very short hole in the west of England. The green is beset by bunkers and semi-plateau. Even so, you really ought to get your 3. At the 8th, on the other hand, your longest hitting is needed. Even from the forward tees, it's 450 yards and there's out of bounds in waiting for going right with either drive or second shot.

The 11th is an awkward driving hole. There's an out-of-bounds wall along the right with the fairway sloping that way. Play well left. You next come to a series of holes known as 'The Valley'. The 13th is a long par 3 which needs good judgement of distance on the day for it's played from way up above the green. The 15th is one of the few examples in British golf of a hole with a wall as a hazard of play. This one runs diagonally across the direct line from the tee to green and, of course, must be carried. From the forward tees, however, the hole is just 260 yards, so you can think in terms of trying to drive it. The last of 'The Valley' holes, the 16th, tests your accuracy with the drive and your nerve on the approach shot. There's out of bounds on the right but the ground slopes left to another kind of problem – a rough hillside and valley. If you are well left, your second shot will have to carry a grassy quarry to the elevated green. You finish with a par 5 which isn't particularly long, but both gorse and trees can block you out from the green.

£ £19	M a handicap certificate	🚗 from the M5 take the A369 for Bristol from Junction 19 and turn right at first traffic lights. The club is on the right after about 1 mile
✗ snacks and lunch daily; dinner can be arranged for visiting parties		

BROADSTONE ⛳

Wentworth Drive, Broadstone, Dorset BH18 8DQ
☎ *Broadstone (0202) 692595*

I quickly grew to love this course in my youth. The only hole I don't much care for is the 2nd, a par 4 which can seem rather a long and dull slog uphill. Otherwise the course has great variety, with its great strengths being the excellent par 3s and several par 4s of over 400 yards.

It was originally laid out by Tom Dunn, and Harry Colt was called in to update the course just before the First World War. Work had to stop when the army commandeered all the horses in use!

The first nine are protected from the wind to some extent and then for several holes you're up on open heathland with splendid views of the Channel, Poole Harbour and rolling Dorset countryside, before you come home to the clubhouse over the last two holes. The course is crossed by two railway lines, now long closed which used to belong to the Somerset and Dorset Joint Railway in the days when men of prime ministerial stature used to play here – A.J. Balfour, Bonar Law, Ramsay MacDonald and Winston Churchill, for example.

The 7th is the first of its top-rank holes. The tee shot is over a valley and you need to find the left side of the fairway to have much chance of hitting the green with your second. This has to carry another valley to an elevated green. The far side is set with bunkers and plenty of heather and wiry grass.

There then follows a very testing par 3 indeed, at a little over 200 yards – something of a monster, you'll find, if the wind is against you. It is very well guarded by bunkers, which tend to gather the ball, so you must carry all the way to the green.

The 11th, though a little shorter, is thought by many to be the hardest par 3 at Broadstone. The green is long but narrow, with bunkers right followed by heather and gorse. To the left, there is a steep, heather-covered bank.

The 13th is one of the really classic par 4s. After carrying a road and ditch, which force you to go right, you then play across a valley to a green that is a little like the famous Redan hole at North Berwick in that it too slants across the line of play. There is a drop to the left, followed by bunkers the rest of the way. Many people are tempted to play along the right and try to make sure of a 5 with a pitch for their third shot. It is really satisfying to see your long approach sailing in on target.

💷 £20	🍴 *snacks, lunch and dinner daily*
Ⓜ *a handicap certificate*	🚗 *Turn off the A349 Poole to Wimborne road at Dunyeats Road and follow signs*

BURNHAM AND BERROW ⤴

St Christopher's Way, Burnham-on-Sea, Somerset TA8 2PE
☎ *Burnham (0278) 785760*

The greens at Burnham and Berrow were magnificent, summer and winter, when I used to play there in my youth, and I believe they still are, if Christie O'Connor's thoughts are anything to go by. After winning the Senior's Championship in 1983 he said: 'I wish I could dig them up and take them back to Royal Dublin.'

They feed them with traditional stuff – bone meal, blood, hoof and horn and, occasionally, iron. It works very well, as it always did.

Some very famous professional names have been associated with Burnham, J.H. Taylor most of all. He was brought up at Westward Ho!, where he became a greenkeeper, and his first full club professional's job was at these links. Taylor was renowned for his skill and accuracy with mashie (5 to 6 iron) approach play which he felt was honed by the need for extreme precision to the undulating and tiny greens of the course in the 1890s.

The course has been much visited by amateur events: the English Amateur Championship and the Brabazon Trophy on several occasions and the Ladies' Championship on three occasions, as well as by other premier competitions. One of the most interesting of these is the West of England Matchplay, held here, with many famous names on the cup, since 1912.

This is a place of high dunes and billowing, broken fairways. There are some blind shots, though these have been much reduced by course changes, and the greens, though larger than in Taylor's days, almost always demand exact iron play.

From the 1st tee you see dunes in all directions; you drive down an avenue. You may get a helpful kick back to the fairway from the slopes to the side if your tee shot is not too wild but the fairway narrows to only 15 yards. Don't let your shot to the green drift too far right as you'll run down a bank and into the Burnham buckthorn.

Though there's more room for your tee shot at the 2nd, and the carry over a pit oughtn't to be a problem, your second shot must hit and hold a plateau green. The 3rd green is more kindly. There are banks all around which may well shepherd your shot onto the putting surface, which is set in a saucer. Your approach will probably be semi-blind, over a hump.

If the scoring hasn't gone well, the 4th, a short par 5, gives you a chance to get one back. There are views of Wales and the Bristol Channel from the tee. If you can ignore the rough ground and sandhill right, biting off some of the dogleg in this direction will give you a good chance of finding the green with your second shot – or taking 7. Ground falls away all around the green.

The 5th is the first par 3, and a very good one, well bunkered, with the elevated tee at about the same level as the green.

The 6th is just about the most difficult hole, stroke index 1 in fact, and right into the prevailing wind. It doglegs left around some intimidating country which includes a mere but you have to stay to the left to shorten the hole.

The 7th is a long, rather boring flat par 4 – and a difficult one. There are bushes all along the left and a dyke to the right. It's more of a threat to your second shot, when it comes quite close to the green. The dyke is rather closer up on the next hole, not a long par 5 but with a tight shot to the green.

At the 9th, a short hole, you are at your farthest from the clubhouse. Here the tee is above green level, which is well bunkered indeed. If your shot plummets down into the soft, fine, Burnham sand, you could have difficulty even finding your ball.

The 10th is a truly old-fashioned hole. You walk down into a pit and drive upwards, hopefully more or less over a marker post. If your tee shot goes very much right, abandon hope, while a long straight drive can find a bunker in mid-fairway. However, the falling ground may well flatter you and give a very short pitch to the green. The 11th is a long flat par 4, played with a road along the left. The green is narrow and protected.

The 13th is the last of the par 5s, and a most attractive one. It is possible to get home in two, but the green is difficult to hit from any distance. It's long, narrow and set up in the dunes, with the ground falling away to the right. Little more than a hundred yards away to the left is the church. The 14th is one of two par 3s in the last five holes. This one is all carry. If you're going to miss, miss on the right for the ground falls sharply away left and there's a hollow in front of the green.

The 15th has an extremely tumbling fairway and is played towards the lighthouse. Well over 400 yards, it's a fine two-shotter. Much the shortest par 4 on the course comes next, and there's even a choice of two fairways to aim at, the 'wrong' one shortening the hole but leaving you with a far more demanding pitch to play. The 18th is as difficult a home hole as you'll find anywhere, a spectacular dogleg left with a typically Burnham fairway full of humps, hollows and sweeping undulations. If you're prepared to settle for a 5, it's safer to plod along the right, but you must be left to get up in two for your par.

This may just be the finest course west of Bristol and, with a few hundred yards added, would be of good enough quality to host an Open Championship. Even so, it's still over 6,600 yards from the back tees. There is a good nine-hole course also, not short at nearly 3,300 yards.

£25 M must have a handicap of 22 or under

X lunch and dinner daily

starting sheet in operation daily

dormy house with four twin rooms

leave the M5 at Junction 22 and bear right at Young's Garage on the roundabout. After about a mile along Berrow Road, look out for St Christopher's Way on your left

CAME DOWN

Winterbourne Came, Dorchester, Dorset DT2 8NR
☎ *Upwey (030581) 3494*

Golf has been played on the chalk downlands here since the 1880s and Came Down Golf Club dates from 1906, on a course originally designed by the great J.H. Taylor and later re-designed by H.S. Colt.

Came Down is very much associated with the names of the famous Whitcombe brothers. Their father was 'Keeper of the Dunes' at Berrow in Somerset, a grand-sounding title which meant he was responsible for keeping the rabbits under control. Ernest arrived at Came Down as professional in 1910, with his brother Charles as his assistant and his mother as stewardess. When Ernest went off to the war, his other brother, Reg, took over as both greenkeeper and professional.

As the highest point on the course is 500 feet, Came Down can be very windy indeed and bitterly cold in winter, a time of year that can also show it at its best because of its quick-drying qualities. Most of the holes are open to the winds, although a couple, the 3rd and 10th, are well wooded. It's undulating, though none of the climbs are stiff. There are views of Dorchester, Maiden Castle, Weymouth, Poole Harbour, Portland and Hardy's Monument. To the east, Thomas Hardy's Egdon Heath is also visible from the 18th fairway.

Some of these have produced names for the holes – the 1st 'Casterbridge', the 7th 'Maiden Castle', the 8th 'Hardy' and the 12th 'Diggory Venn'. Two of these are amongst the finest on the course. The 7th is quite a difficult par 4 of more than 400 yards. You drive here to the top of the hill and are then faced with, say, a long iron to a two-tiered green with a large bunker guarding the approaches at the front right. The 12th is a fairly testing par 3 of some 190 yards, with bunkers left and right and the green sloping so as to drift your ball right.

The 16th is another good par 4, a dogleg right of about 400 yards with a boundary wall all along one side. The 18th, a rather long par 4 at over 400 yards, settles many a match and is just about the most exposed hole of all.

£ *£14, £20 at weekends*

M *none*

Ⓛ *juniors pay half green fees*

✗ *lunch daily, dinner daily except Mondays*

🚗 *2 miles south of Dorchester east of the Dorchester to Weymouth road (A354)*

COTSWOLD HILLS

Ullenwood, Cheltenham, Gloucestershire GL53 9QT
☎ *Cheltenham (0242) 522421*

Although the club dates back to 1902, the course here is fairly recent. Set high up in the Cotswolds, it's undulating but there aren't any steep climbs. There are panoramic views for much of the time and it always gives the feeling that you are well away from it all.

The course itself was designed by a former club champion and measures some 6,600 yards, with the standard scratch one more than the par. Not many years ago it started an open amateur ladies' event, the Cotswold Gold Vase, which soon became established as a scratch event that was highly desirable to win. The English Ladies' Closed Championship came here in 1981, and the course has also been used for a county championship. Two quite well-known names hail from here, Peter Berry, a tournament player, and Beverly Huke, who was a Curtis Cup player in 1972 and English champion three years later. She became a tournament winner as a professional and in 1982 was one of only two British players to hold a US LPGA card. The next year she was leading money winner on the WPGA European circuit.

Trees are a great feature of the course. Many are long established but thousands have been planted to enforce accurate tee shots.

The 3rd is a very good long par 4 with a rather frightening drive through a long avenue of trees and out of bounds along the left. For your second shot, you'll usually need a wood, uphill, to a tightly bunkered green set on a plateau. The 8th is a shorter par 4, doglegging to the right, where there's also an out of bounds. The green is small and again well bunkered.

At the 15th, you reach the highest part of the course, before the descent back to the clubhouse. This is a long par 3 and the green away there on the horizon looks a very small target indeed. A Cotswold drystone wall and trees on the left don't add to your confidence.

The 17th is the best amongst the finishing holes, a medium-length par 4, which plays a lot easier if you can get a long drive away. Otherwise, the small elevated green is hard to hold with anything more than a pitching club.

£ *£20*   M *none*   🚗 *3 miles south of Cheltenham on B4070*

✗ *lunch and dinner daily except Monday, when snacks are available*

EAST DEVON ☘

North View Road, Budleigh Salterton, Devon EX9 6DQ
☎ *Budleigh Salterton (03954) 3370*

Although close to the sea, East Devon is not links but very much heather moorland in character. Set at about 400 feet, it has a wonderful array of views. In one direction along the coast are Sidmouth and Seaton, followed by Lyme Regis. Portland Bill will be visible on a clear day, some 40 miles away. The cliffs closer at hand are red, gradually shading to white chalk. In the opposite direction along the coast there is a series of jutting headlands ending at Start Point. Inland, there are views of the River Exe and the mass of Dartmoor beyond. The club claims to have the finest variety of land and seascapes in England. Few would argue with them.

I used to hold the course record and competed in the West of England Championship at East Devon, but my deeds have been long eclipsed – I'm a little sorry to say. In 1990, George Ryall went round in a record 64. Despite this low score, the par of 70 is seldom bettered. As with so many of our older courses, some old par 5s in the 450 to 460 yards range have become 4s. There are now two par 5s, the 6th and the 12th which was recently made into a doglegged par 5 of some 480 yards.

Wind usually has a great effect on the playing of a course, but in the case of East Devon a shift of just a very few degrees over West Down much changes the playing qualities of the holes. Each is strongly individual in appearance and there are frequent changes in direction. Only the 1st and 2nd run parallel and the only sequence of holes following the same direction is the last three back to the clubhouse.

The flora and fauna may be of interest to the golfer having an off day. There are wild thyme, hare bells, wild orchids and large numbers of deer. The club takes the pheasant as its emblem, for they too are plentiful in the gorse and heather.

Two shortish par 4s set one off fairly comfortably, though a precise shot to the 2nd green is needed, which is on no fewer than four levels. The 3rd is quite stern stuff at a little over 400 yards into the prevailing wind. The fairway narrows towards the green, which has a track to the left and gorse on three sides.

The 6th was a favourite of Henry Cotton's. There's an out of bounds all the way down the right, with the fairway unkindly sloping towards it. A grassy hollow eats into the fairway on the approaches to the green, which though large is difficult to hold.

Stroke index 3 follows immediately. The second shot is demanding. A low-flying shot is likely to run through, so it's best to pitch short and hope to run on from the left. On the 9th, Vernon Haydon managed a drive of 430 yards some fifty years ago, no doubt helped by the fact the hole plays downhill. The 11th is an interesting driving hole across a deep valley, where the player must decide how much he dares to bite off. The 15th is the highest part of the course, and the views here are at their finest. For its playing qualities, however, the 17th is much admired. It's a long par 4, yet long hitters must stop short of the gorse which begins about 250 yards out. Your second shot has to carry a deep valley or you'll be pitching blind from the bottom. As you continue downhill for the end, your nerve may be tested by interested observers of the golfing scene at the clubhouse.

There is a putting green, good-sized practice ground and a practice green and bunker.

£ *£20, £25 at weekends*

M *membership of a golf club and a handicap certificate*

✗ *lunch and dinner daily except Monday and Saturday, when snacks are provided*

🚗 *leave the M5 at Junction 30 for Budleigh Salterton and turn right at the first junction, following signs thereafter*

FERNDOWN

119 Golf Links Road, Ferndown, Dorset BH22 8BU
☎ *Ferndown (0202) 872022*

This is where it all began for me, my real introduction to both golf and life. My father came here as professional just before the war when I was seven. I may have swung a golf club before, but Ferndown is where I learned to play the game. A very important part of my education and 'growing up' came from all the conversations I had with members both wise and knowledgeable.

I stayed there as assistant to my father until 1957, when my brother and I took over as joint professionals at Parkstone.

The conversations I've mentioned took place mainly when strolling the fairways. I wasn't allowed in the clubhouse until 1953. When it seemed likely I might make the Ryder Cup team that year, a few voices were raised suggesting that I might be a fit person to be allowed in. Caution prevailed for a while: 'Let's wait and see if young Alliss *does* get in' was the majority opinion. In due course, Alliss did cross the threshhold and there's now an 'Alliss Corner', with relics of the many years my father and I spent there.

The course was designed by Harold Hilton who had two unique distinctions in his golfing record. He was the last British amateur (the American Bobby Jones did it later) to win our Open Championship and he is the only Briton to win the US Amateur Championship, something he achieved in 1911.

Ferndown has become fairly familiar from TV as the Hennessy Cognac Cup was staged there in both 1982 and 1984. For today's professionals it's not a very severe test. At 6,400 yards, Ferndown is not quite long enough for them but quite good players find the length very nearly ideal. Not many people enjoy courses with eight holes around the 450-yard mark, when they also have to reach for a wood at every 'short' hole.

The shape of the ground is also ideal. There are no real uphill trudges yet it's not flat either, just gently undulating. One good feature for the visitor is that, from the forward tees, you're still playing the course more or less as it was designed. Only the 5th and 11th are quite a lot shorter.

Ferndown is, and always has been, in very neat and tidy order. The fairways are superb. The 3rd is one of the most testing holes, a longish par 4 which doglegs to the right and is slightly uphill. There are two very attractive short par 4s, both heavily bunkered, the 8th and 16th. At the latter, your drive is blind and then you have to cope with the three-tiered green. All the par 3s are excellent and I am very fond of the 13th, which was designed by my father after a part of the course was sold for housing.

However, for me it's the feel of the course that's more important than any individual hole. I love the pines, silver birch and purple heather. Ferndown is simply a marvellous place to spend a day.

There is also a 'relief' course which is very pleasant, nine holes, with two sets of tees to alter the character of many of the holes quite a lot. This new course is a good deal shorter than the original.

£ £27 for the Old Course and £17 for the new, £35 and £25 at weekends

---

M a handicap certificate

✗ snacks and lunch daily; dinner may not be available on Friday and Saturday when members are 'dining in'

🚗 take the A31 Bournemouth road and the clubhouse is behind the dormy house, about 1 mile from the centre of Ferndown village

---

HIGH POST

Great Durnford, Salisbury, Wiltshire SP4 6AT
☎ *Salisbury (0722) 73356*

This downland course is set on Wiltshire chalk with good walking underfoot and views over Salisbury Plain. I suppose there aren't many courses left where I still hold the record but High Post is one – a 65.

A very strong feature of the course is that banks and slopes surround most of the greens, sometimes helpful but more often not. The course is not particularly long – just over 6,200 yards from the medal tees and just under 6,000 from the forward ones – so it can be very suitable for a thirty-six-hole outing. A couple of the par 4s are testingly long and none of the four par 3s ask for a wooden club shot from the tee, except the 17th if the wind's in your face. Together with the 17th, the best holes are the 9th, 12th and 18th.

The 9th is a sweeping dogleg where you'll usually have a hanging lie for your second shot to the green. When Henry Cotton visited the course some years ago he declared it the best hole on the course.

The 12th hole, 430 yards, is arguably the most difficult. Your tee shot has to be well placed to hold the fairway and you are then confronted by a slope and cross bunkers about 70 yards from the green, which itself has slopes leading up to the putting surface. The 18th makes for a good finish, a par 4 of more than 400 yards with trouble both sides and also through the back. Although it's the last hole, it's still rated as stroke index 6; clubs usually seek to avoid a low number on the last so that a stroke isn't given in matchplay.

£ £18, £22 at weekends

M a handicap certificate at weekends

✕ lunch and snacks daily

🚗 on A345 4 miles north of Salisbury and 4 miles from Amesbury

---

KNOWLE

Fairway, Brislington, Bristol, Avon BS4 5DF
☎ Bristol (0272) 776341

Prospects are pleasing when you arrive at this parkland course: fairways with both the 18th and 9th greens close at hand and players attempting the short 10th. The putting green is excellent and set amongst trees, rose bushes and shrubs.

Quite a few famous professionals have been associated with this club, Syd Easterbrook, for instance, who was only a stroke away from first place in the 1933 Open Championship and was a member of the victorious Ryder Cup team of the same year. Today, Gordon Brand presides over the pro's shop, while his son, after many achievements in his amateur career, quickly made good on the European Tour.

The club was formed in 1905. The course was designed by Hawtree and Taylor and has been developed, rather than drastically changed, over the years. It begins with a short par 4 of about 320 yards. The short pitch to the green, shaped like a pork chop, has to be quite precise. It's cut into the hillside with a steep, short rise to the green and is well bunkered. However, you ought to get your par, which is much less likely on the 2nd.

This is a monster 4 at 471 yards and plays its full length. You must get a long drive away to have any real chance of getting home in two but the out of bounds all the way along the right can be a deterrent to opening the shoulders. Assuming the good drive, you're still left with a lot to do. Your second has to be played through quite a narrow gap between the out of bounds on the right and a large spinney to the left. The green is then set on a rise and is two-tiered.

Off next to an elevated tee and a dogleg to the right where you have to decide how much you dare shorten the hole by carrying an out-of-bounds corner.

There's another elevated tee at the 4th where you have to play through a gap with hedges and water on either flank, followed by an uphill second shot to a green set on the crest of a hill. This is rated stroke index 2, though it is not as tough a par 4 as the 2nd.

There are some short par 4s in the holes which follow but usually with plenty of potential trouble in the shape of out of bounds, the fall of the ground and tight bunkering.

The finish is quite severe, with three par 4s of more than 400 yards in the last five holes. The 14th is stroke index 1, a dogleg to the left with out of bounds on that side and a spinney to the right. Many bunkers guard the green. The 16th is a par 4 of about the same length, 426 yards this time to an elevated green and setting similar problems. The finest, however, is the 17th. This is a 403 yards, played from an elevated tee to a rising fairway. There are eight bunkers on the hole and the green is quite difficult to find, cut into a hillside and difficult to get at from the right side of the fairway.

The last hole, 551 yards, is much the longest on the course. Your drive is blind and in hard, running conditions must be long or held well left if your ball isn't to career with the left-to-right slope into a ditch on the right of the fairway. The hole is fairly plain sailing otherwise, with prospects of getting home in two.

£ £16	**🚗** about 3 miles south of Bristol on either the A4 Bath road or the A37 Wells road turn into West Town Lane and look for the turning marked 'Fairway' after about ¼ mile
M a handicap certificate	
✗ snacks and lunch daily, dinner daily except Sunday	

LONG ASHTON

Long Ashton, Bristol, Avon BS18 9DW
☎ Long Ashton (0272) 392229

Long Ashton was founded in 1893 with membership, for a short time, restricted to residents of the parishes of Long Ashton, Barrow Gurney, Flax Bourton and Wraxall. This may sound rather a quaint idea but wasn't at all uncommon.

The present course dates from 1937 and was designed by Hawtree and Taylor. An important addition came in 1966 when what is probably the best practice ground in the area was added, which now includes a practice green complete with bunkers and a chipping green. The course was eventually bought from the owner in 1957 for less than £5,000 – what a bargain. I wonder if the club thought so then.

Long Ashton has produced a number of good players, the best known being two ladies. Ruth Porter won everything in the area for years and was also English Ladies' Champion in 1959, 1961 and 1965, while Katrina Douglas was British Ladies' Champion in 1982. Spurned by the Curtis Cup selectors in 1984 she turned professional and, though she didn't head the Order of Merit, was undoubtedly the year's best player on the circuit. Ian Patey, English Amateur Champion in 1946 is an honorary member and Andrew Sherborne and David Ray have been internationals in recent years. Both are now tournament professionals.

The course is set on Ashton Hill and overlooks the city of Bristol. Turf, which is excellent, is of downland type with such good drainage that it remains playable both winter and summer, even after prolonged downpours.

The course is not particularly long at 6,051 yards, mainly accounted for by the fact that several of the par 4s are just a drive and a pitch. You begin with one of these, 316 yards. The 2nd, just 128 yards, has the unusual feature that the green is situated in what was once an iron mine. Though short, the green is small and there are rocks behind. There are only two par 5s on the course, the first of these being the 4th, a bit under 500 yards. Rough and gorse along both sides of the fairway may be the main problem but there's also a small pond to catch drives too far left.

The 6th is stroke index 1. Though only 383 yards, it's into the prevailing wind and the fairway is narrow and falls away to gorse and rough on the right. There is more of the same to the left and also a pond. The second shot is difficult to judge on a first visit because there are no bunkers or other features to help you gauge distance.

The second nine is the longer by about 500 yards and includes at least two stiff 4s. The 14th is 450 yards but the 433-yard 15th is probably the more difficult of the two. Again it's into the wind most of the time and also slightly uphill. Bunkers short of the green on either flank call for an accurate and long second – very often a wood.

£ £18, £25 at weekends

M a handicap certificate

✗ snacks, lunch and high tea available daily until 6pm

🚗 leave the M5 at Junction 19 along the A369. Turn right along B3129 and follow signs

MINCHINHAMPTON

New Course, Minchinhampton, Stroud, Gloucestershire
GL6 9BE
☎ *Nailsworth (045383) 3866*

Founded in 1889 on common land, Minchinhampton was for a time the only course between Malvern and Westward Ho! It first came to public notice through the deeds of Lady Margaret Scott. In 1892, she won a competition there in which all the other competitors were men, and the following year became the winner of the first Ladies' British Open Amateur Championship. Minchinhampton was one of the first clubs to have a ladies' section, with their nine holes opening at just about the same time as an eighteen-hole course for men. Why two courses do you ask? Well, this was in days when golf for women was largely thought of as requiring something not too demanding – despite Margaret Scott.

The fact that golf was on the common was later to prove fatal for the Old course. With the development of car ownership, the weekends became purgatory for club members. There were picknickers, pirates parking their cars and nipping onto the course without troubling themselves to pay green fees, and horses ridden over the greens. Car parking on the course itself was also a problem. At one point, a ditch was dug to keep the enemy at bay – but to no effect. Overnight, enthusiasts for commoners' rights filled it in!

The club looked for suitable private land and bought the present Cotswold upland site. This New course was designed by Fred Hawtree and opened for play in 1975. Stones and a thin infertile soil were the main problem on the course but fairway lies have improved. There was also a lack of trees, and about a dozen elms were all stricken with the Dutch disease. Today they are stark scarecrow figures, but have been reinforced by a major tree-planting programme.

The course today is 6,675 yards from the medal tees and has the feature that you can see the bottom of nearly every pin for your shot to the green. Seven of the holes are doglegs; no greens slope away from the player although some are flat, conforming to the shape of the ground. The Hawtree taste for doglegging is very evident, and the correct line from the tee is often vital. The greens themselves are usually large so precise club selection is doubly important.

The first outstanding hole is the 5th, a par 5 with a right-angled dogleg, followed immediately by the first stroke hole, a par 4 of 400 yards doglegging right which is very heavily bunkered. Bunkers are again the main hazard at the 7th, a short hole played to an island green. The next short hole, the 11th, offers similar bunker problems but the green is welcoming, strongly tilted from back to front. At the 10th, 13th and 17th, tee shot placement with regard to the day's pin placement is always vital and the course ends with the challenge of a par 5 where you

184

can hope to get home in two – if you avoid the humpy ground about 30 yards short of the green.

There is a very attractive clubhouse, which was converted from a tythe barn and extended.

£ £18, £22 at weekends	🎯 a skittle alley
M membership of a golf club	🚗 head for Avening from Minchinhampton and the clubhouse is on your left after about 1¾ miles. From Avening, it's on the right after ¾ mile
✗ snacks, lunch and dinner daily	
✉ need to book in advance	

PARKSTONE

Links Road, Parkstone, Dorset BH4 9JU
☎ *Canford Cliffs (0202) 708025*

I had my first full club professional's job here, in partnership with my brother Alec. We followed Reg Whitcombe, Open champion in 1938, who had been at Parkstone many years. I stayed thirteen years before moving to Moor Allerton in Yorkshire.

I enjoyed my time there enormously. A lot of this was to do with the members, who were a wonderful cross section of society. I also never tired of playing the course, set in pine, heather and silver birch country. Some think it a little unorthodox because it has five par 3s and five 5s with the last hole being a 3. However, it's the quality of the holes that should count and not the numbers on the score card. One feature of the par 5s is that each offers the long hitter the challenge of getting on in two and yet there are just two bunkers on the lot.

It's a fine winter course, because of sandy subsoil, and is seldom really bleak in winter or too bouncy in summer, one of the problems, for instance, with almost all links courses.

After a fairly quiet start, with some birdie chances, the 5th, though not particularly long at 373 yards, is the first key hole, with a road and trees along the left and on the right more trees and bunkers. The green is set amongst trees with one of Parkstone's lakes close at hand.

The 6th, a dogleg left, is played round lakes and pines, and the drive from the back tee is a tough one where you will be aiming to reach a flat lie at the top of a rise. The green is elevated and two-tiered.

The 7th is one of my favourite amongst the par 3s, uphill all the way with a cross bunker and a slope set with rhododendrons behind the green. The green is on three levels so the wrong choice of club is very likely to lead to three putts.

Pause for a while on the 8th tee, and savour the views of Brownsea

Island and castle in the middle of Poole Harbour. Long hitters can then try to shorten this short par 4 even further by carrying the silver birch along the left, which will reward you with a very short pitch to the green.

The 9th, not a long par 5 at 505 yards, has the threat of out of bounds along the right and this becomes close in the green area. The next par 5 is the 11th, with many folds in the ground a little short of the green which can kick your ball away into the woods on the right.

The 13th, played from a high tee with superb views, has a green with a large cross bunker but you should carry this with ease as the hole is only 361 yards. The 15th can be difficult. At about 220 yards a drive can run away left and you'll usually be playing your second from a sidehill lie. There are pine trees right of the green and quite a steep drop on the left.

There are now two par 3s and a 5 sandwiched between them to finish with. The 16th needs a high downhill pitch with out of bounds at the back. On the 17th, 530 yards, shorter hitters should aim for the plateau along the left, known locally as 'Old Man's Alley', while a long shot can be aimed up the hill in front of the tee and over the guide marker.

The 18th is a fine finishing hole of 190 yards and has decided many a match. You must try to go right, if anything, for there is a heathery slope on the left and it's very difficult to save your par from there.

Parkstone was originally laid out by Willie Park in 1910 and James Braid and J.R. Stutt extended the course in the 1930s.

£ £25

M membership of a golf club or a handicap certificate

✗ snacks, lunch and dinner daily

🚗 from the A35 between Bournemouth and Poole turn into St Osmund's Road by the traffic lights and church

✉ need to book in advance

ST ENODOC

Rock, Wadebridge, Cornwall PL27 6LB
☎ Trebetherick (020 886) 3216

This is a popular course, and was much loved by the Poet Laureate Sir John Betjeman, who is buried nearby. He even wrote a poem on the delight he felt at a rare birdie 3 scored here, on the 12th.

Golf was first played here, on a very casual basis indeed, in the late 1880s. Soon, a few holes were laid out amongst the huge sand dunes at Rock and in 1890 the present club was officially formed. James Braid laid out an eighteen-hole course in 1907 and revised it in the 1930s.

St Enodoc is basically hilly links over broken country with water hazards more common than is usual in natural links country.

The start is a par 5, played over really rolling and tossing ground within a valley, as is the 2nd, where the drive is over a crest with the second shot to a plateau green. The 3rd, another long par 4, gives you an amusing second shot, over both a road and stone wall to the green set around the corner of a hillside. The 4th is a short par 4 which has been much praised. Only some 270 yards or so, it can be reached from the tee but is a little uphill. You must carry an out-of-bounds fence to the right, while there's a Valley of Sin and much worse trouble to the left.

The 6th is famous for the Himalayas sandhill and bunker. Bernard Darwin thought it the highest he had ever seen on a golf course. Actually, all you have to do is play just an ordinary respectable iron over the top but the penalty for lifting up on the shot is very severe – you should probably try to play out backwards, if you are lucky enough to be able to find a stance on the steep slopes!

At the 7th you play back over it, this time from an elevated tee, but it is not really a frightener, unless your nerve has gone. The green is set close by the shore of the Camel Estuary. The 10th, rated the hardest hole on the course, has a massive slope on the right and a brook all down the left-hand side. You then play a short loop round St Enodoc Church, once buried by wind-blown sand from the beach. In the graveyard there is a tombstone to Dr Theophilus Hoskin, who leased some of the land for the course to the club. For a good many years after his death his widow refused to allow golf around the church loop on Sundays, which reduced play to just twelve holes.

The 12th tee gives superb views of Daymer Bay and was one of Sir John Betjeman's favourite places. He relished 'the prospect of the fairway with the sound of the Atlantic on the shore behind'.

The 16th runs along the Camel Estuary; the fairway is full of folds and undulations, with a hollow in front of the green to catch a long second which doesn't quite get there, or a weak pitch. By this time you're making directly for the clubhouse. You finish with a stern par 3 of more than 200 yards to a raised-up green and much rough country if you don't get there.

The last is a long two-shotter played from an elevated tee with a large bunker to carry and thence to a valley full of bumps, hollows and slopes.

There are those who don't like links golf. St Enodoc has changed many minds on this score. Those who were already enthusiasts have casually discovered St Enodoc and thereafter have looked nowhere else for their annual golfing holiday.

There is also a short course with nine par 3s and mostly short par 4s. A bit daunting to go round it in 64 and find yourself over par!

£ £22

M a handicap certificate

✕ lunch daily

🚗 from Wadebridge, take the B3314, turning left for Rock at St Minver. Through Rock, turn right at Roskarnon House Hotel

THURLESTONE

Thurlestone, near Kingsbridge, South Devon TQ7 3NZ
☎ *Kingsbridge (0548) 560405*

Thurlestone was founded in 1897 on a massive rabbit warren, covered with scrub, brambles and gorse. Put another way, it was almost the ideal for golf – once the fairways had been carved through, and greens laid.

Once this had been done, many balls were still lost but some provision was made for this. A device was kept in the clubhouse to stamp members' initials on golf balls, and any found were supposed to be handed in to the professional. Original owners could then buy them back for a fee of twopence.

Today, with much of the club's revenue coming from summer visitors who can also enjoy the three hard and eleven grass tennis courts, most of the rough has been cut down in the interests of speeding play, particularly in the crowded summer holiday season.

Despite this paucity of rough, the wind over the cliff tops is often a major factor. The 17th, for instance, though only 152 yards from the medal tees, can cause even quite long hitters to reach for their drivers.

The course begins with what is known as 'Boozers' Loop', six holes of modest length after which the day's exercise can be considered honorably underway.

However, the 1st, only 271 yards, is by no means an easy starting hole with both a stream and out of bounds in play, and at the 2nd the drive must clear a quarry in front of the tee. The 6th, 148 yards, is a nice well-bunkered short hole and then you are out onto holes far more open to the wind and usually longer.

The 8th, 9th, 10th and 16th are all par 4s of well over 400 yards and there is the oddity of three par 5s on the second nine and none on the first.

£ *£18*	🚗 *leave the A379 Plymouth to Salcombe road at any of three Thurlestone signposts. Go through the village towards the beach and the clubhouse will be obvious*
M *a handicap certificate*	
✗ *snacks and lunch daily*	

TREVOSE GOLF AND COUNTRY CLUB

Constantine Bay, Padstow, North Cornwall
☎ *Padstow (0841) 520 208*

If the Fates are kindly, the best time of all to arrive at Trevose is on a clear summer evening, when the sunset over Trevose Head and Booby's Bay is quite magnificent. The views from the clubhouse, which sits overlooking the whole course, are exceptional – it really is situated in just the right place.

Golf came to Trevose early this century, as a result of the unusual enthusiasm of the owner of the land, Dr Williams. He enjoyed building bridges.

They're needed on a golf course crossed by streams so this gave him an excuse to practise his hobby!

The present course was laid out by Harry Colt in 1924 and, except for a couple of holes and new tees to give more length, has been basically unchanged ever since. It's sand-based and fairly flat though there are slopes and undulations. Drainage is very good and the course has its own water supply, vital in the long rainless spells that can occur around the Camel estuary. In 1984, for instance, they had no measurable rain for many months.

There's little rough, so play is not held up on what can be a very busy holiday course in the high season, and the present owner, Peter Gammon, tries to ensure that visitors play at a crisp pace. The turf and greens are good and the bunker sand very fine. There's just one blind shot on the course and few bushes, except for the tamarisk, which are thought to be unique to the area.

As you climb the 1st tee, built of Cornish stone, you have the feeling of playing straight down towards the sea. You drive between hillocks to a green set in a natural dell. At 443 yards, it's a long par 4 to start off with but there's some help from the run of the ground.

The 4th is a long par 4 of 450 yards for you but a par 5 from the back tees for professionals and a birdie opportunity. The hole runs along with the sea on the left to the sound of breakers, doglegging slightly left and with a blind second shot. The green could hardly be nearer the beach.

The next hole, a stiff par 4, is played directly away from the sea, with a gem soon to come, the 7th. This is a very slight dogleg right of 371 yards with the setting of the green being the prime feature. It's on the top of a rise, with two big bunkers in the upslope. A precise iron shot is needed.

The 9th takes you back quite near the clubhouse and is a long 4, played from an elevated tee to rising ground. There's a bunker in mid-fairway to catch a short second shot, and at the green the ground falls sharply away to the left. Another difficult par 4 begins the second nine. The drive is from an elevated tee to a sloping fairway with a stream running across, only reachable in fairly extreme conditions. The second shot is a lot further than it looks.

The 12th is stroke index 1, a big par 4 of 448 yards, swinging left with bunkers at the elbow. The 13th is the only par 5 from the white tees and there's a chance of getting on in two, especially if you play close to the out of bounds on the left, leaving a carry of about 220 yards for the second shot. This hole is a birdie opportunity and so are the next two, both short par 4s.

These are followed by a tough finish, with a long par 3 of 225 yards played between two bunkers and two difficult par 4s. At the 17th the drive is narrow and a stream fronts the green. The 18th plays as a 4½. Keep your drive to the right for it's a very testing shot to reach the green over a dip from the left.

There's a very good par 3 course also and a large practice ground.

I won one of my four West of England Professional titles here, and my son Gary was once the professional here.

£ *£18 to £25 dependent upon season*

M *a handicap certificate*

✗ *snacks, lunch and dinner daily*

🎾 *tennis, table tennis and a heated outdoor swimming pool*

🏠 *a wide variety of self-catering accommodation*

🚗 *from outskirts of Padstow head for St Merryn and take the Constantine Bay turn off right, looking out for the clubhouse, which will come into view on your right*

WEST CORNWALL

Lelant, St Ives, Cornwall TR26 3DZ
☎ *Hayle (0736) 753401*

This is the most westerly course in Great Britain. It first became known for the deeds of Jim Barnes. 'Long Jim', as he was known, was born in the little village of Lelant and came to golf as a caddie and later assistant before emigrating to America. During the 1920s his name was only slightly lower in status than Jones, Hagen and Sarazen, and was in his time Open Champion on both sides of the Atlantic. At Lelant, the Jim Barnes Cups, open meetings held during May, help perpetuate his memory.

Lelant is a true links course with a few holes at a lower level by the river. The greens are usually fast and true and much of the course winds through dunes, using the shape of the ground to full advantage. Fairway turf is excellent.

The course is fairly short, at 5,854 yards, and if you're a good hitter you won't be using fairway woods very often on a still day. You'll probably need one at the 1st, however, a long par 3 getting on for maximum length with a road on the right and a fairly narrow fairway. Aim at the church tower and hope to keep it on line.

The 2nd is one of the best holes, a par 4 of 389 yards, swinging slightly right around the sandhills. The green is raised and to find it you must play through a narrow gap in the sandhills, with the sea beyond.

So far, a tough start, and soon after you come to what is locally known as 'Calamity Corner'. This begins with a par 3 of 191 yards, where you really must hit the green, and a couple of short 4s with a 3 in between. It all shouldn't be too difficult but many cards are ruined on this stretch. They look more simple than they are.

The 9th is a very difficult hole of 438 yards to play in par. It's uphill to a raised green with a natural valley to the right and dunes left. The views at about this time may make you forget the golf: St Ives Bay, Godrevy Lighthouse and much of the North Cornish coast.

Your concentration must return for the 11th, however, perhaps the best hole on the course. It measures 381 yards, with a railway along the right. The second shot is very demanding. You must carry sandhills to a green at the foot of hills covered by gorse and also avoid a large bunker in a hollow just short of the green. If that's not enough, remember that you must always keep right of the pin.

The 12th tee reveals fine views of both beach and ocean and you drive to a plateau followed by a downhill second at this 520-yard hole. The 13th should give you a chance of a birdie. A really straight drive from an elevated tee may well find the green, 272 yards away.

If so, you now face a very long par 4 of 460 yards in dune country. You should try to find the gap in the dunes from the tee and then your second shot, even if long enough, may be thrown off either left or right.

The 16th is a true par 5, slightly uphill all the way and 533 yards. The finish is then complicated by a long par 3, with a quarry left and road right and a downhill 394-yard last hole with out of bounds again a threat and a hollow near the green which traps many shots.

So, only 5,854 yards, but long enough to be testing. Perhaps this is because there are only two par 5s. Four or five of them always bring the yardage up, yet tend to make a course a little easier. On most of these, the pros will be cross if they can't get home in two and reasonable players expect to be playing a pitch for their third stroke.

£ £12

M a handicap certificate

✕ snacks and lunch daily, dinner daily except Monday

snooker

at cross roads in centre of Lelant bear right for the church and then left at the church and look out for clubhouse on right after 200 yards

WESTON-SUPER-MARE

Uphill Road North, Weston-super-Mare, Avon
☎ *Weston-super-Mare (0934) 633360 or 626968*

Weston was formed in 1892, and was originally designed by a prolific man of the day, Tom Dunn. I do believe his fee of £4 for the twenty-seven holes is the lowest I've come across in my researches for this book – and out of that he had to pay his expenses!

However, it must be admitted that 'experts' were called in just to decide the general shape of the course, where each tee and green should go and perhaps a few bunkers here and there. The rest was up to the greenkeeper and keen hands on the committee, or even just one enthusiast. However, that is not the course of today. It was redesigned by Dr Alister Mackenzie, and a very enjoyable course he created. It can test long hitters but isn't too discouraging for others.

It starts with a fairly short par 4, made rather more difficult by a fairway narrowing towards the green. The 3rd, a short hole, demands that you make sure to be up because there's much broken ground and a hollow just before the green. The 5th is a good long par 4, with the out-of-bounds sea wall to the right and a narrow entrance to the green.

The 8th is a par 5 of some 480 yards with a high bank which traps many second shots, while at this point there are also a couple of bunkers to miss. The 11th is a difficult par 3 of over 200 yards, the entrance to the green being two sandhills. This hole begins the second loop.

Two quite long par 4s follow and then a good very short hole of little more than 120 yards with plenty of natural hazards.

The 15th is undoubtedly the 'star' hole at Weston, and it has often been compared to the famous Road Hole at St Andrews. Instead of driving over the outline of old railway sheds, at Weston there's a ridge to be cleared with much the same out-of-bounds problems. There's also a pond, trees and a large bunker on the left in the hole's 455 yards. The plateau green has slopes which shrug anything worse than a very good shot indeed into a bunker immediately left.

The 18th makes a tough finish to the round. Re-measurement probably is the cause of its no longer being a par 5 as it was in my youth. It takes two mighty straight blows to get up in two, especially with the out of bounds on the right.

Weston-super-Mare has that rare facility, indoor practice nets.

£ *£17.50*

🎱 *snooker*

M *handicap certificate required at weekends*

🚗 *head for the south end of Weston-super-Mare and the beach*

✕ *snacks, lunch and dinner daily*

YELVERTON

Golf Links Road, Yelverton, Devon PL20 6BN
☎ *Yelverton (0822) 852824*

Yelverton is one of the finest courses in the West of England. It's not long, 6,325 from the medal tees, yet the standard scratch score of 70 has rarely been broken over the last twenty years or more.

This is heathland golf of a high standard over a course similar to Walton Heath but without trees and some 600 feet above sea level. Situated on the edge of Dartmoor, the members would give you an argument if you claimed more beautiful views were to be found anywhere else. If Walton Heath was architect Herbert Fowler's masterpiece, Yelverton is really only its inferior in terms of sheer length.

You start with a long par 3 of just over 200 yards, followed by a difficult 418-yard par 4. Here the tee shot has to carry a ravine, with hillocks and bunkers the hazards for the second shot. Another long par 4 comes at the 7th, where placement of drive to the right is essential because of a large bunker on the left, besides gorse and heather all the way.

Next, you reach the longest hole on the course, a very long par 5 of 573 yards, but sheer length, which can be daunting enough, is the only real problem here.

You now encounter a piece of history, Drake's leat. Sir Francis lived at nearby Buckland Monachorum and one of his public-spirited actions was to build a watercourse to supply Plymouth. Today it comes into play at several holes, particularly the 9th, a short 4 of 285 yards, where it discourages attempts to drive the green. On the 10th, a long par 4 of 425 yards, you could find it with either first or second shots.

The 13th, 440 yards, is the longest par 4 at Yelverton and the difficulties of length are reinforced by a deep ravine which crosses a few yards in front of the green. The same ravine has to be negotiated with the tee shot at the next hole and again at the 16th with the shot to the green, a long one.

The 18th is an excellent finishing hole of 386 yards where, if you've not got a particularly good drive away, the ravine in front of the green is again a formidable hazard.

💷 *£14, £18 at weekends*

Ⓜ *membership of a golf club and a handicap certificate*

🍴 *lunch and dinner daily except Tuesday*

🎱 *snooker*

🚗 *turning close by Moorland Links Hotel on the A386, 5 miles south of Tavistock and 8 miles north of Plymouth*

LONDON & THE HOME COUNTIES

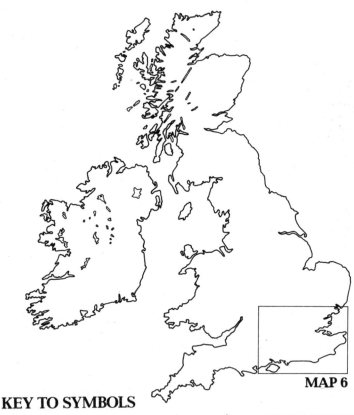

MAP 6

KEY TO SYMBOLS

PARKLAND	TELEPHONE	CATERING PROVIDED
LINKS	NEED TO BOOK IN ADVANCE	ACCOMMODATION PROVIDED
MOORLAND	APPROXIMATE COURSE FEE	RESTRICTIONS ON LADIES AND/OR YOUTHS
HEATHLAND	MEMBERSHIP REQUIREMENTS FOR VISITORS	
DOWNLAND		OTHER SPORTING FACILITIES
UPLAND		DIRECTIONS

ADDINGTON, THE   ⅃

205 Shirley Church Road, Croydon, Surrey CR0 5AB
☎ *Croydon (081 777) 1055*

This used to be one of Henry Longhurst's favourite inland courses. Though only 12 miles from London, it is in ideal golfing country with a wealth of silver birch, bracken and heather. It is one of the relatively few courses of quality in the immediate London area where a member would have time to play a full eighteen holes after a day at the office.

The course was laid out by the legendary J.F. Abercromby just before the First World War and he continued to develop it over many years. If he thought golfers were 'getting away' with relatively poor shots here and there, a problem would be added. Abercromby was very fond of par 3s, probably the reason why there are six of them at The Addington. Very good most of them are too.

You begin with a par 3, perhaps the weakest of them, medium-length and uphill. As Henry Longhurst once wrote: 'Addington really begins at the 2nd.' This, 557 yards, is easily the longest hole on the course and very few players can get home in two. There follows an excellent par 3, perhaps best played not from the very back of the medal tee, where many people have little hope of getting on with their tee shot.

With two long par 4s in succession, the start is tough indeed, and then there's a formidable pit to avoid, just short and right of the green on the doglegged 6th. The 7th is a very much respected par 3 with bracken and hillocky ground to catch a poor mid-iron.

The 8th is a very difficult 4, with an uphill tee shot which must be kept to the left. No bunker lies in wait for the second shot – there are already difficulties enough in the run of the ground. The 12th, just a couple of yards or so short of par 5 length, needs two very good carrying shots. The drive is across a large valley to a level stretch of fairway before the ground slopes away, and then there's another valley to surmount to reach the plateau green.

The 13th is one of the best par 3s in British golf. Henry Longhurst went even further, declaring: 'I swear it to be, with the exception of the 5th at Pine Valley, near Philadelphia, the greatest one-shot hole in inland golf. To see a full shot with a brassie, perfectly hit and preferably with a new ball, sail white against a blue sky, pitch on the green and roll up towards the flag, is to know the sweetest satisfaction that golf has to offer.'

Henry also felt that long demanding shots to greens were a characteristic which helped make The Addington stay in the mind when the details of many courses might have been quickly forgotten. It is a metropolitan gem.

Abercromby, did his work well. Since his time only the 18th has been substantially changed mainly to enable better practice facilities to be fitted in. He was a dictator, albeit a benevolent one. If a member asked for the suggestions book, he would say, 'I am the suggestions book.'

£ £25	**⇐** *from East Croydon Station, follow Addiscombe Road then the dual carriage-way, going straight on at the roundabout. Then take the first left into Shirley Church Road, after which the clubhouse is on the right after about ³⁄₄ mile*
M *membership of a golf club*	
✗ *lunches daily*	

ASHRIDGE 🌳

Little Gaddesden, Berkhamsted, Herts
☎ *Little Gaddesden (044 284) 2244*

Berkhamsted and Ashridge are near neighbours, but as different as chalk from cheese. Ashridge is laid out in parkland of great beauty, though only one hole, the 13th, was actually carved through woods. Founded in 1932, when times were hard, a high level of membership was hard to achieve but in 1937 Henry Cotton was retained as professional. It did the club no harm at all when he went off to Carnoustie that same year and won the Open Championship with the US Ryder Cup team all in attendance. The four woods he used are still on display in the clubhouse. He built himself a large house near the course, which he called Shangri-La, and introduced a professional's shop of a standard not dreamed of at the time. Clubs were displayed in glass-fronted cabinets, and seats were covered in zebra skin!

As a whole, the course offers safe routes for those content with being one over par but it's testing for the more ambitious. Most of the fairway bunkering is in the 200 to 250 yard range, on the tiger lines which give the best approaches to the greens. Condition is excellent.

The 1st is a gentle start, with a tee shot hit off line often being gathered back into the bottom of the valley. The 9th, 'Cotton's' is played downhill and so called because Henry found a line where he could drive the green. He contrived a low hooking shot that would just catch the fairway and then skidded and curled onto the green – more than 350 yards away. However, the normal route is left and you should be neither too long or too short. The long drive gives you a hanging lie for your approach to the plateau green and the short creates problems as well. It is often spoken of as one of the best short 4s in the country.

The 14th offers some of the same problems as the Road Hole at St Andrews. The green is set diagonally across the line of play and is banked. There's a bunker at the left and a road beyond. However, it is nearly a hundred yards shorter.

The last hole is downhill with the approach played across a shallow valley to a two-tiered green where it's very easy to three-putt.

£ *on application*

M *a handicap certificate or letter of introduction*

✕ *lunch daily*

🚗 *from London take the M1 to Hemel Hempstead then the A41 through Berkhamsted and then the B4506 for about 3 miles. From the reverse direction, still aim for B4506*

BEACONSFIELD

Seer Green, Beaconsfield, Buckinghamshire HP9 2UR
☎ *Beaconsfield (04946) 6545*

After being professional at the Wannsee club in Berlin for six years it was to Beaconsfield that my father, Percy Alliss, returned early in the 1930s when I wasn't even at the toddling stage.

He entered from this club when, having finished third at Carnoustie in 1931, he had an even better chance of winning the Open at Prince's, Sandwich, the following year. His play through the green was at a peak but, alas, he couldn't have putted them into a bucket. It was at about this time that I first swung a golf club, though my first memories of actually playing golf begin not at Beaconsfield, but from when we moved to Ferndown in the 1930s. Beaconsfield is a delightful parkland course, mildly undulating with a stiffish climb at the 8th hole. Fairways are mainly defined by trees – maple, oak, chestnut, beech and various evergreens. It was designed by Harry Colt in 1924 and bears most of that very busy architect's trademarks, such as his use of the ravine on the 6th fairway. Here you have that choice of whether to lay up or go for the carry. The 4th is a good doglegged par 5. The green has a well-guarded entrance, so you must be bold and accurate with either a long second or a little pitch for your third.

A ravine comes into play again on the 10th, a dogleg to the left.

On the 17th your mind is almost made up for you; it is a dogleg right par 5, where your shot to the green has to elude a large and well-bunkered pit. Probably best to play short and pitch over.

£ *£25*

M *a handicap certificate and a letter from your club secretary*

✕ *snacks daily during the day, lunch daily except Saturday*

🚗 *leave A40 along A355 for Amersham and turn for Seer Green at sign. The clubhouse is about 1/2 mile on*

BERKHAMSTED

The Common, Berkhamsted, Hertfordshire HP4 2QB
☎ *Berkhamsted (0442) 865832*

Set 600 feet up in the Chilterns, this is one of the few courses that are totally without bunkers. And why not indeed? A purist could argue that you should only have sand bunkers on links courses and that otherwise the architect should make use of the shape of the ground and other natural features to create difficulties.

In the case of Berkhamsted, just such a feature is provided by Grim's Dyke; this ancient earthwork comes into play at seven of the holes, sometimes as an obstacle for the tee shot and at other times for an approach.

This latter situation is the case at the 1st hole where, after a comfortable drive, the way is barred about 20 yards from the green by the Dyke, 6 to 8 feet high and, more important if you miss your shot, with a grassy bottom about 4 feet deep.

It's there again at the second, a heather-clad shoulder on the left of the green.

From this point on, we are out into fairly open heathland for a series of holes laid out by James Braid in the 1920s, when the course was lengthened.

The 6th is a famous dogleg hole round a fine clump of trees, well over 250 yards away and once carried from the tee by Ted Ray, Open Champion in 1912.

The 9th is another most attractive hole, a shortish par 4 at 353 yards. The drive is from an elevated tee over a shallow valley with a road at the bottom and a steep bank beyond. It's no great carry but many are relieved to reach the fairway beyond. This completes the first nine and also gets us back to the clubhouse. If all has gone reasonably well so far, beware, for most players consider the second loop the more difficult of the two.

The 11th is a really long par 5 of 568 yards. Once again, Grim's Dyke comes into play to catch your ball after two long woods or, perhaps, your weak third. It's about 40 yards short of the green. The 13th is another good hole, this time quite a short par 4 but with a drive between two sets of mounds. If you negotiate this successfully, keep your head down on the second shot. There's a tangle of rough to carry just short of the green and a hawthorn tree may also be on your line of fire. The 16th is perhaps the last demanding hole. The out of bounds right may tempt you too far left. This leaves the player to make a long carry over gorse. The approach area to the green also sets a stiff examination. The fairway narrows and the green itself is guarded by a solitary, and dense, May tree to the left and a grassy depression the other side.

Now you meet the Dyke for the last time. As long as you clear it with a straight one (it's a carry of about 150 yards) you should be home and dry.

All in all, it is, as Bernard Darwin once wrote, 'a course which always makes the spirits rise'. To play it at its best, come when the gorse and furze is in full bloom, though it's also an excellent dry winter course.

Since 1960, the Berkhamsted Trophy has been played here, one of the top amateur events of the golfing year.

🅴 £30	🚗 north along the A41 to Berkhamsted, turn right up Raven's Lane and then left at the crossroads. The clubhouse is then some 300 yards along on the left
🅼 a handicap certificate	
🍴 snacks daily	

BERKSHIRE, THE

Swinley Road, Ascot, Berkshire SL5 8AY
☎ Ascot (0344) 21495

Golf clubs with thirty-six holes are comparatively rare. Often, the second eighteen is an afterthought, created to relieve pressure on the main course. Not so at the Berkshire. It was thirty-six from the beginning: the Red and the Blue. It is said these neutral names were chosen so that neither course was singled out as the better.

Both courses share the characteristic that almost all the holes are separate, wandering through heather, pine, birch, chestnut and lime, over rolling heathland. The Red occupies the higher ground and the going is a little steeper but the springy turf makes thirty-six holes a day no great matter.

The Berkshire is the home of one of Britain's premier amateur events, The Berkshire Trophy, and has hosted the English Amateur Championship. The ladies too haven't been forgotten: the Avia Foursomes, a very popular event, was held here for a good many years in the very early spring, some tribute to the recovery powers of the course in a wet season.

The Red is unusual, even odd, in having six par 3s and six par 5s. Of the short holes, the 10th and 16th are the most difficult. The 10th, 187 yards, demands a good carry over heather, and there's a very severe drop to the right of the green. The 16th, a long par 3 at 220 yards, demands a very straight hit down a tree-lined avenue to the green. Here, there's a steep upslope with bunkers left and right. You might find this the right opportunity to wager your opponent won't find the green with his tee shot! The 17th is the longest of the par 5s and a difficult hole to birdie. The green has two tiers and is well guarded. Of the par 4s, the 6th is an extreme dogleg and the 8th a long curving hole with trees

199

invading along the right. The 11th is a very good short par 4 where you have to judge your approach nicely to a very small plateau green.

It's sometimes said that if the Red is all 5s and 3s, by contrast the Blue is all 4s. Well, that's not true. Here we are much more back to the average with four 3s and three 5s, none of the latter being as long as 500 yards. Perhaps the 1st, a par 3, is the most difficult hole of all on the Blue. The green is set on a hump with heather all the way, so the tee shot must carry all the way. The 13th is a most attractive short hole, with bunkers eating into the green all the way around. Ditches come into play on a few holes, notably the par 5 6th, where you must clear one with your second shot; the 11th where another zigzags across the fairway between 200 and 100 yards of the green; and the 16th where you must miss a fairway bunker on the left with your tee shot and clear the ditch with your long second to the green – a difficult hole this.

Professional events are not encouraged at The Berkshire which some people find rather a shame because, though neither course is of full tournament length, both are a severe test of driving; the wayward shot is unlikely to escape without punishment. There is also no course record, amateur or professional – 'Records are not kept'. The reason is simple and hard to argue with. The club considers that scoring depends very much on conditions, so a 72 one day could well be more of a feat than a 66 on another.

£ £45, £30 per round	**✗** snacks and lunch (famous at The Berkshire) daily except Monday
M a letter of introduction or a handicap certificate	**🚗** on A332 between Bagshot and Ascot

CAMBERLEY HEATH

Golf Drive, Camberley, Surrey GU15 1JG
☎ Camberley (0276) 23258

Camberley is another of Harry Colt's creations, now Japanese-owned, set in excellent golfing country. It has heather in abundance, gorse and broom and many fine pines, silver birch and rowan.

Camberley caused quite a splash when it was opened in 1913. The clubhouse alone had cost £4,000 and the whole project £15,000. It was widely thought to be the most expensive club ever. Bernard Darwin complimented Colt highly on his work: 'It bears all the unmistakable marks of his characteristic genius.' It has, however, over the years been somewhat overshadowed by its very famous neighbours, although it is as good as them. Perhaps they are better known because they have the facilities to host tournaments.

The course has a grand start. A few paces only from the clubhouse you have a downhill drive to a slanting fairway. It's not really the place to open your shoulders because placement is vital. You must be as far left as you dare, in order to shorten your long iron to the plateau green, which has a sharp rise in front of it to defeat a shot not quite up.

An excellent par 3 follows immediately, with a sweep of heather leading to an encouragingly large green – but it's three-tiered, and we all know what problems that can cause for putting.

The 5th, a par 5, is played from an elevated tee over a dip with the fairway swinging left almost at right-angles. There's plenty of space to aim at but make sure you reach the fairway. Then comes a short par 4 of some 280 yards, where a splendid army golfer, W.H.H. Aitken, followed the policy of thrashing a fairway wood into the bank at the rear of the green, hoping to see it run back close to the hole.

The 8th is another of Camberley's excellent par 3s, around 200 yards. You start from an elevated tee over a shallow valley to a green set near the beginning of the rise in the opposite slope. It's all heavily bunkered to either side with the ground falling away left. Decide whether to play a high carrying wooden club or a lower long iron, which should swing in with the run of the ground from the right.

The 11th is another par 3 of much the same length but is very different in character. You must cross a ravine to a green set at the top of a steep upslope with the front blocked out by four bunkers. There are trees and bushes to either side and through the back.

At the 13th you drive over an expanse of heather to a wide fairway rising to a crest. You have to reach it if you hope to get on in two at this par 5. The green is set on the same ridge as the clubhouse, so the shot must carry.

A quiet phase of the course follows, before the grandstand finish of the 17th and 18th. The 17th is a fairly long par 4, with thick heather to clear with your drive. To the left is an out of bounds and this is the side you should tend towards. To the right you may well run with the flow of the ground into dense heather. The green is narrow and there's a sand cliff you may have to clear before you reach it.

Of the last, it's said that W.H.H. Aitken once put down six balls and had four of them on the green with the other two just missing on the left. 'Unbelievable,' you may say looking at your scorecard and noting that the length of the hole is some 370 yards. Yes, it has been lengthened. But it still used to be well over 300 yards and all carry. If you hit a reasonable drive, don't fall just short with your shot to the green or you'll see your ball run back down the ridge into one of the bunkers set there just for that.

£ *£17 per round*

M *introduction from a member*

✗ *snacks and lunch daily*

🚗 *situated on the A325 between Frimley and Bagshot. First take the A30 if travelling from Bagshot, and if from Farnborough turn up Golf Drive about a mile past Frimley Park Hospital*

COOMBE HILL

Golf Club Drive, Kingston Hill, Surrey KT2 7DG
☎ *London (081) 942 2284*

Coombe Hill has been associated with famous professional names for most of its history. Craig DeFoy is the current standard-bearer, having succeeded Ken Bousfield, who stayed for more than forty years. Other famous names have been Neil Coles, the 1939 Open Champion Dick Burton, Henry Cotton, Sandy Herd – the first Open Champion to use a wound ball in 1902 – and Arthur Havers, who beat the great Walter Hagen at Troon in 1923, being the last British winner for eleven years.

Like Addington, Coombe Hill was designed by J.F. Abercromby. Thinking what you are trying to do with every shot is a good deal more important than just blazing a drive straight down the middle. Many of the drives down tree-lined fairways are quite tight.

Trees and rhododendrons are almost always a feature, making it easy to forget how near London you are, with the Kingston bypass close at hand and a view of the Telecom tower from the 8th green over what look to be continuous woodlands.

The 1st hole ought to be easy enough, only 300 yards downhill. If you think you can make the green, good luck, but perhaps your chances of a 3 are better if you play an iron down the left. The 2nd, 50 yards or so longer, is again downhill, so you really ought to start with a couple of pars for things now become rather more difficult. Next is a 400-yard dogleg left where you must try to be close to the elbow if you are not to have a lot more than a mid-iron to the green. Once on the putting surface, tread warily. It's very fast from the back left to front right and there are some tricky borrows.

The 5th has been shortened by a few yards in recent years to make it a par 4 and you'll need two of your best blows to get on. The second shot is uphill all the way. You need to play right of the flag, for there's a sharp slope from the right to the left on the green.

Abercromby was fond of par 3s and there are four very good ones at Coombe Hill, the 6th being the first. Judgement of club can be difficult with this green set well below the tee.

The first nine finishes with another good par 3, played across a valley to a tightly guarded green with a bunker ready to catch anything short.

The 11th is a longish par 4, made more difficult by a false horizon short of the green that makes one play short. The club laid a two-tier green in 1984. This has not eased the difficulty one jot!

Ken Bousfield considers the 12th the finest of the par 3s. There's a severe fall-away on the left of the green so try to 'fail' to the right.

The next two are short par 4s and Bobby Jones considered the 14th 'one of the finest holes of its length I've played'. With too long a drive you can run out of fairway, and the tee shot should be kept well right, which will make your pitch to the small green amongst the humps much easier.

The 15th is a good driving hole. It gives you options. 'Shall I try and play straight down the middle or cut the angle of the dogleg by carrying the large trees on the right of the fairway?' My advice is to go for it. Far better to try for a big whack when there's some real point.

The 16th again needs a long uphill second shot, which is rather a feature of Coombe Hill, and it is followed by the last of the par 3s. You're dead through the green on this one. The last hole puts some pressure on the tee shot. There's no 'safe' side for the drive. Go too far right and you're out of bounds; left and you're little better off, scrabbling in the rhododendrons. If you come to rest more comfortably, remember that the blind second shot needs a little more club than you think.

💷 £45

🅜 a handicap certificate, no visitors at weekends

✖ snacks and lunch daily; dinners can be arranged for visiting parties

🚘 on the A3 (Kingston bypass), turn for Kingston along the A238 and look out for Golf Club Drive after about ½ mile at the top of a rise

---

CROHAM HURST 🌳

Croham Road, South Croydon, Surrey CR2 7HJ
☎ *London (081) 657 2075*

This course is very popular with visiting societies, partly because it is always in good condition. It's fairly flat also, making walking easy, and the club's policy is to keep rough to a minimum. As a result, Croham Hurst does look quite undemanding but this can be deceptive. The main hazard on the course is that the fairways tend to be tree-lined.

You are right in at the deep end on the first two holes, both well over 400 yards. The 2nd is a dogleg with trees to either side and a well-bunkered green. However, a couple of short par 4s follow immediately, where you can hope to atone for a poor start.

There are three more par 4s of over 400 yards, all on the second nine. The 15th is a very difficult hole and stroke index 1. It's over 460 yards long, from both medal and the yellow markers, and the fairway is extremely tight. Your second shot has to pass through converging lines of trees and then hold the green, which has a pronounced slope to the right. This is followed by a long par 3 of some 220 yards. It doesn't quite play that length because the green is lower than the tee but it is very severely bunkered.

Harry Weetman was professional here for some years before moving on to Selsdon Park Hotel.

The clubhouse has a long enclosed verandah, used as a solarium, which gives good views of the course.

£ £25   M none

✕ snacks and lunch daily

🚗 take Croham Road from South Croydon Station for 1 mile and look out for the club on the right when Croham Road ends and Croham Valley Road begins

DUNSTABLE DOWNS

Whipsnade Road, Dunstable, Bedfordshire
☎ Dunstable (0582) 604472

Dunstable Downs is set on chalk downland, and with some justice claims to have some of the best fairways in Britain. It dries wonderfully well in the winter. There is an upper and lower level, and quite often the winds blow free: indeed this is a popular gliding area. However, don't go in a bitter north-easterly.

The course was designed by James Braid early this century and changes were made by Tom Moore, who was secretary for forty years. The firm of Alliss/Thomas has also left its mark, producing two new holes some years ago.

The lower nine is undulating, with the holes quite well separated by trees—beech, chestnut and birch—while there are also bushes in plenty. The upper section is, of course, more open to the wind and again undulates. The views are superb, particularly towards the Vale of Aylesbury, and you can see six counties from the 11th hole.

You start with a relatively short par 5 and then the only other par 5 follows rapidly as the 3rd. After some reasonably short par 4s, there comes the 8th, nearly 450 yards off the medal tees, and often played against the prevailing wind. The 9th is a highly rated short hole. Though you may need only a wedge, the green is very well guarded.

The 11th and 12th are again two long par 4s, each more than 450 yards. Both are well bunkered and there's an out of bounds along the left of the 11th. Four fairly short par 4s ease the journey home, though there is another long and difficult hole as well, the 16th. Fairly unusually, the fourth par 3 completes the round.

Practice facilities are much above average: two large areas and also a practice bunker and approaching green and a putting green.

£ £25   M a handicap certificate

✕ lunch and dinner daily except Monday

🚗 leave the M1 at Junction 11, taking the A505 through Dunstable and then the B4541 to the course

GATTON MANOR

Standon Lane, Ockley, near Dorking, Surrey RH5 5PQ
☎ *Oakwood Hill (030679) 555*

The manor from which the course takes its name was built in 1728 and has been in the Heath family for three generations. In the 1960s Bob Heath decided to create a golf course and later a hotel on the estate. With his son David, he travelled widely in both Europe and the USA, studying the design of both courses and individual holes to learn both the art and nuts and bolts of creating a course of championship standard. He wanted a course that could also be enjoyed by golfers of fairly high handicap, depending on the line chosen to the green.

Perhaps as a result of his American experience, much use was made of water hazards. They come into play on fourteen of the holes. The choice of tees is very much according to modern principles. For ladies the length is a fairly stiff 5,492 yards, and for men the medal tees produce a course of 6,145 with the yardage going up to 6,611 from the tigers. At full tournament stretch the course can measure just over 6,900. This increase makes for some interesting contrasts. The par 5 17th, for instance, is 525 medal, 580 tiger and – wait for it – 625 championship, longer than any hole on an Open Championship course by about 50 yards. There's a similar sort of contrast at the five par 3s. From the forward tees, none are really much more than a mid-iron, but most become at least a long iron from the back tees. One, the 10th, is 73 yards longer from the back tees than the front, 228 as opposed to 155 yards.

Most men play the course from the medal tees, so these are the distances given.

The 3rd is a very interesting hole of 395 yards. Your tee shot is played through woods with your second having to carry over one of two ponds to a well-bunkered green. The 6th, 357 yards, is another excellent hole. Again, the tee shot has to thread through woods and then lands on sloping ground which can take you into the river. Your second shot has to carry a meander of the same river, which you might also find if you're too long and go through the green. The 7th is also a good hole, a par 3 with a stream winding across the fairway about 50 yards from the middle of the green. At this distance it oughtn't to give you much trouble. The 11th is a really short par 4 of only 265 to 277 yards, depending on which markers you play off so, one might think, very drivable indeed. However, you will have to take account of that river, again twisting across not far short of the green.

The 18th is a grand finishing hole. How often this just isn't so, with the course designer content just to get us back to the clubhouse. Here, you are faced with a tee shot over the river, and your second has a stream to cross some 50 yards from the middle of the green, with quite a steep upslope immediately beyond. The green is bunkered front left and right and there are woods close by as well.

Trees, indeed, are one of the delights of the course, which was carved through dense woodland. There are many very fine specimens and a mass of rhododendrons, magnolias and a huge tulip tree. There's a great deal of bird life also and otter, badger and roe deer.

£ £12	**M** none	**🚗** from A24 turn along A29 for Ockley. At south end of village take turn at Old School House pub and carry on to T junction and turn left, following signs thereafter
✗ snacks, lunch and dinner daily		
🏨 golf/hotel packages available		
🏊 fishing, bowls and tennis		

KNOLE PARK

Seal Hollow Road, Sevenoaks, Kent TN15 0HJ
☎ *Sevenoaks (0732) 452150*

For very many years this was the home club of Sam King, third in the 1939 Open Championship and a contender on many other occasions, notably in 1948, when he caught the maestro, Henry Cotton, during the final round but then faded.

The club was founded when the Wildernesse estate was about to be sold in 1923 and a country club set up. Some of the members of Wildernesse Golf Club objected to the plans and sought the agreement of Lord Sackville to build a clubhouse and the present course. This has the fairly unusual number of six par 3s, perhaps because one of the course architects, J.F. Abercromby, was particularly fond of designing them.

You begin with one, not particularly difficult except that it's the first hole, nearly 200 yards and a little uphill to a green well-protected by bunkers.

Long par 4s are also a feature. There are six measuring at least 400 yards and two come early, the 3rd and 4th. The latter is a very attractive hole where the drive is from an elevated tee and the fairway doglegs left along a valley. The 11th is perhaps the most difficult hole, 426 yards with a very demanding drive. The fairway doglegs sharply right round some tall trees and the drive has to be both long and well positioned if your second shot isn't to be more than 180 yards.

The 18th makes an excellent finish. It's a 400-yard hole where the drive is blind and must carry bracken and reach a plateau. From there, your second is to a green at the bottom of a slope, guarded by bunkers on the left and a pond on the right. A par is often good enough to win it.

The course is built on light soil and the many trees are usually the remains of the original forest which covered the area. Bracken and, less common on our courses, ant hills of unknown age punish drives off line, while there are nine ponds, two of which, on the 13th and 18th, are not visible from the tee.

£ *£22*	*snooker and squash*
M *verbal confirmation is required that you are a member of a golf club with a handicap*	*turn down Seal Hollow Road from Sevenoaks High Street and continue ¼ mile*
snacks and lunch daily, dinner daily except Sunday and Monday	

MOOR PARK

Moor Park Mansion, Rickmansworth, Hertfordshire WD3 1QN
☎ *Rickmansworth (0923) 773146*

They do say you remember a golf course with special affection if you've played it well, and that's certainly one of the reasons for my liking Moor Park. In the 1964 Esso Golden Tournament I played the best golf of my life. I hit the ball well throughout, hardly missed a short putt and holed not a few long ones as well. It was a round robin matchplay event with a selected field. You played everybody. I won all my matches except for a half with Kel Nagle and a loss to Christy O'Connor, who both finished with birdie 2s.

Moor Park has been seen a great deal on TV in recent years, with the ill-fated Bob Hope Classic and its successor, the Wang Four Stars event, being held here. It's also been the venue for four PGA Matchplay Championships, the Uniroyal twice and the 1979 Tournament Players' Championship, which gave Michael King his first and only major victory. Long ago, the tournament season used to start off here, with the long-gone Silver King and Spalding events.

The first thing you notice at most golf clubs is the clubhouse, and Moor Park's may just be the most magnificent in the land, a Grade 1 listed historic building. Historic it certainly is. In the thirteenth century the house was known as the Manor of the More and later Cardinal Wolsey, Henry VIII and Catherine of Aragon lived there. A peace treaty with France was signed within its walls in 1525.

In 1679 James, Duke of Monmouth, the bastard son of Charles II, bought the estate and had a new house built. He didn't live long to enjoy it, however. In 1685 he headed a rebellion to seize the throne against his uncle James II, but was defeated at the Battle of Sedgemoor and executed on Tower Hill. He was, of course, playing for high stakes against a golfer!

What you see today basically dates from the early eighteenth century, when a profiteer in the South Sea Bubble scheme brought in Giocomo Leoni to restyle the house. Later, Capability Brown laid out the parkland. Much later still, in 1919, the estate was bought by the soap magnate, Lord Leverhulme and this led, in 1923, to the laying out of three golf courses by Harry Colt. One of these is now a municipal course; the others are the High and the West.

The next non-golfing brush with history came in the Second World War. The mansion was headquarters of the 2nd Airborne Division and saw the planning of the Arnhem disaster.

But what, you may be saying, about the golf?

I always found the High extremely difficult, at just over 6,900 from the blue championship tees, with several long par 4s, but five par 5s to ease the way.

The lst is uphill and, though not particularly long at some 370 yards from medal tees, is quite a tough start. It is followed by a hole some 50 yards longer, a sharp dogleg right. The 3rd is a good par 3, and the excellence of the short holes is indeed the strongest feature of the course. The most difficult hole on the first nine is the 8th, a very long par 4 where you must be either centre fairway or just left of centre to have a chance of getting home in two. Watch out for the pond on the left of the fairway about 120 yards short of the green. The first nine is completed with a shortish par 5 of 480 yards, with a grove of beech trees along the left. The 12th is an outstanding long par 3 of 210 yards, played across a valley and all carry to the two-tiered green with three putts a near certainty if you alight on the wrong level. It's the first of a run of the three most difficult holes, where pros are delighted with 3, 4, 4. The 14th has another difficult green, big and undulating, and at the 15th it's no easy matter to play your second to the green over the road and stay on. The 16th is the best of the three par 5s, slightly uphill and with trouble for a tee shot to the right. Few players seem to birdie it. The last hole is a par 3. It's played from a high tee to a green protected by falling ground on the left and back, with trees and a bunker to the right. It was here in 1963 that the South African Harold Henning, now making a new career on the US Senior Tour, holed in one during the Esso event and was £10,000 the richer – a huge sum then.

The High is 6,675 yards from the medal tees, standard scratch 72, and despite the quality of the players who have competed here, the amateur record stands at 69. Early in his career, Bernard Gallacher went round in 63, with an eagle and seven birdies.

The West course must be considered a great deal easier, if only because it's more than 800 yards shorter. There are two big par 4s, however, the 7th of 457 yards and the 15th, 434. However, there are several par 4s of around 330 yards or a lot less, and no doubt you'll be trying to get on with your drive at the 10th, 264 yards, and the 17th, 267.

£ £27   *snooker and tennis*

Ⓜ *handicap certificate or a letter of introduction*

✕ *snacks and lunch daily*

🚗 *just off the A404 in Rickmansworth at Backworth Heath Hill, or alternatively by leaving the A404 along A4145*

ST GEORGE'S HILL

Weybridge, Surrey KT13 0NL
☎ *Weybridge (0932) 42406*

It may well have been W.G. Tarrant who invented the idea of a 'golf estate', where there is, ideally, a splendid course with building plots of substantial size all around. This concept has done very well for developers in America for many years, and since the Second World War has caught on in parts of Europe too. Less so in Britain, though, where St George's Hill and the Wentworth estates are the most notable examples. Tarrant was largely responsible for both – and was bankrupted by Wentworth!

The raw material, the land itself, was very well suited to golf at St George's Hill. It was said in 1660 that it was: 'A bare heath and sandy ground and fit for no other kind of improvement but only for the breed of coneys' [rabbits]. That was a view of the area for *farming*. But through the eyes of Bernard Darwin it was very different: 'By a merciful dispensation of providence, fir trees, sand and heather, which are beautiful things in themselves, are the ingredients from which inland golf courses should be made. The prettiest courses are also the best and certainly one of the prettiest and the best is St George's Hill.'

Work began on the course in 1912, with H.S. Colt as architect. What a prodigious task it must have been to carve a golf course through what Darwin called 'a huge primeval forest' with the help of a team of horses, hand saws and one steam engine. Oh yes, and explosives – 7,000 stumps were blown out of the ground.

The club quickly became very fashionable. George VI, when Duke of York, was a frequent visitor, as was the Prince of Wales, captain in 1933–4. A certain Herr von Ribbentrop was an honoured guest in 1937!

Great players came too. In 1926, for instance, St George's Hill saw the final thirty-six holes of a £500 challenge between Walter Hagen and Abe Mitchell. Bobby Jones beat Cowan Shankland, one of the club's best-ever players, in the Amateur Championship in 1930, going on to win what was to be the first leg of his Grand Slam of the Amateur and Open Championships of both Britain and the USA in 1930, a feat never achieved before or since. Shankland achieved a lifetime eclectic score over St George's Hill of 43 – with only one hole in 1.

The course is laid out in two loops, the 1st and 10th tees actually being back to back. Most of the fairways are heavily tree-lined and the placement of tees, as in so many of Colt's designs, is a great feature. Here they are often set into hillsides, giving the view of an expanse of heather to be carried before the fairway.

The 1st provides a reasonably easy start, though the pitch to the green has to be played up to a kind of saddle up above. The 2nd is a long par 4, though the drive is a little downhill. The 3rd is a long par 3. Hit the right half of the green as a ridge divides it.

The 4th is one of those delights of golf, a really short par 4 of about 270 yards, but carry all the way if you think you can drive it. Bunkers totally screen the front, so there's no way to run it in.

The 6th is stroke index 1, rightly so. From the tee there's a long carry over heather and you must find the line if you're to get on in two strokes.

Shortly thereafter comes one of the great par 3s of world golf. In still air the 8th may need just a well hit 4 iron, but you play over a valley to a green set on top of the rise with three huge bunkers set into the upslope. Bernard Darwin chose it as one of the holes in his favourite eighteen.

The 10th gives you a blind tee shot over a crest and the green is partly masked by a ridge and large bunkers, a very good two-shot hole, followed by a really short par 3 of 115 yards or so, cocked up on a hill with a ravine in front, behind and to one side. Yes, just a wedge but...

For the remainder of the second nine, perhaps the 16th is the finest hole, a long 4 with a line of cross bunkers to catch the second shot which doesn't quite reach the elevated green.

Without doubt, St George's Hill is in the highest category of Britain's inland courses and with no clear superior for variety of holes and beauty.

£ *£40*

M *a handicap certificate or introduction by a member*

⊠ *bookings should be made in advance.*

✗ *snacks and lunch daily*

🚗 *from the A3, take the A245 towards Byfleet. The turning for the club is on the right after 3/4 of a mile*

STOKE POGES

Park Road, Stoke Poges, near Slough,
Buckinghamshire SL2 4PG
☎ *Slough (0753) 26385*

This is a first-class parkland course of over 6,600 yards. Bernard Darwin wrote of it more than seventy years ago: 'Never was there a better instance of the art of forcibly turning a forest into a golf course than at Stoke Poges. The beautiful old park turf was always there, cropped from time immemorial by generations of deer but in every direction there stretched thick belts of woodland and yet a golf course was made and opened in less than no time.' As you'd expect, this means that every hole except the short 7th is tree-lined, mostly by oaks, and there's that good sense of the separateness of each hole as you play along.

It is one of relatively few courses of real calibre to the north of the Thames, close to London, and has hosted the Matchplay championship three times (won here in 1937 by my father), the most recent occasion being in 1977.

The clubhouse is vast, and is much used by film and TV companies. It dates from the 1720s. Bernard Darwin once wrote: 'The clubhouse is a gorgeous palace, a dazzling vision of white stone, of steps and terraces and cupolas, with a lake in front and imposing trees in every direction, while over it all broods the great Chief Justice Coke, looking down benignantly from the top of his pillar and gracefully concealing his astonishment at the changes in the park.'

In general, the course is flat, with hillocks here and there. Brooks cross several of the holes.

The 3rd is very heavily bunkered and slopes upwards from tee to green; there's a brook in play too. On the 5th, cross bunkers intimidate many people and lead them to play too far left. Do this, and you're often through the green and left with a very difficult shot back.

The par 3 7th has damaged many a card. There are problems to both left and right, with heavy banking and a brook. Few players feel entirely convinced they've chosen the right club. The 9th, one of several long par 4s, has an uphill drive with fairway bunkers very much a threat.

The 12th is stroke index 2 with both a brook and diagonal cross bunkers the main problem, apart from the length of the hole. Yet another long par 4 comes at the 14th. Here you must keep your tee shot right while bearing in mind the bunkers that are hidden on that line.

The 15th, apart from the difficult green, is perhaps the most testing hole on the course. If you play 'safely' left, you find you've no feasible shot in. The answer is to go right but not too far, otherwise you'll be in the car park or secretary's office – definitely out of bounds.

£ £20

M a handicap certificate or a letter of introduction

✗ snacks, lunch and dinner daily

Ⓛ ladies may play only if invited and juniors must be accompanied by an adult

♨ sauna

🚗 leave A4 at Slough and take the B416 to Stoke Poges. Turn into Stoke Poges Lane on your left and continue for about 1½ miles looking out for clubhouse on the left

SUNNINGDALE

Ridgemount Road, Sunningdale, Ascot, Berkshire SL5 9RW
☎ *Ascot (0344) 21681*

This is one of my favourite places to play golf. Naturally that is partly because of the superb quality of the courses, but for my own golf the surroundings are every bit as important as the standard of the course, and I relish its sandy character and the heather, bracken and silver birch. I was brought up in fairly similar terrain at Ferndown but some of my early golf education might well have come at Sunningdale. My father was offered the professional's job a little after the war and thought long and hard about it. In the end he decided he was well settled in Dorset so the Ryder Cup player Arthur Lees moved down from Dore and Totley in Yorkshire and remained happily for the rest of his working life. He still plays at Sunningdale and can give good account of himself though in his eighties. He regularly 'betters his age' and is still a scourge of young bucks fancying their chance against the old master.

The first design for the famous Old course was the work of Open Champion Willie Park, though there have been many changes over the years, with Harry Colt responsible for many of them in the 1920s. He also designed the New course in 1922.

The Old quickly became a fashionable place to play, helped by the PGA Matchplay Championship coming here in 1903. In the 1920s one of the most famous rounds of golf ever was played by Bobby Jones in a qualifying round for the Open Championship. He had a 66, 33 out and 33 home. He played 33 strokes through the green and had 33 putts (rather a lot for a low score by today's standards). He reached all the par 4s and 5s in two strokes and missed only one green, on a short hole, but got his par 3 there as well. It was regarded as golf of an impossibly high standard for, because of the equipment of the day, he was hitting woods or long irons into the majority of the greens.

His card hangs framed in the club dining room as does his portrait. The 66 was no flash in the pan for he went round in 68 the next time out. However, others have bettered his scoring in later years, including the Australian Norman Von Nida who had a 63 in the Dunlop Masters shortly after the Second World War and Manuel Pinero years later in 1982 when he stormed through the field on the last day to win the European Open, an event frequently played here.

The Old Course

By today's standards the Old course, at 6,341 yards, is by no means a long course, and from the yellow tees it's even less of a slog. However, it's a subtle test and usually asks a player to have command of every club in the bag.

212

The 1st hole, 494 yards, is a comfortable enough start, slightly downhill with many players looking to get home in two on firm ground with a helping wind. However, you can start disastrously as there is out of bounds along the right and one or two large bunkers to the left.

At the 2nd you first encounter one of the features of Sunningdale, the long par 4s of over 400 yards, of which there are seven in all. This one is particularly difficult and perhaps none too good a hole for visitors with a blind drive to a slightly angled and raised fairway and blind second to a rather shelf-like green. Judgement of distance is difficult.

The 3rd offers another Sunningdale feature early on. It's the first of three very short par 4s and is only 296 yards, but it's well bunkered along the right and has heather in plenty to the left.

After an uphill par 3 to a plateau green, you come to one of Sunningdale's most famous holes, the 5th. Most professionals play safe with an iron from the tee. The best line is along the left while the pond is an obvious magnet for the second shot of handicap players. Two more medium-length two-shotters follow, the 6th being a beautiful one, the fairway running between pine woods. The 8th, in a cross wind, can be a very difficult par 3 of some 170 yards, especially if you just miss the green, for your ball will run far away to the right and bunkers and out of bounds are tight on the left.

The first nine ends with an encouraging very short par 4 with an open approach to the green. By all means have a go at covering its 267 yards with one mighty blow but perhaps a gentle 4 wood and a very precise pitch when the pin is at the back produce more birdies.

The inward nine begins with the much-loved and photographed 10th hole where an inviting fairway sweeps first down and then up towards the green with the prospect of a pause for refreshment in the famous hut just beyond.

The main feature of Sunningdale Old is the stern finish. After a relatively easy par 5 14th of under 500 yards, most players will need wood for the par 3 which follows, 226 yards long with bunkers everywhere. Long second shots are the feature of the last three holes, each considerably more than 400 yards. Aim to have handicap shots in the bank before tackling them as a finish of 4, 5, 5, 5 is very likely. The 18th with its huge oak tree by the green is a beauty. At least one of the bunkers is the result of a wartime bomb.

The New Course

The fame of Sunningdale Old has detracted from the merits of the New, though many would argue that the 'reserve' eighteen holes are the best, even if the course as a whole is less easy on the eye and would have benefited much from an energetic pine and birch tree-planting programme over the past thirty years. Where the Old tends to run through valleys, the New occupied higher ground, along ridges, overlooking Chobham Common. The New is about 300 yards the longer and is perhaps a couple of strokes more difficult. It has five par 3s, the shortest being 175 yards and much the same number of long par 4s as the Old course. Three par 5s offer some relief to the handicap golfer though one of these is over 550 yards.

£ £58

M letter of introduction

✗ lunch daily except Monday

🚗 ¼ mile from Sunningdale Station. Travelling west along A30, turn left 100 yards after the level crossing

✉ need to book in advance

TANDRIDGE

Godstone Road, Oxted, Surrey RH8 9NQ
☎ Oxted (088371) 2274

One of the many fine courses in Surrey, Tandridge is less well known than the Sunningdales and Wentworths but it's still excellent golf, played in thick woodlands, with one of the most attractive clubhouses in the country.

The club dates from 1923, when the great Harry Colt designed the course.

I would guess that he intended the start to be a couple of reasonably comfortable par 5s but changes to par ratings several years ago mean that you're pitched straight in at the deep end nowadays, with two par 4s of near maximum length. At the 1st there are fine trees along the right, with the fairway slanting towards them and bunkers to catch a drive too far left. The 2nd is slightly downhill to the green, so it may be easier to reach, but you have first to find a narrow exit for your tee shot and cope with a two-level green later.

The 5th is perhaps an even better par 4 of just under 400 yards. There are problems for your tee shot, with trees and bunkers to either side of the fairway, and the green is well protected by bunkers and a hollow in the front. It's rated stroke index 2.

The remainder of the first nine is easier going, with the 9th being a well-designed short par 5 of 476 yards. Here your drive must be in the left fairway because trees come into play for your next shot otherwise. There are hillocks for about the last 80 yards up to the green.

You begin the second nine from the clubhouse with another good par 4 of 431 yards, one of five par 4s of this length or more. The 13th is the most difficult of the four par 3s and measures 215 yards. There's a plateau green with the ground falling away to trees on the right and several bunkers to catch shots steered away from this trouble.

The 14th is stroke index 1, over 450 yards. You play from a high tee to a fairway well below, a Colt trademark, which then slopes up to the green, protected by a line of bunkers which should catch anything not well struck. The 17th is a similar hole and contrasts with the last hole where the drive is played uphill with the ball tending to run away to the right. Keep left.

£ £35

M a handicap certificate or a letter of introduction

✗ snacks and lunch daily

🚗 on the A25 Godstone to Westerham Road and 2 miles from Godstone. If on the M25, turn along the A22 for East Grinstead and shortly turn off along A25 signposted Oxted, Westerham and Sevenoaks

WALTON HEATH

Dean's Lane, Tadworth, Surrey KT20 7TP
☎ *Tadworth (073 781) 2060*

The Old course at Walton Heath is one of the sternest tests of inland golf in the British Isles. Indeed, the members claim that play on any other course seems easy after the unremitting demands of this heathland, 700 feet above sea level and open to the winds.

Chalk lies beneath the sandy subsoil so the course dries quickly and gives the turf a distinctly links quality. The ball never seems to sit up begging to be hit. Instead you must either squeeze it between clubhead and turf or nip it off clean. Precise striking is always needed, with little margin for error. There are often quite severe carries from the tee over heather, bracken and gorse, but once you reach the mown areas there's some run to be had. Bunkers are punishing and on the Old course often look rather threatening. Always in plain view, they tell you what you have to do. The rough used to be frightening in days gone by, and it's still severe today but is more graded. Some forty years ago James Braid used to advise: 'If you can't get a spoon [3 wood] to it, take a niblick [8 iron].'

Walton Heath came fairly early in the London golf boom and was the result of property development and the desire of one man, Herbert Fowler, to design a golf course. The Old course was very probably his first attempt and his masterpiece, though he went on to do work on others, notably Westward Ho!, Cruden Bay, Saunton and Yelverton.

How to go about designing a golf course is very much a matter of individual taste, though most these days seem to think in terms of two loops of nine, each finishing at the clubhouse. More often architects think first of the longer holes, so the par 3s often become just links in the chain of the whole course, which doesn't produce many good par 3s. Not so Herbert Fowler. He went out looking for a couple of short holes. He found the ideal sites, he felt, in the original 6th and 12th, and filled in the rest of the course in various directions from them.

215

Walton Heath rapidly became something of a parliamentary course. In 1913, for instance, twenty-four MPs were members and twenty-one members of the Lords. Lloyd George was a frequent visitor and he used to say of his game, with his reputation for deviousness in mind: 'Unlike what may be imagined, I am always straight.' Winston Churchill became a member in 1910, often playing with his Welsh friend, but he was not a keen player.

James Braid was at Walton Heath right from the start. Before the course opened, he had already won one Open, and wrote from his club in Romford, asking if he might be of service. His offer was accepted, and he spent the rest of his life until he died in 1950 at Walton Heath. He is commemorated by a Braid room in the clubhouse and it is said that during his thousands of rounds over the two courses, he managed to do all the holes in 2 or less, quite an eclectic score!

Walton Heath has been the scene of many great golfing events, the News of the World Matchplay Championship in particular, held here more than twenty times. Several amateur championships, for both men and women, have taken place on the Old course and, for professionals, the European Open several times and the 1981 Ryder Cup. The course is altered a little for these events, with three holes of the New course being used.

Old Course

The 1st gives quite a stern start. It's a long par 4 but this is followed by a short 4, 289 yards from the medal tees, drivable and with the green merging into the fairway.

Good hitting becomes increasingly necessary from this point on. The 3rd is a long flat par 4 of 443 yards and the 4th is one of Walton Heath's best holes, a par 4 of 391 yards. The drive is downhill but the run of the ground will tend to take your ball towards bunkers on the left. Go too far right, however, and you're either in heather or a hidden bunker. The shot to the plateau green must avoid deep flanking bunkers and the green itself is fraught with subtle borrows. Many a visitor past the flag has putted off the green and into those bunkers.

Some straight holes follow but variety is added by the 9th, a dogleg right of 395 yards to a green set on an upslope, not an easy target by any means. There is a new 10th hole, a par 3 of 160 yards, which is followed by a 380-yard par 4. The 12th, called Cotton's hole by many of the members, is a 371-yard par 4, bending to the right with a slightly downhill drive landing on a fairway banked rather like a race track.

You are now into the last nine, a sequence Tom Weiskopf once said was the best to be found anywhere and certainly everybody finds the last six very testing, with three par 5s, a couple of very good 4s and a long short hole.

The 16th is the best of those par 5s and one of the great holes of world golf. Long ago Bernard Darwin wrote of it: 'First, we must hit a long tee shot with heather threatening on the left and heather on the right. Next we see the green at the distance of another full shot ahead of us, perched defiantly on a crest, with a most cavernous bunker eating into its right-hand side. And that second shot must be hit quite truly and must be held up. If there is a trace of cut in the shot, if there is even a suspicion of weakness of hitting, into that bunker the ball will go.' The fairway slopes right to left so you must either place your drive or hit one with a left-to-right flight to avoid the heather on the left and a long bunker. If you've no real thoughts of getting home in two at this 510-yard hole, the pitch to the shelf-like green is still no easy one.

The 17th is a par 3 to an island green of 181 yards and is followed by a good 4 to finish with. There's some carry from the tee. Cross bunkers guard the green on this 404-yard hole, with dead ground between them and the green. It's always one more club than the visitor may think.

New Course

Like the New at Sunningdale, Walton Heath's New course is not clearly inferior to the Old but is undeniably a little shorter at 6,659 to 6,813 yards; it's also slightly softer and more inland in character. It has rather more variety, with some greens set in hollows and others on plateaux.

The 3rd is a stiff par 4 of 424 yards with a rather damnable bunker in mid-fairway which catches many a good drive. There's a deep pit left of the green and a deep bunker at the right entrance.

The 6th is one of Walton Heath's best par 3 holes at 169 yards, played to a plateau green.

On the 12th you have to find a drive which avoids the heather on the right. Even from a good lie, it will be all but impossible to find the green at this 426-yard par 4. From the left, only a very precise shot will hold the narrow putting surface; from centre fairway, the shot is still fraught. There are bunkers to the front left and right and a shot a little too long and to the right will plunge away and leave an almost impossible little pitch back.

The 14th gives a splendid downhill drive, followed by an exacting shot up the rise to a plateau green, some 400 yards from the tee.

After James Braid, Harry Busson was professional for many years. Now retired, he still produces superb handmade woods and putters.

£ £45

M a letter of introduction

✕ snacks daily 12.00 to 3.30pm, lunch and afternoon tea available

🚗 leave the M25 at the Sutton/ Reigate exit and head along the A217 for Sutton, taking the B270 after 2 miles into Mill Lane and then left along B2032. Dean's Lane is on the right after 1 mile and the clubhouse on the left shortly thereafter

WENTWORTH

Wentworth Drive, Virginia Water, Surrey GU25 4LS
☎ *Wentworth (0344) 2201*

This must be the best-known course of all to TV viewers, with the World Matchplay Championship being held here in the autumn for so many years. I refer, of course, to the West course, also known as the Burma Road, but it must be said that the East, though at 6,176 yards nearly 800 yards shorter, is also a course of tournament standard, and contains both the best par 3 and best par 4 on either. Harry Colt designed both, the East in 1924 and the West a couple of years later.

The East hosted a match between the professionals of Great Britain and Ireland and those of the United States in 1926, when the Ryder Cup came into being. Six years later the first Curtis Cup was held there. The West later staged the 1953 Ryder Cup, and many major tournaments.

The 1st is a stiff par 4, despite the generous width of the fairway, for at 462 yards from the medal tees and a dip to clear before the plateau green, a long drive is needed to give any hope of getting the green with the second shot. Even the longest-hitting professionals are struggling, once there's more than a very light breeze against. The 2nd, 137 yards, needs a precision shot to the rather shelf-like green. Many shots hit just short and tumble back down the bank in front. The bank at the back means the best strategy is to overclub a little.

The 3rd is again a long par 4. The drive is along a sort of wooded valley, with good placement needed to avoid fairway bunkers, before playing a second shot to a two-tier green backed by woods. The par 5 4th offers some respite; it's not long, with the ground favouring you on the blind drive. At the 5th, a par 3 of 167 yards, the green is set almost at eye level, which shortens the look of the hole a little. Bunkers surround it.

On the next three holes, all par 4s of no great length, the professional will be hoping to improve his score before facing the 9th, one of the West's most difficult holes. The drive is to a shelf-like plateau, with out of bounds close by on the left and a narrow green to hit. It's well over 400 yards from the tee and stroke index 1.

The short 10th has another shelf-like green, a feature the architect Harry Colt often used, and the 12th, 468 yards, has a fairly unusual feature, a line of trees across the fairway which must be carried. Unusual because although trees often dictate correct placement of a drive, or cover a green from one side or the other, we are seldom asked to make a frontal assault, as here. It's an obvious feature to use at a par 3 but encircling bunkers tend to be the choice.

Soon, you reach the famous West course finish, beginning with the 14th, an uphill par 3, where finding the right level of the two-tier green is part of the problem. The 15th gives a bit of run to the drive normally but it's a long 4 with a diagonal ditch to avoid with the second shot to a green set in the woods.

The 16th, a shorter par 4, should be relatively easy but many people get themselves too tight along the left and trees then block the shot to the green. The 17th is one of the great par 5s of inland golf in Britain, 571 yards for tournaments and 538 from the medal tees, with a sharp dogleg to the left. The drive must be kept left, especially if the ground is hard, or the ball will run too far right. The Open Champion Alf Perry took 7 here in his final round in a pre-war tournament but still managed to break 70 in every round.

Another par 5 ends the course, a left-to-right dogleg which has seen many dramatic finishes, not least a long pitch and run by Seve Ballesteros which enabled him to catch Arnold Palmer when he holed out in the 1983 World Matchplay. Greg Norman eagled the hole to beat Bernhard Langer by a single stroke in the 1981 Martini International, after a birdie on the 17th.

Like the New at Sunningdale, the East course should not be missed, just because you have heard and seen so much of the West. In the 4th it has the best par 3 of the lot and a case can be made out that the 11th is the best par 4.

There is also a good short course of nine holes, with length ranging from 340 yards to 113. There are also a first-class driving range and a large practice ground. Bernard Gallacher has been the professional for some years, having followed another Ryder Cup player, Tom Haliburton. He has an excellent shop. He and Gary Player were consultants on the John Jacobs designed Edinburgh (South) course which opened in autumn 1990.

🅴 *West £100, East and Edinburgh £75*	✗ *snacks daily, lunch and dinner daily except Saturday*
Ⓜ *a handicap certificate, unless booking in advance*	🚗 *leave A30 at the Ascot turn-off by the Wheatsheaf Hotel in Virginia Water*
🏨 *11 double, four single rooms available*	

WEST HILL ⛳

Bagshot Road, Brookwood, Surrey GU22 0BH
☎ *Brookwood (04867) 2110*

In ideal heathy country with a profusion of heather, pine and beeches, this is an excellent inland course. Alec Bedser, a member here for many years, considers it a sterner test than Sunningdale from the back tees.

West Hill is the home of the very popular annual father and son foursomes and would be good enough to be a full tournament test of professionals were it not for the fact that it's on the short side at just over 6,300 yards.

It is one of the few courses that owes its foundation to a woman, Mrs Lubbock, who found in those more sexist times just after the turn of the century that few clubs in the area would allow women as members. She instructed her architects, Willie Park and Jack White, to ensure good carries from the tees and fairly severe penalties for those who could hit neither straight or a good length.

The start is not an easy one, a par 4 of nearly 400 yards, with trees encroaching in the drive landing area and then a ditch to be carried by your second shot. The 3rd, some 50 yards longer, sets similar problems and a par takes some getting, again with a stream short of the green.

At the 5th, one of just two par 5s, heather is very much a threat and is immediately followed by the stroke index 1 hole, 419 yards. You drive slightly uphill and the second shot makes this hole, played to a green below you, with trees and heather to the right and a big bunker eating into the green on the left.

There are more good par 4s at the beginning of the homeward nine. The 10th, has a broader fairway than you usually find at West Hill, while the 11th asks you to make a good carry with your tee shot over thick heather. The 12th is a subtle short par 4, where you'll often need plenty of backspin with your little pitch to hold the green. The 14th demands two full-out shots to cover the 462 yards.

This brings you to the 15th tee and West Hill's most famous hole, a par 3 of 212 yards with trees all along on either side and also through the back. The green is set at the top of a rise with bunkers to catch anything not quite up. Bernard Darwin once rated it the best long par 3 in the country. To land a 3-wood or long iron fair and square on the green provides a moment to savour.

The last hole, 440 yards, is in view from the clubhouse all the way. There's a cross bunker to carry with your second shot to a large flat green that's well bunkered.

£ £25   **M** none   ✗ *snacks and lunch daily, dinner for larger groups only*

Ⓛ *juniors fees are only £4.00 per round currently*

🚗 *on A322 just south of crossroads with A324*

WILDERNESSE

Seal, Sevenoaks, Kent
☎ *Sevenoaks (0732) 61199*

·This is a parkland course well-known for its natural beauty. It has many trees, which makes your long shots feel tighter than they really are. How often the appearance of a hole, rather than how it actually plays, affects the nerves of a golfer! There is a relief from such feelings, however, on the 10th to 14th holes, which are more open.

In fact, the first nine holes and the last five are played around a 60-acre wood, and overall the 6,478 yards of Wildernesse are a good enough test to have been used by the R and A for regional qualifying for the Open in the very recent past.

After the comfortable start of a quite short par 4, you're plunged into the thick of things at the 2nd. This is a 437-yard par 4 which doglegs right. There's quite a tight drive and your ball needs to move from left to right to fit the shape of the fairway. You need quite a long tee shot mainly to make your next easier. The green is narrow and heavily guarded to the right. On the right, there's a pond about 100 yards short of the green which should only come into play if your tee shot has been weak.

Your best chances of building a good score will probably come on the four par 5s, none of them particularly long.

In contrast, however, the 9th is a monster par 4, at 475 yards with out of bounds all down the left, making you feel you can't really let fly with gay abandon. The 16th is another long 4 with a tight drive and plateau green, difficult to hit with a mid- to long iron.

The 17th doglegs to the left and your drive will need to be near the angle and reasonably long to give you sight of the green.

All in all, this is a well-balanced course with par for both nines being 36. There are several short- to medium-length par 4s which may yield birdie opportunities, and three of the par 3s, in still air, are no more than mid-iron shots.

£ £20	**✗** snacks daily, lunch daily except Tuesday and Saturday, dinner can be arranged for visiting parties of 50 and above
M proof of handicap	
🎾 tennis	
✉ need to book in advance	**🚗** on the A25 between Sevenoaks and Maidstone turn off for Seal and club is signposted thereafter

WOBURN

Bow Brickhill, Milton Keynes MK17 9LJ
☎ *Milton Keynes (0908) 370756*

The Duke's course, opened for play in 1976, and the Duchess, a couple of years later, are two of the best courses to enjoy the limelight in recent years. The ground was once farmland which was later forested, and these two courses are basically carved through pine forest with heather and rhododendrons in profusion.

The Duke's in particular has become very well known through television, featured on my *Around with Alliss* programmes and also on the *Men versus Women* series held there in recent years.

Now the permanent home of the Dunhill Masters, Woburn has been used for several other major events including the Dunlop Masters twice, in 1979 and 1981, the Brabazon Trophy, the Ford Ladies' Classic, and the Women's British Open.

From the men's medal tees, the Duke's course measures 6,914 yards and is a little out of balance with the inward nine being the longer by more than 500 yards. The Duchess is about 250 yards shorter and has some fairly short par 4s, unlike the Duke's layout. Both nines are just over 3,300 yards.

The 3rd hole on the Duke's has been much photographed and is almost always featured in television coverage. Only 134 yards from the medal tees, it should be easy enough, but the tee is set high above the green and clubbing often causes problems. The rhododendrons which surround the green may well lose their charm when a ball plunges into them!

The 4th, stroke index 3, is indeed testing, a right to left dogleg and uphill all the way through a valley for its near 400 yards. The next hole, the second of the four par 5s, again doglegs left. At 488 yards, it has often been reached in two but the second shot is challenging, with a ravine to be carried. However, it is possible to aim for a narrow strip of fairway along the right.

Perhaps the most difficult hole on which to get your par is the 7th, again a dogleg to the left and over 460 yards in length, played to a green with a Norman church behind. The green has a big step through the middle.

A ravine or gully again comes into play on the 13th, 419 yards, with a fairway sloping left amongst tall stands of pines. The gully must be negotiated by your second shot.

The 14th, 565 yards, has been acclaimed as the best par 5 in Britain and is played through the pine forest. If either tee shot or second shot wanders near the edge of the fairway, trees will often block out your next shot. Judgement of distance must be exact for the approach to the two-tier green or three putts are very likely indeed.

£ *by arrangement*

M *membership of a golf club and a handicap certificate*

✗ *breakfast, lunch and dinner by arrangement*

🚗 *leave M1 at Junction 13 for Woburn Sands and follow signposts to the club for about 4 miles*

✉ *need to book in advance*

SOUTH
OF ENGLAND

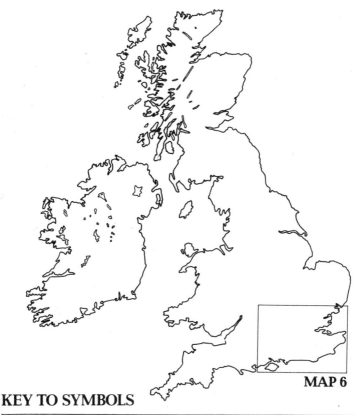

MAP 6

KEY TO SYMBOLS

🌳	PARKLAND	☎	TELEPHONE	✗	CATERING PROVIDED
🚩	LINKS	⊠	NEED TO BOOK IN ADVANCE	🏠	ACCOMMODATION PROVIDED
🌿	MOORLAND	£	APPROXIMATE COURSE FEE	Ⓛ	RESTRICTIONS ON LADIES AND/OR YOUTHS
⚓	HEATHLAND				
🏴	DOWNLAND	M	MEMBERSHIP REQUIREMENTS FOR VISITORS	▶	OTHER SPORTING FACILITIES
🏔	UPLAND			🚗	DIRECTIONS

BLACKMOOR 🍴

Firgrove Road, Whitehill, Bordon, Hampshire GU35 9EH
☎ *Bordon (0420) 472775*

This is the home of a premier amateur competition, the Selborne Salver, played each April. Competitors sometimes go on to greater things and in the past several years winners have included such current European Tour players as Sandy Lyle, Gordon Brand from Bristol, Paul Way, Paul Hoad and Ronan Rafferty.

Although this is quite a short course at 6,213 yards, only once has anyone done better than two under the par of 69. In a word, it is yet another of Harry Colt's excellent designs, which has needed to be little modified since he supervised construction in 1913.

Like many others in this Surrey/Hampshire belt of superb golfing country, it is heathy in character, though this had tended to change quite a bit in the last thirty years or so, since the decimation of the rabbit population. The pine, silver birch and oak have had more of a chance and the woodland is quite rich. However, heather, bracken and gorse still punish the golfer who cannot keep to the fairway.

The feel of the ground is gently undulating and the subsoil is sandy. In the winter mats are not needed and neither are temporary greens. Both members and visitors ought to rejoice.

There is a gentle start to the course, to which few people would object, with two shortish par 4s. Two considerably longer ones follow. The 4th is stroke index 1 and justifies its rating, usually being into the prevailing wind, with out of bounds and heather to the left to punish the shot that fails to hold the ideal line of tee shot, which is left of centre. The 9th requires right judgement of club. It will not do to be far through the green, and a cross bunker should deter anyone hoping to run on their tee shot to this 140-yard hole, having cleared the heather first.

The 15th is another well-known par 3, but this time much longer, with the green elevated and flanked by deep bunkers to left and right. The 18th is fit to settle many a match. From an elevated tee, your drive is threatened by heather to either side of the fairway. For the second shot, bunkers right and left protect the green with a deep quarry also, behind the right-hand bunker. The green is invitingly large, but the undulations mean that you'd do well to get your ball reasonably close, if you're not to three-putt.

💷 *£27.50*

🍴 *lunch and dinner daily*

Ⓜ *a handicap certificate, only members' guests at weekends. Ladies' day Tuesday*

🚗 *take the A325 for Petersfield from Farnham for 8 miles to Whitehill. There, turn right into Firgrove Road*

FRILFORD HEATH ﺍﻟ

Frilford Heath, Abingdon, Oxfordshire OX13 5NW
☎ *Frilford Heath (0865) 390428*

Here are two heathland courses of very high standard indeed, it being a matter of dispute among the members as to which is the better. This is the reason why two 'neutral' names are used, as at The Berkshire, the 'Red' course and the 'Green'.

However, the Red measures over 6,700 yards, while the Green is about 750 yards shorter with a standard scratch of 69, four lower than the Red.

On the north side of the city it's rare to find land as well suited to golf as this until much further from London. Indeed, Bernard Darwin once said of Frilford that it was 'a wonderful oasis in a desert of mud. The sand is so near the turf that out of pure exuberance it breaks out here and there in little eruptions.'

Probably the best time to visit is spring and autumn for, like nearly all heathy courses, it can become rather dusty after long periods without rain.

Red Course

The first two holes are medium-length 4s, both right-hand doglegs with plenty of trouble in the form of rough and trees just off the fairways. In fact at Frilford, you'll sometimes be better off if you're really wild off the tees rather than just inaccurate, for you can quite often land up on a neighbouring fairway. The 4th is a long-iron par 3 and is very tightly bunkered.

You may be hoping to reach the 5th, not a particularly long par 5, in two, in which case there are cross bunkers not far short of the green which, of course, you must carry. There's a similar problem on the next, again a par 5. The 8th is a very stern hole, over 470 yards with a narrow fairway and a tight line into a green with difficult borrows. The 9th takes you back to near the clubhouse with a pond between the tee and the green.

The second nine begins with a par 5 of some 550 yards and a challenging tee shot where you will probably feel you can't carry sand on the right and try to place your drive between it and the trees along the left.

At the 12th, the last of four par 5s, you reach your furthest from the clubhouse. It's one of the only holes on the Red that's not a dogleg. The setting of the green is splendid, with a high stand of trees behind the green. The 13th is a right-angled dogleg over a stream that shouldn't really come into play. The green is attractively set in a saucer.

Rather surprisingly, there are two rather short par 4s in the last three holes. Both are little over 300 yards and in a favourable wind are drivable, but the 16th asks for carry all the way, and at the last, with the out-of-bounds wall of the car park in the driving area to the left, it's much safer to play your tee shot for position.

Green Course
The par 3s are especially good and the 6th, about 150 yards, has been singled out for high praise. The most difficult holes are the 7th and the 16th, both long par 4s. There are five par 4s of about 340 yards or less to provide the main birdie opportunities.

£ *£28 and £38*

M *handicap certificate essential*

✗ *snacks and lunch daily, dinner for visiting societies only*

🚗 *4 miles west of Abingdon on the A338 Oxford to Wantage road*

LA MOYE

St Brelade, Jersey, Channel Isles
☎ *Jersey (0534) 42701*

La Moye's setting is spectacular, some 250 feet up above St Ouen's Bay on the south-west promontory of the island, with views of Guernsey, Herm, Sark and Jethou away to the north-west. The club was started in 1902 by George Boomer, headmaster of La Moye School. Two of his sons, Percy and Aubrey, became professionals of note, especially the latter who won the French Open five times, three other national championships and was a Ryder Cup player on three occasions. Mr Boomer's course was revised by James Braid and final changes followed in the late 1970s, mostly to provide more length. In tournaments it can now be stretched to 6,700 yards, but the golfing holiday-maker will find it 400 yards or so shorter and enjoy the Continental feeling.

The 2nd is a good par 5, with the tee shot having to find a narrow fairway which doglegs among the dunes; the green is narrow too. The 4th is another dogleg with views of nearly the whole course, the bay and then the islands beyond. The 5th is said to be the most demanding par 3 in the Channel Islands. The shot is all carry over pot bunkers and a bank, while if you are too strong, the ground drops away sharply at the back of the green. At the 6th you have to carry sandhills from the tee with gorse and broken ground as well.

The 8th again gives you fine views and the prospect of having to find a green set on the very edge of the cliffs. On the 13th, out of bounds are a

226

threat to both the tee and second shots. The parallel 14th fairway is not in play, nor is a clump of trees to the left that can easily catch the fairly long second shot. The 16th is a good driving hole where you should find the left half of the fairway in order to ease your second to a narrow plateau green.

All the greens are excellent.

Tony Jacklin is an honorary member, and won the 1981 Jersey Open over the course.

£ £40 (including lunch), £25 per round, weekly terms are available

M a handicap certificate

✕ snacks, lunch and dinner daily

♦ snooker

🚗 off the Route Orange, at La Moye School

LITTLESTONE ⚑

St Andrew's Road, Littlestone, New Romney, Kent TN28 8RB
☎ *New Romney (0679) 62310*

Littlestone is hard by the English Channel with views of the marshes, the cliffs of Folkestone and Dover, with France in sight on clear days.

One of the very first British Ladies' Championships was held here. More recently it has hosted the English Ladies' and Open qualifying rounds, when the championship comes to Royal St George's.

It is a bare links course with hard fast greens and sand dunes. The wind is very often a factor and the fairways have rather fewer bumps and hollows than such other Kent links as Deal and Royal St George's. It's both fun and a good test of golf of over 6,400 yards.

As with Royal St George's, Laidlaw Purves is given the credit of being the first to see the possibilities of the links in 1888, when he became the first captain. Sandy Herd and, later, James Braid made many changes to the original design.

The short par 4 1st hole, just 297 yards, may lead you to assume Littlestone easier than it is. Such an idea will soon be dispelled by the 2nd, quite a long par 4 where your second shot is played blind over a hill. On the next, a hole of similar length, you have to carry a bunker from the tee, with a testing shot to the green, set up in the sandhills. The 8th takes you to the far end of the course and is a very likeable hole. You drive over a dune and the second shot is to a particularly well-bunkered green. Bunkers and dunes sometimes have to be carried at the next few holes. Then you come to Littlestone's very fine finish.

At the 14th, a good 183-yard hole, be sure to be well up with your tee shot for the green gathers the ball. The 15th is not a long par 4 but is one of the few doglegs, and again you must go for the heart of the two-tier green. The 16th is Littlestone's finest hole and a very long 4 at 468 yards. The second shot is to an elevated green on the horizon, with a water tower beyond.

The 17th tee may give you sight of France before you tackle this very fine par 3 of about 180 yards to a green set on a ridge. It's one of the best short holes in the south of England.

The last hole is a flat one of 488 yards but plays a good deal longer into the prevailing south-west wind. In still air there's a chance of getting home in two but the green is elevated and well bunkered, so both your shots must be very good ones.

£ *£25, £18 per round*

M *membership of a golf club and a handicap certificate*

✗ *snacks daily, lunch daily except Tuesday*

🎾 *tennis*

🚗 *from Ashford take the A2070 to New Romney, Littlestone and follow club signs. From Hastings or Folkestone take the A259 for New Romney*

OLD THORNS

Longmoor Road, Liphook, Hampshire GU30 7PE
☎ *Liphook (0428) 724555*

Although having opened as recently as 1982, this is a course which was part of my life for a good few years. It started off as a partnership enterprise with the Alliss/Thomas Golf Construction Ltd, Patrick Dawson and Ken Wood, of electrical equipment fame, and, incidentally, it was one of the reasons for my move down from Moor Allerton in Yorkshire to this very pleasant corner on the Hampshire and Surrey borders.

I might then be thought to be a bit biased in its favour! However, many people find that the greens are particularly good, though not as lightning fast as they used to be.

The first thing you'll probably notice on driving up to this country club is that the centrepiece of the original Old Thorns farmhouse is very

228

attractive indeed. Inside, there is relaxed elegance, not austerity. Decor, furnishings and even the locker rooms are all a visiting golfer could wish for.

A few years ago, the whole project was sold to Japanese investors – one of the first to take this path – and its name was briefly changed to London Kosaido on account of this.

The course itself runs through a landscape that is typical of this part of England – birch and pine trees, heather, brooks and ditches with good use made of lakes in David Thomas's design on several of the holes. The 3rd is challenging and interesting, a long par 4 with an all-or-nothing second shot which has to carry a deep ravine in front of the well-bunkered green. The 8th is also testing, with a narrow driving area, out of bounds all along the left and water both on the right and then biting into the front of the green. A lake again comes into play on the 10th, a fairly long par 3 over water up to about 30 yards of the green. Take enough club here. The round ends with another very good hole, an exception to the fact that many 18ths are just a way of getting players back to the clubhouse, which in this case is just behind the green.

The course has already been used for several pro-ams and for a Women's Professional Golf Association event.

💷 *£27, £18 per round*	🏠 *32 twin-bedded suites*
Ⓜ *none*	🚗 *on the A3 from London in Liphook turn right at the first small roundabout along the B2131 (Longmoor Road). After about 1½ miles turn left for the clubhouse*
✗ *snacks and dinner daily*	
🏊 *swimming pool*	

OSBORNE

Club House, Osborne, East Cowes, Isle of Wight
☎ *Isle of Wight (0983) 295421*

Osborne is a charming nine-hole course running through the grounds of what used to be Queen Victoria's favourite home (perhaps because it was designed by Prince Albert), and features a wealth of trees and fine shrubs.

The course opened in the 1890s with just three holes and a pavilion which overlooked the Solent. It became a golf club proper in 1903, with use reserved for officers from Osborne House and local gentry. The membership base was broadened after the Second World War.

While playing here you can expect to have views over Osborne Bay, of the Solent and of Osborne House.

Constructed in a fairly tight area, there are few holes when out of bounds are not a threat, sometimes close at hand on either side. This helps to make the short 3rd more difficult, where the green is also well ringed with bunkers and has a severe slope. The 7th tee is elevated and you must keep straight to avoid an out-of-bounds fir plantation right and deep woods left, with a water hazard also in the driving area.

The 8th features an unusual hazard. Directly in front of the tee there's a circular stone pit, known as 'the elephant bath'. If you top your shot into it, it costs you two penalty strokes.

In its way, Osborne is as attractive as Leeds Castle, near Maidstone.

£ £14

M a current club handicap

✗ lunches daily

🚗 make for Osborne House in East Cowes and take the main entrance, bearing right past the house itself for the golf course

PRINCE'S, SANDWICH

Sandwich Bay, Kent CT13 9QB
☎ Sandwich (0304) 612000

As the years go by all too quickly, my memories of tournament victories grow dim. Two of them, however, are still bright – my first, which was in the DAKS at Little Ashton more than thirty years ago, and my last. This came at Prince's in my last full tournament season, 1969. The event was the Piccadilly Medal in a form of matchplay. It was head to head all the way but each round was settled by having the best strokeplay card, instead of by winning and losing of holes. I was particularly pleased to knock out Tony Jacklin, fresh from his triumph in the Open Championship at Royal Lytham and St Annes, in the semi-final, and went on to beat George Will in the final on the 37th hole.

I was very pleased to return to open their new clubhouse nearly sixteen years later, on 14 July 1985 to be exact. It is part of a development which has made Prince's a centre for golf holidays, package deals, conferences and overseas visitors. There are three loops of nine holes, the Dunes, the Himalayas and the Shore, with the clubhouse at the centre of it all, making it an ideal place to visit.

Yet this is by no means a new course. It was first opened for play in the summer of 1907, the third of a formidable trio, with Royal St George's and Royal Cinque Ports, playing over much the same kind of linksland. Prince's, however, was to suffer in the two World Wars. In the first it was used as a training ground and the buildings were taken over by the military. Little serious damage was done, however, and golf soon resumed. But in 1939-45 the links became a battle training area, complete with minefields and tank traps. Afterwards, there was a strong possibility that it might become a Royal Marines rifle range. But happily work began in 1949 to reconstruct the course and the clubhouse, which had been used for house-to-house fighting.

The aim, as at Augusta, Georgia, was to produce a course that, as the architect Sir Guy Campbell wrote, 'would enable players of all calibres to sample and enjoy *comparatively*, their attempts at solving the same problems. They would play the championship course arranged in accordance with their respective capabilities.'

With the changes that have happened over the years, the result is probably the most likely course in England to be added to the Open Championship rota. Although so near to Royal St George's, it is much flatter, with fewer uneven stances for shots from the fairway.

At Prince's, many of the fairways run between sand dunes so there are no 'old-fashioned' carries except, occasionally, over cross bunkers. A far more common hazard, however, are the dyke and smaller ditches which come into play on half-a-dozen or more of the holes. Consult your yardage charts!

Good iron play, as at so many links courses, is vital at Prince's. Nearly half the twenty-seven holes are raised, either tucked up on a plateau or only a little above the surrounding terrain. An iron shot which is not quite good enough will dribble away off the putting surfaces.

The difficulties of the shots to the greens allowed the architect to use greenside bunkering fairly sparingly so that fourteen of the holes have none. Visitors whose bunker play is poor may well rejoice but will find themselves severely tested on the short pitch and chip shot by the difficulties of the subtle upslopes to the raised greens. The tee shots, however, are seldom daunting. Fairways are wide and start more or less from the tees.

There isn't a bad hole on the course, and there are some outstandingly good ones. The 1st on the Dunes, for instance, usually played into the wind, often needs a couple of woods to get up in regulation, and sometimes there's still something left to be done. The 2nd on the Himalayas is another excellent par 4. At 415 yards it's of no great length but fairway bunkers at driving range to the left and right mean you must get a straight one away. The hole then doglegs left more or less at right angles. For the right-handed player, fade is very helpful for the second shot which must hold against a right to left slope with a fall-away on the right of the green.

The 6th on the Himalayas is a true par 5 of little less than 600 yards. The drive is between bunkers left and rough and bushes on the other flank; your second shot needs to avoid bunkers on the left. The green itself is bunkered to left and right. As the hole plays into the prevailing wind, you will often need more than a short pitch for your third shot.

The 7th is perhaps the best of the par 3s. Depending on the wind, you'll need anything between a 6-iron and a fairway wood to cover the 195 yards. The raised tee is hard by the beach and the green both small and difficult to hold. If you miss, a 4 is the best result you can reasonably hope for.

At the 4th on the Shore, a par 4 of 413 yards, you must get your tee shot well away otherwise your second shot will be menaced by a cross bunker in front of the green. Into a stiff prevailing wind, this is probably the most difficult hole to par of the twenty-seven.

As you play, you may well marvel at the recovery from all that mortar practice in the Second World War, which Lord Brabazon of Tara described as 'like throwing darts at a Rembrandt'. In the same war, a man who had grown up at Prince's, Battle of Britain pilot Laddie Lucas, used his local knowledge to land his stricken Spitfire on one of the fairways.

£ *£25, £30 at weekends*

M *a handicap certificate*

✗ *light snacks, lunch and dinner are available every day and practice facilities are good*

🚗 *make for Sandwich Station and turn into St George's Road, close by a level crossing. Follow signs to the course*

ROYAL ASHDOWN FOREST 🏌

Forest Row, Sussex RH18 5LR
☎ *Forest Row (0342 82) 2018*

Ashdown Forest is one of those few courses that prove that golf can be quite testing enough without any bunkers. There's not one on either the main or the New course.

When Ashdown Forest was first laid out in the late 1880s, they were not considered a compulsory feature of golf. If sand was not freely available on site, the architect did without them. Instead he tried to make maximum use of the shape of the ground and what natural hazards there might happen to be in the way of streams, ditches, trees, perhaps a quarry, and heather.

Heather is the main hazard, but, as Bernard Darwin wrote in 1910, 'Nature had been kind in supplying a variety of pits and streams to carry and so we certainly do not notice any lack of trouble or incident.' He also praised the course for having 'not a single hideous rampart' in sight.

The 11th is a good example of the terrain. The tee shot to this long par 3 has a backcloth of Sussex countryside beyond. First we must carry heather and bracken; the ground is then well folded short of the green and falls away both left and beyond. At 249 yards, there's no need of a bunker.

Earlier the short 6th, famous as 'The Island Hole', has a stream as the hazard. It's only 126 yards and the green is large but water protects the front, half way round the right, and all of the left. The next, a not overlong par 4, asks you to carry a formidable amount of heather and fierce rough with your drive, and to find a narrow green.

Some of the relief at Ashdown Forest is provided by the fact that there are several shortish par 4s, but you can hardly have one much longer than 472 yards, the 17th. This used to be a par 5, slightly downhill, that invited you to go for the green with your second, if you dared the trouble on either side, but it was shortened by some 40 yards and is today a much more severe hole to play to par.

That left three par 5s, the 12th being the best. It's long, at 558 yards, with carries over heather for both your drive and second shot.

This is a most unusual and excellent course with a long and interesting history. One particular feature of this is that Jack Rowe served as professional for 55 years from 1892. He was succeeded in 1947 by Hector Padgham, brother of Alf Padgham, the Open Champion of 1936, who learned his golf here. At last account, Hector was still there, although he has now retired: two professionals in almost 100 years.

€ £27.50

M a letter of introduction or county card

✗ snacks and lunch daily, limited catering on Mondays

✉ advisable to phone in advance

🚗 on the A22 south of East Grinstead turn left onto the B2110 then turn right into Chapel Lane after about ½ mile

ROYAL CINQUE PORTS

Golf Road, Deal, Kent CT14 6RF
☎ Deal (0304) 374007

Deal is an Open Championship course which, for one reason or another, like Prestwick, is almost certainly off the rota for ever. The first championship was held in 1909 and the second in 1920. It was scheduled for Deal on three further occasions, 1915 during the First World War, 1938, when high tides damaged the course, and 1949, when again the salt seas burned the greens and fairways. In both these cases the championship moved down the road to Sandwich.

Deal, however, is still a championship course for amateurs. The Amateur Championship was here in 1982 and the English Open Amateur Strokeplay in 1984. It's a severe test. It was said in 1903 that 'this course is the second most difficult in the kingdom' while Henry Cotton declared in 1938: 'It is possible at nearly every hole to place a ball bang in the middle of the fairway and then find yourself in such an awkward position that a successful second shot can scarcely be played. What is more galling than that?'

This is hardly high praise, so let's hope Henry meant that there was an ideal line for every drive and that this was not necessarily down the middle.

As Cotton's remarks imply, though the course looks flat enough, many of the fairway lies are up, down or sideways and there are many dunes both large and small. In fact, there is one continuous dune all the way from the 1st tee to the end of the course. Play is even more affected by the wind than is normal on links. In the prevailing south-westerlies you just have to make a reasonable score over the first eleven holes. The return to the clubhouse, difficult at the best of times, will be apt to mean a salvo of 5s, even for players of championship quality.

The 1st gives you a quiet enough start, a par 4 of not much more than 300 yards, though there is a ditch in front of the green which shouldn't really trouble you. The 2nd is a little longer, where the drive must be held along a ridge, with the second shot played to a green protected and half-hidden by another. The 3rd is a long 4 but the fairway is broad. The blind green is in a hollow, helpful to a second shot that seems to be not quite getting there. At about the 300 yard mark, the ridge set with two large bunkers may be a problem if you've got a poor tee shot away.

The 6th takes you down to the sea. It's a short par 4, less than 300 yards, but you'll have to avoid some stern rough to the right and bunkers. If all goes well, you should be left with a very short pitch to the plateau green which is hard by the shingle beach. Annoying to take 5, even 6, here with the far longer second nine to come.

The 10th is a splendid par 4. It's by no means a monster in length, around 360 yards, but the approach into the green is narrow with a hollow left and inviting bunker right. It doglegs left and is easier played from a tee shot right of centre.

At the 12th, you turn for home and into the prevailing wind. This and the next will prove long enough par 4s for most of us. The 14th, about 200 yards, is by far the stiffest of the par 3s. A redoubtable Irish member was once grabbed by a photographer and asked to knock an iron towards the distant green. Obligingly he did so and holed out, thought to be the first hole in one ever photographed.

And so to Deal's famous finish, which many people have thought the most difficult in championship golf. The 15th demands that you avoid two large fairway bunkers on the right; if you've driven well, your second shot will still be blind and has to carry a moderate sandhill. It's as well to be fairly bold on hard ground for if you pitch short and catch the downslope, your ball will probably scuttle through the green.

The 16th is a great hole, easily the longest par 4 on the course, at over 450 yards. Cross bunkers shouldn't catch your tee shot unless it's a poor one or played into a rather stiff wind. It was designed as a par 5, with a second shot intended to come to rest in a valley with bunkers before the green, perched quite high on a plateau, which demanded a neat pitch. But the thrill is to hit a good drive and see your second soar towards the flag on that distant plateau – and little chance of that with even a stiff breeze in your face.

The 17th is nearly a hundred yards shorter but the fairway is full of ups and downs and the green is a very small target amongst more tumbling ground. The last, just a touch under 400 yards, is mostly a matter of the second shot. If you can manage it, a low runner will probably serve you best, one that skips up the slope to the green. Pitch into that slope and you'll almost certainly come back down again, while a carrying shot is very likely to go through.

£ £35

M a letter of introduction or a handicap certificate

✗ snacks. Lunch and dinner by reservation

🚗 off A258 just north of Deal along the seafront

ROYAL ST GEORGE'S

Sandwich, Kent CT13 9PB
☎ *Sandwich (0304) 617308*

This course is now very much in favour again for the Open Championship, but once it seemed the greatest days were gone for ever.

The championship was first played here in 1894, the first time the event came outside Scotland, and it returned in 1899. It was then a regular venue until 1949 when the great days departed as access to the course was poor for large crowds. However, it continued to be used for great amateur and some of the professional events which attract smaller crowds than the Open Championship. It was here, for instance, in 1959, that Jack Nicklaus won his first event in England, the St George's Challenge Cup, and here too that he was knocked out in the quarter final of the Amateur Championship, his only entry in the event.

When the championship at last returned in 1981, many people were nervous about how it would work out but the R and A's superb organization foresaw all the possible problems from catering, minor injuries and toilets on course to traffic flow in getting there. It worked so well that it came back in 1985 when Sandy Lyle recorded the first British victory since Tony Jacklin's in 1969.

The origins of the course are lost in time, but it does seem that a certain Laidlaw Purves ascended the tower of a Norman church in Sandwich once and liked what he saw. He formed the Sandwich Golfing Association and may also have laid out the course, perhaps with the assistance of the first professional, Ramsay Hunter, in 1887. The course has remained substantially the same ever since, except that Frank Pennink made a few changes some fifteen years ago with a view to making it more suitable as a championship venue.

Royal St George's has been called 'the St Andrews of the south' and is a sterner test than the old lady of Fife, mainly because there are no holes

235

as 'easy' as a few of the short par 4s at St Andrews.

You start with a drive to quite a wide fairway, but it's a long par 4 and unreachable in anything of a wind. The first par 3 comes at the 3rd and it's difficult and long, with a slope up to the green with bunkers left and a bank on the right. It'll be a wooden club for most players. The 4th is a frightener. There are huge bunkers which may be in your driving distance along the right and another left at the angle of the dogleg. If you get on in two, it's very easy to three-putt if you land in the dip and hollow at the front of the green.

The 5th is no easier and can be unplayable if your drive is 20 yards off the fairway. It's followed, from the medal tees, by a huge par 4 of 475 yards at the 7th, with bunkers at the right to catch your drive and others to catch a second that's not quite getting up. Undoubtedly, it should be easier for a championship field when it's a par 5 of just under 530 yards.

Over the next three holes you can at least hope to improve the look of your score card. Each is a par 4 of reasonable length, but then comes a monster par 3 of much the same length as the 3rd. Both are too long because you immediately need a driver if there's a wind in your face. The 12th is a medium-length par 4 with a drive to a ridged fairway with bunkers, followed by several more scattered in the approaches to the green. The 13th may well be the most difficult hole on the course. There's a blind drive, but just aim for the middle of the old Prince's clubhouse and you won't go far wrong. There are plenty of bunkers near the green, which has two ridges. The 14th, 'Suez Canal', is a famous hole but a little dull for all that. It ruined Gene Sarazen's chances in 1928 when he topped a couple of wooden club shots. You drive over sandhills and need to be far enough, if the wind's against you, so as to be in no danger of finding the Canal, over 300 yards from the tee, with your second shot. Many people have actually driven into it, but only with a following wind. In 1985 it ruined the hopes of several championship contenders, but Lyle's birdie in the last round set him up for victory.

Unless there's a following wind, the 15th is one of the most difficult holes in golf. There's a long carry to the fairway, which is of generous width. The second shot, to a small humpy green, has to carry deep cross bunkers only just short of it. You may well not be sorry to finish just short and hope to pitch and single putt.

The 16th is the best of the short holes, not too long at 165 yards, but with eight bunkers either to the side or in front. It was here that Tony Jacklin achieved the first hole-in-one on TV in the 1967 Dunlop Masters. The green itself is big but with slopes and hollows.

After a little flat golf, the 17th is right back amongst the humps and bumps and, though well over 400 yards, doesn't seem to play its full length. The plateau green, eaten into by bunkers, has a back which can throw your ball on to the green again.

The last is a hole fit to decide a championship, and has done so many times. Par 4s were very rare in the 1983 PGA Championship, which Seve Ballesteros won, having missed the green in his first three rounds but making no mistake in his last. Ken Brown showed how the hole should be played with a drive up to the left followed by a low chasing long iron to hold against the slope of the green. It gave him a birdie putt to tie the Spaniard, but he narrowly missed.

Even more than on most links courses, you must expect not to get too many flat lies in the fairways – perhaps none at all. As José Maria Canizares said during that PGA: 'Is too blahdy difficult for me.' Seve was also said to dislike it at one time, perhaps a result of two high scores and a missed cut in one of his first appearances in Britain.

The clubhouse, converted from a Kentish farmhouse, has great charm and a wealth of old leather sofas and books.

£ *£45, £30 per round*

M *a letter of introduction and a handicap certificate no higher than 18*

L *ladies may only play with a member and with handicap limit of no more than 15*

✗ *lunch daily except Tuesday, when snacks are available*

🚗 *at Sandwich follow signs for Sandwich Bay for 1 mile and turn left at the district sign for Worth*

SEAFORD

East Blatchington, Seaford, East Sussex BN25 2JD
☎ *Seaford (0323) 892442*

Designed by the five times Open Champion J.H. Taylor, Seaford is one of the most delightful downland courses, with views of both sea and downs from all parts of the course.

Founded in 1887, it is one of the oldest clubs south of London. The golf used to be on Seaford Head but the move to the present territory came in 1907.

After J.H. Taylor's early work, J.S.F. Morrison, who used to be Henry Longhurst's partner in the Halford-Hewitt Trophy, a public schools foursomes event played annually at Deal, made some alterations, and it's now a formidable 6,600 yards or so from the back tees.

There are many holes of character. On the 6th there's a deep pit just beyond tee shot range but very much in play for the second shot on this par 4 of over 430 yards. The 7th, a par 3 of about 160 yards, is defended by a pit short of the green with bunkers to the right, and the 8th is a good long par 4, doglegging to the left. The 11th, a good two-shot hole, runs along Cradle Valley, and there's another two-shot hole at the 17th where you aim your tee shot at an old Sussex barn. At the last, another good par 4, you drive across the valley.

£ *£20*

M *a club handicap*

🎱 snooker	🚗 in Seaford, turn inland at the war memorial and keep going for about 1 1/4 miles until you can go no further. You'll then be at the clubhouse
✗ snacks, lunch and dinner daily	
🏠 a dormy house with six single and six double rooms	

STONEHAM

Bassett, Southampton, Hampshire SO2 3NE
☎ *Southampton (0703) 768151*

Stoneham is one of many courses originally laid out by Willie Park, in 1906, in what was once a deer park. The sandy and peat subsoil mean that the course is quick-drying. One of the main attractions is that belts of trees and gorse between the fairways make each game feel separate and well away from the rest of the world. Although it's only some 3 miles from the centre of Southampton, there's scarcely a house to be seen.

Although by no means long, 6,300 yards, Stoneham has been used for many professional tournaments, including the first Dunlop Masters, held in 1946 and won by Bobby Locke and Jimmy Adams (no play-off in those days).

It's a course with great variety. Take the lengths of the holes, for example. You have a couple of very short par 4s but one very long one; a very short par 3 and an equally long one. There are a generous number of par 5s, none of which is very long.

At the 1st, you drive across a diagonal valley to a broad fairway and may get off to a good start by reaching the green in two.

The 2nd will then ask you to play a good long iron. It's some 190 yards with out of bounds on the right and trees close up all the way along the left.

The 4th can be very difficult. It's some 460 yards and rated stroke index 1. If you get a long one away from the tee, you should get the benefit of a downslope and then play across a stream in the valley bottom – but may find you need to play short of it.

Cross bunkers twice come into play at the 6th, a par 5. Those in the driving area are supported by a tree on the left, which blocks the line to the green from this side. Having cleared the second cross bunkers, you'll probably finish in the bottom of the valley, which makes reaching the green in two difficult even for long hitters.

The 8th is the best of the short holes. It's not particularly difficult but it looks right, with the tee shot of 160 yards or so having to carry over a valley, stream and cross bunkers. The 11th is a very fine hole indeed.

There are cross bunkers about 150 yards from the tee followed by another on the right about 30 yards further on. For your second shot, you carry over a grass gully and over a heather-faced slope to a plateau green with bunkers on either flank.

The 15th is rather an oddity. At 255 yards it's almost a par 3 and the sort of hole that it's irritating not to birdie. The drive is blind and needs to be on the right line to ease your little pitch to the green. Those trying to drive the green will be bunkered as often as not.

The 15th gives you a downhill drive, always exhilarating, but try to keep it right at it's easier to find the green from this line. The finish at Stoneham begins with a short par 3 of 120 yards to an island green, then a right-hand dogleg at the 17th. For the 18th there is a fair carry from the tee over a rough valley and a gully all along the right by the approach to the green which catches more shots that perhaps it should. The green itself is tightly bunkered so it's a real achievement to get home in two.

£ £24

M a handicap certificate

X snacks daily to 6pm, lunch and dinner daily except Sunday

🚗 on the A27 on the left about ½ mile from Chilworth roundabout

WALES

MAP 5

KEY TO SYMBOLS

PARKLAND	☎ TELEPHONE	✕ CATERING PROVIDED
LINKS	✉ NEED TO BOOK IN ADVANCE	⌂ ACCOMMODATION PROVIDED
MOORLAND	£ APPROXIMATE COURSE FEE	Ⓛ RESTRICTIONS ON LADIES AND/OR YOUTHS
HEATHLAND	M MEMBERSHIP REQUIREMENTS FOR VISITORS	OTHER SPORTING FACILITIES
DOWNLAND		
UPLAND		🚗 DIRECTIONS

ASHBURNHAM

Cliffe Terrace, Burry Port, Dyfed SA16 0HN
☎ *Burry Port (05546) 2466*

Ashburnham was founded in 1894. A few years later Harry Vardon said of it: 'This is the course I like best in Wales. It is one of those excellent links which require very little attention.' How revealing a remark this is! Here was the greatest player of his day saying how important low maintenance was to a club's well-being. No wonder golf was so cheap all those years ago.

The course was first laid out as nine holes over 2,809 yards. The performance of the guttie is well illustrated by the fact that par (they'd have called it 'bogey') was 45. One of the holes of 188 yards was rated as a 4, while 243 merited a 5 and there were bogey 6s for two holes measured at 445 and 491 yards.

I played my last PGA Championship as a tournament regular at Ashburnham in 1969, and the club also hosted that event in 1959 – really hosted it, for this was the last occasion a club had to put up all the prize money. It cost them £2,000. Although the course was a good deal shorter in those days at 6,500 yards, against 7,016 from the tournament tees today, only five players in the field managed to break 70. The late Dai Rees was one of them, and his 70 and 69 on the last day saw him home by six strokes for his first win in Wales.

Ashburnham is a true links course, and overlooks Carmarthen Bay and the north Gower coast. The rough on many holes consists of bramble as difficult – even suicidal – a stuff to play out of as I know. Some holes are tree-lined on one side.

You begin with quite a long par 3, one of the most difficult starts in golf, and you'll probably have a wind blowing you towards the out of bounds on the right. You are then plunged into a long par 4 (a regular feature here), again with an out of bounds. To start with two pars is very difficult. A much shorter 4 follows and then one of the most difficult holes, a 400-yarder doglegging to the left. The 5th is the shortest of the four par 5s and perhaps your best chance of getting home in two.

The 6th is the best of the four par 3s. The green is elevated with a bunker left and a steep drop to the right. Only a very truly struck long iron will do the job for you. With the 10th you turn for home and, with the out-and-back Ashburnham pattern, the prevailing westerly should be with you for the longer homeward march.

You begin with a very long par 5 of almost 560 yards and the 400-yard par 4 11th, where the prevailing wind makes for a difficult tee shot. The 15th is another very long par 5, again almost 560 yards. It doglegs right, with the blind second shot having to clear a high ridge. Either second or third shot has to find a gap to the green between high banks. The 15th may just be the most difficult hole at Ashburnham. Drive short of an embankment and you'll probably then need at least a long iron to the

241

green, set in an old quarry where there's trouble left, right and through.

The last hole ruins many cards, although it's only a medium-length par 4. The green is set high up on a ridge. Miss and a 5 becomes just about certain – or worse, which will take away some of the enjoyment of the glorious view of the estuary spread out below you.

£ £15-20, £20-25 at weekends	🚗 5 miles west of Llanelli. Take the A484 towards Carmarthen and turn left at Chivers Corner Filling Station
M a letter of introduction	
✕ snacks daily, lunch and dinner daily except Monday	

CLYNE

118 Owls Lodge Lane, The Mayals, Blackpill, Swansea, West Glamorgan SA3 5DR
☎ Swansea (0792) 401989

If my father had not been a travelling man, I might well have been brought up here. Having moved from Yorkshire, he began his professional career at Royal Porthcawl as an assistant and then became Clyne's first professional in 1920. The course was officially opened in 1921 with the Mayor of Swansea invited to perform the inauguration ceremonies. Alas, his worship missed the ball at his first attempt to drive in and my father had to give him a quick word or two of advice on his golf swing.

At that time, Clyne was a place of very narrow fairways, often lined by thick gorse bushes. One of the members is said to have become so irate at the number of balls he was losing that he decided to take appropriate action. It was simple enough. When he got into it, he 'punished' the offending bush by setting fire to it, thus relieving his feelings and improving his prospects on the next visit. Sometimes, there'd be several fires going to mark his day's journey.

Clyne begins with a couple of short par 4s and then a par 5 where you may be able to get home in two if you can carry the bunkers at the angle of the dogleg. There's a similar choice at the 5th, a short dogleg par 4. Here you can cut the corner off, which involves a carry of more than 180 yards over an out-of-bounds hedge. Playing more safely left gives you a much longer second shot and the chance of being bunkered.

Two difficult par 4s follow, both more than 400 yards. The 6th needs a fair carry over a sea of gorse and fern, while the 7th is a little uphill all the way, to a small green with a narrow entry. The 8th and 12th are good par 3s. The first needs a long iron at least to a large green, with several bunkers almost certain to trap a shot pitching short. At the 12th the ground falls away around most of the green and there's an open ditch right. The 13th is a well-designed short par 4. Once again, you're asked for a reasonable carry from the tee and there's a gully in front of the green.

At the 16th, where there are fine sweeping views of Swansea Bay and Mumbles Head, the main difficulty will be sheer length, some 460 yards. This is followed by the last short hole and perhaps the best, made by a ravine on the left and ground falling away on the other side.

Back we go to the clubhouse, with a tee shot that needs to be placed left, to cope with ground sloping right, a common feature of tee shots here.

£ *£15, £20 at weekends*

M *membership of a golf club*

✕ *snacks, lunch and dinner daily except Monday*

🎱 *snooker*

🚗 *from Swansea make for Mumbles and turn right up Mayals Road after 3 miles*

GLAMORGANSHIRE, THE

Lavernock Road, Penarth, South Glamorgan CF6 2UP
☎ *Penarth (0222) 701185*

Only about 5 miles from the centre of Cardiff, the higher ground on this course commands splendid views over the Bristol Channel to Weston-super-Mare and the hills of Somerset.

Founded in 1890, the Glamorganshire was one of the first clubs in Wales and hosted the Welsh Amateur Championship as far back as 1897. Several members have indeed been champions, H.R. Howell one of the finest amateurs Wales has produced, on eight occasions. For a bet, in 1926, playing just with a marker and timekeeper he went round the Glamorganshire in 63 from the medal tees. Howell took 68 minutes, perhaps the best combination of low scoring and high speed ever achieved on a golf course.

If you visit, you'll not be expected to set such a cracking pace but be forewarned: the score card does declare: 'SLOW PLAY IS DEPLORED'! So if your best pace for a friendly fourball is five hours you could be gently admonished.

Doglegs are very much a feature of this course, appearing in about a dozen holes. This is partly because the Glamorganshire is laid out around the undulating plateau of Downs Hill. Most of the holes are either on flat ground or land falling away from the hill.

You start off with quite a demanding par 4 of 400 yards. You'll do well to get home in two if you haven't played a few 'looseners' first. Then comes a very short par 3, say a wedge to a shelf green that's tightly bunkered. Next are a couple of par 5s which dogleg around the wood in reverse directions. The 4th is a particularly good 5 with a drive downhill. Keep fairly well right to give yourself much chance of being on the small green in two. It's guarded by a bunker left and a tree right.

The 5th is a very sharp dogleg indeed, played downhill from a high tee and then left around a clump of trees. It is only a little over 300 yards, so you should try to make sure at least of a par before facing the 6th, stroke index 1. Drive right to ease your long second shot to the green. The first nine ends with a third par 5, trees right and a bunker left threatening the second shot. That problem safely negotiated, you are left with quite a tricky little pitch to a green set into a slope.

The 11th is the last of the four par 5s and it's another good one, shortly followed by an excellent par 3 of some 160 yards. Here you have to play an iron shot from a high tee down on to a long narrow green, well protected by bunkers with an out of bounds uncomfortably close on the right. After a very short par 4, just a yard or so away from being a 3, comes the long slog of the 15th, uphill to a two-tiered green and difficult to reach in two. The round ends with a stiff par 3, either a long iron or a wood, with out of bounds threatening and maybe too many interested observers for your taste.

£ £20

M a club handicap certificate

✗ snacks, lunch and dinner daily

🔄 squash and snooker

Ⓛ one of the bars is open only to men

🚗 on west edge of Penarth on the right of the A4055 for Barry

---

MONMOUTHSHIRE, THE 🌳

Llanfoist, Abergavenny, Gwent NP7 9HE
☎ Abergavenny (0873) 3171

'All things bright and beautiful' is a hymn we all grew up with. It is thought that the poet C.E. Alexander based his feelings on the view from the site of the present 1st tee. Yes, I know, he makes no mention of golfers. They came later but the mountain he refers to is The Blorenge and the river is the Usk, which runs alongside the 5th and 6th fairways.

The poet wasn't exaggerating. This is one of those places, never mind how you're playing on the day, where it is very pleasant to be.

There are six par 3s, four of them on the second nine, and four 5s, three of which are in a row, from the 6th to the 8th.

The lst offers a very long hitter the chance to drive the green across the left-hand dogleg, but for the first shot of the day most people are more concerned with avoiding the brook, which can catch a wayward shot to either side.

The 4th is one of the more difficult holes. You will certainly not wish to be over the steep escarpment that runs down to the river on the right, while keeping well left involves a fair length of carry over rough which then rewards you with a fairly open shot to the green.

At the 6th the River Usk comes fully into play. You have to carry it, but a drive left will almost always find the river, while one too far in the other direction is likely to be in rough. The river bed is regarded as out of bounds but the foreshore is playable. If your shot to the green is of any real length, beware the dip in front, while too firm a shot may run away into the Usk.

The 16th is always a testing hole, a par 3 of 234 from the medal tee. You play from a high tee over a valley, carrying the left edge of a dewpond while bunkers guard the right-hand side.

£16, £22 at weekends

a handicap certificate

snacks daily, lunch and dinner daily except Tuesday

from a London direction along the M4, leave at Junction 26 for Abergavenny. From the Midlands along M5 and M50 leave for Ross-on-Wye and follow the A40 to Abergavenny. From there, take the Llanfoist road for 2 miles and turn into Gypsy Lane

PYLE AND KENFIG

Waun-Y-Mer, Kenfig, Mid-Glamorgan CF33 4PU
Porthcawl (065671) 3093

This is a relatively little-known course, perhaps overshadowed by Royal Porthcawl, fairly near by. However, it's of very high standard and I'm sure its fame will increase with the years, perhaps assisted by the deeds of its star player. This is Patricia Johnson, who has won many major events since 1983, and has been an international since 1984. She was leading European money winner in 1990.

The course has been used for Martini and Coral pre-qualifying and was chosen by the R and A for the British Boys' Plate in 1984.

The course is a mixture of both links and downland, with large sand dunes being a great feature of the second nine. The most attractive holes are the 11th to the 14th. Each wanders through the dunes and is played against the prevailing wind. There are some blind shots which, depending on your personal taste, can add to the fun.

Pyle and Kenfig plays at more than 6,600 yards from the medal tees to a standard scratch of 73. No one has made a nonsense of it, with the professional record being 70 and the amateur also 70.

£ *£20*

M *proof of membership of a golf club and a handicap certificate*

✕ *snacks daily, lunch and dinner daily except Monday*

🚗 *leave the M4 at Porthcawl signs and take the first right after the Esso garage*

ROLLS OF MONMOUTH, THE 🌲

The Hendre, Monmouth, Gwent NP5 4HG
☎ *Monmouth (0600) 5353*

This is the most recent course in the book, opened as lately as 1982, when Greg Norman was attached briefly as touring professional. If its name suggests a well-known make of motor car, there's good reason. The course is laid out on a country estate that has belonged to the Rolls family since the mid-eighteenth century. The present clubhouse has been converted from garages once used as workshops by Charles Stewart Rolls, the founder, with Sir Henry Royce, of the company.

As you'd expect, the course has a parkland lay-out, with plenty of undulation in the ground. Besides the trees you'd expect to find, there are also fine examples of sweet gum, swamp cypress and Corsican pine. There is an arboretum well worth visiting.

The course is laid out in two loops of nine holes, with alternative possible starting points at the 3rd and 5th, which might well prove useful if your visit happens to clash with a society day. Good use has been made of water hazards, which can come into play at about half the holes. There is plenty of space, so there is almost always a feeling of separateness as you play each of the holes. You will have the tree-lined borders of the course around you throughout your round, the pink stone mansion frequently in view, and the Sugarloaf and Skirrid Fawr peaks as backdrops.

You start off with a fairly stiff par 4, and soon find yourself back at the clubhouse, at the 4th green. The 5th tee, finely situated on the mansion's South Lawn, is the start of a good par 5, reachable in two for many from the forward tee. However, the fairway falls away left and large trees are also a hazard to the right, and to get up in two you have to clear a deep swale about 50 yards short of the green.

At the 6th water comes into play for the first time. Depending on which tee you are playing from, there is either a stream or the edge of a lake to be carried, followed by a long second shot. The second par 5 follows, a stern test for those hoping to get on in two because of a stream which crosses the fairway some 50 yards or so short of the green. The lake can also be in play for a shot well left.

At the 9th, a shortish par 4, the stream comes into play for a half-hit shot or one wildly left or right. The approach to the green is narrow.

The second lake comes into play at the 13th, a medium-length par 3, where anything that wanders right is likely to catch a finger that leaks across, short and right of the green. The 15th is the toughest par 4 on the course, and a good driving test. You need to be reasonably long and placement at the dogleg is vital. If you aim too far right, in fear of the out of bounds to the left, your second shot will be almost impossibly long. The green itself is well bunkered and situated in a crook of the old drive, nestling under a lime tree.

The finish is a grandstand one, a par 3 over water and a fitting way to settle a close-fought match. Even from the forward tee, you will need at least your longest iron to cross over the stream and lake.

£ £20 or £24	**M** none	**🚗** take the B4233 Abergavenny road from Monmouth for 3½ miles until the signpost for the club
✖ snacks, lunch and dinner daily		

ROYAL PORTHCAWL ⊸✠

Porthcawl, Mid-Glamorgan CF36 34W
☎ *Porthcawl (0656) 712251*

This club has connections with the Alliss family dating back 65 years and more. My father, a very good cricketer as well as golfer, had been offered a trial by Yorkshire but a letter offering him an appointment as assistant here came first so off he went, shortly after the end of the First World War. It was his first job in golf.

The opening holes will always linger in anyone's memory, tight along the sea shore. On the 1st, in fact, 326 yards, a straight line between tee and green would take you over the beach. Here you'll probably be playing in a left-to-right wind, and if you manage to find the green with your second, three putts can be difficult to avoid, because of the slopes and undulations. The 2nd, however, is a far more difficult hole. There's a good carry from the tee with a cross bunker very much in play, and the second shot is slightly uphill to a green in a hollow, just over the crest of the rise. Go left, and you're on the beach. At the 3rd, a similar length hole of 377 yards, again there's a cross bunker to clear with your drive, and the second shot must clear a little valley to a plateau green with, once again, the beach in wait on the left.

These are the real links holes at Porthcawl; at the 4th you play directly away from the sea. It's 193 yards and the best of the par 3s. There are cross bunkers to catch anything short and other bunkers flanking the green on both sides. The green slopes from back to front, with a terrace. If the flag's at the back and your ball on the front, three putts are almost an achievement!

The 5th is the first of the par 5s and a classic. A boundary wall runs all along the left, and the second shot is uphill all the way to a narrow, saddle-shaped green. The hole's only 476 yards, so as long as the wind's not against you you may be trying to get up in two. But beware, there's a cavernous bunker on the right-hand side of the green. Henry Cotton rated this a great par 5, partly because of the siting of the green.

The 7th really ought to be easy, just 116 yards, but there are bunkers everywhere around the kidney-shaped green and lots of bumps in the ground if you should happen to avoid them. At the 8th you've a blind drive at this 476-yard hole with cross bunkers to clear with your second shot set into a ridge. Though you may be hoping to get up in two, you'll probably be playing into the wind.

The 9th is rated the hardest hole on the course, yet it's not a long par 4 at 368 yards. The green, however, is at the top of a slope and well bunkered. Putting can be very difficult here when the wind's up.

If the first three holes at Porthcawl are thought by many to be the most interesting, the finish, from the 13th onwards, is the sternest stuff.

The 13th itself is quite a long par 4 of 413 yards, doglegged to the left with the green below you for your second shot so as to raise doubts in club selection. The 15th, 421 yards, has bunkers to catch a less than ideal drive, with a good carry from the tee needed. The green is on the brow of the hill and well guarded by bunkers, with a ridge just short of it.

At the 16th you head directly for the clubhouse, encouraged perhaps by a downhill tee shot, but with a line of cross bunkers to carry or play short of. With your next, the shot is uphill, with a bunker at the right front of the green, cunningly placed to gather the ball.

After a par 5 of no particular difficulty, the 18th is downhill. However, the wind is usually against you, and a large gully crosses the fairway in what may be your driving distance on the day. Along the left is out of bounds and the last green is one of the most difficult to read.

After those early links holes, the 6,409 yards of Porthcawl from the medal tees are mostly moorland turf. There's an abundance of heather, bracken and gorse, often very thick in the rough.

There are fine views over the Bristol Channel towards Minehead with Exmoor beyond and across the bay to Swansea and the Gower Peninsula. Most unusually, the sea is in view from every tee and green.

The club has hosted many major events, the first being the 1932 Penfold Tournament. The Dunlop Masters came in 1961 and the Amateur Championship has been on four occasions. Both men's and ladies' Home Internationals have been held here many times, and the Curtis Cup, the European Amateur Team Championship, Vagliano Trophy and British Ladies' Championship once each.

€ £24

M membership of a golf club, a handicap certificate and a letter of introduction

✗ snacks until 6.30 p.m., lunch daily, dinner can be provided for parties of twelve upwards

🚗 leave the M4 at Junction 37 along A4229 for Porthcawl, where club is well signposted

SOUTHERNDOWN

Ewenny, nr Bridgend, Mid-Glamorgan CF35 5BT
☎ Southerndown (0656) 880326 & 880476

I remember this downland course well from playing it in the 1968 Martini International, while a now near neighbour of mine, Colonel Tony Duncan, is the club's president. He also started the Duncan Putter, competed for over 72 holes every Easter, the first major amateur event of the Welsh golfing calendar.

Southerndown overlooks the Bristol Channel and the estuary of the Ogmore River. As all downland courses tend to be, it's extremely exposed and golf here can be a very stern battle indeed against the wind, for there are nine par 4s more than 400 yards in length and only two relatively short par 5s.

The 1st hole, 373 yards, is actually one of the shortest of the par 4s but it plays long, uphill all the way with a good carry needed with your drive to clear a bank and then another for your shot to the green. Henry Cotton once rated it one of the most difficult starting holes he had come across. The 2nd is much longer in terms of yardage, nearly 450, with cross bunkers well placed to catch a second shot not quite well enough hit.

At the 3rd you again have to drive uphill, this time between two mounds. As the 4th is another hole of more than 400 yards, the start at Southerndown will, I hope, bring out the best in you, for there's a great deal more of the same to come!

At the 5th, however, we reach the first par 3, and a very good one it is. To reach the well-guarded plateau green you must clear a deep valley. Into a stiff breeze, its 170 yards can seem a very long way. The 6th, however, may give you a chance to get a stroke back. It's not a long par 5 and very reachable in two with a favourable wind.

However, if you did have some help from the wind, you will turn directly into it at the next, a short hole played downhill of 230 yards or so and perhaps the most demanding of the four par 3s. Downhill or not, you'll often need a driver to get home.

The first nine ends with the shortest par 4 on the course, but there are bunkers along the left to catch your drive and the green is well bunkered

249

at the front. The 12th, a slight dogleg left, has a demanding drive, with heavy gorse in wait to either side of the fairway. At the next, a short par 5, there's a fairly long carry to reach the fairway but, despite bunkering in the driving area, you should be thinking in terms of getting on in two, unless the wind's in your face.

The 15th, downhill, does not play its full 377 yards, but the approach to and surrounds of the green are the most heavily bunkered on the course. There's a quartet slanting across the fairway and another five on the sides of the green.

The finish at Southerndown, consisting of three long par 4s, is as tough as anything that's gone before. Features are an uphill drive at the 16th, with trouble which includes a deep hollow right of the green, a right-to-left slope of the narrow 17th fairway, and a drive to a two-tiered fairway from an elevated tee at the last. This is one of the best holes on the course.

The 6,600 yards of Southerndown are arguably the most testing of this kind of golf in Britain.

£ £24	✕ snacks, lunch and dinner daily
M a handicap certificate	🚗 take the M4 to Bridgend and then A48 until the Ogmore turn-off. Then turn left at the Pelican Inn
🎱 snooker	
✉ bookings should be made in advance	

TENBY

The Burrows, Tenby, Dyfed SA70 7NP
☎ Tenby (0834) 2978

Though the 8th and 9th greens are furthest from the clubhouse, Tenby by no means follows the typical straight out-and-back pattern. You change course quite often, some pairs of holes being in opposite directions, while others are played either directly towards the sea or inland.

Founded in 1888, Tenby is the oldest club in Wales and lies in what has become the Pembrokeshire Coast National Park.

The course is very much links in quality except for the 15th, 16th and 17th. To get to them you cross over a railway bridge and find yourself in something much nearer parkland.

Long par 4s are very much a feature, seven of these being over 400 yards. There's only one par 4 that could be called short, and only one par 5, so scoring can be very difficult, helped a little, perhaps, by normal links run on the ball. If you can play to your handicap over the 6,333 yards, with the Standard Scratch of 69 being three below the par, it'll be an achievement.

The start is a difficult one, with three long 4s in the first four holes. The 1st is 466 yards over undulating ground with little chance of being up in two against even a mild breeze. The 2nd is nearly as long and the narrow green is a difficult target. However, the 3rd, though much shorter at 382 yards, is rated as stroke index 1. This is because great precision is required for the second shot to the very small plateau green, with a bunker to catch anything just short and steep falls to either side.

No chance to relax at the 4th, a big par 4 again, of 447 yards, with sand dunes to the left and a narrow fairway; the second shot to the green, hidden amongst steep banks and sandhills, is blind. This green is close by the sea, as is the 5th tee, with superb views over to Caldey Island.

Of the par 3s, the 12th is the best, 199 yards with your ball needing to carry all the way, with a deep grassy hollow followed by the beach to the right. The 17th, however, 174 yards, is also good, with a tee which overlooks almost the entire course and the green, with much trouble surrounding it, below you.

There's another elevated shot at the last, a spectacular hole. You drive from very high up, hoping to sail serenely over the roof of a cottage below. Out of bounds is also at hand all along the left-hand side to the green, which is over 400 yards away, and also through the back.

£ *£12-15*

M *a handicap certificate*

✕ *snacks daily, lunch and dinner daily except Tuesday*

♙ *snooker*

🚗 *from Tenby town centre follow British Rail signs and thereafter signs for the golf club*

NORTHERN
IRELAND

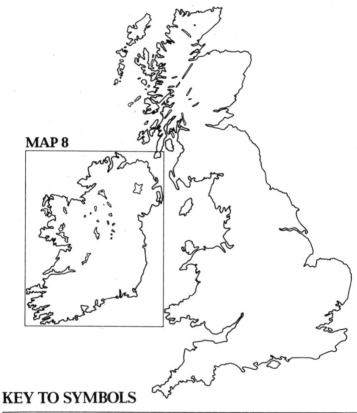

MAP 8

KEY TO SYMBOLS

🌳 PARKLAND	☎ TELEPHONE	✗ CATERING PROVIDED	
LINKS	⊠ NEED TO BOOK IN ADVANCE	🏠 ACCOMMODATION PROVIDED	
MOORLAND	£ APPROXIMATE COURSE FEE	Ⓛ RESTRICTIONS ON LADIES AND/OR YOUTHS	
HEATHLAND	M MEMBERSHIP REQUIREMENTS FOR VISITORS	OTHER SPORTING FACILITIES	
DOWNLAND			
UPLAND		🚗 DIRECTIONS	

MALONE

240 Upper Malone Road, Dunmurry, Belfast BT17 9LB
☎ *Belfast (0232) 612758*

This is a relatively long and very handsome parkland course. Although the club itself has been in existence since 1895, the course itself is fairly new, and was designed by Fred Hawtree.

Trees feature considerably, beginning with mature limes which flank the approach to the clubhouse, a fine stone building dating from about 1800. There are three nines. The 'Inner Nine' is a relief course measuring 2,892 yards, which can be played twice.

The main course is set out in two nine-hole loops. For play on the second nine, a 20-acre lake is a great feature. The first real test of your nerve comes at the 3rd, a par 5 of 486 yards with a chasm to be carried immediately in front of the green. The 7th is a very long 4, just below the maximum distance with a bunker to be carried just before the green.

Two par 3s are amongst the most testing of the remaining holes. One, the 12th, is close on 200 yards and all carry – there's a bunker blocking a running shot. The 15th causes some knuckles to whiten on the club. It's just a pitch with an 8 or 9 iron but there's water to carry to an island green.

There is a good-sized practice ground, a putting green and an approaching green.

🅴 *£17, £20 at weekends*	✉ *need to book in advance*
Ⓜ *none*	🚗 *take the Malone road south from Belfast and after about 4 miles turn on to Upper Malone Road. The clubhouse is on the left after 1½ miles*
✖ *snacks and lunch daily, dinner daily except Sunday*	

ROYAL COUNTY DOWN

Newcastle, County Down
☎ *Newcastle (03967) 23314*

This is among the most admired courses in the world. In 1982, Royal County Down made the top twenty-five courses in the UK in a *Golf World* survey, and in 1984 rose into the top ten. The American *Golf* magazine rated it even higher. When they did a ranking test in 1983 of all the world's courses, their panellists rated it number three, below only Muirfield and Pebble Beach.

It's rare indeed to find such unanimity, as tastes for golfing country and design vary so much.

Part of the reason for its great appeal is simply that Royal County Down is a beautiful place. The course is set in classic links country with sand dunes by the score, often covered in gorse, whins and heather. All along the eastward boundary there is the long curve of Dundrum Bay. But more than this, it is actually the place 'where the Mountains of Mourne run down by the sea'. The foothills begin immediately behind the town, which is next to the course, and you can see Slieve Donard, which rises to nearly 3,000 feet.

In such a setting, Royal County Down is bound to be well liked in much the same sense, for example, as Gleneagles. However, the golf here is altogether more difficult. The distinguished American golf writer, Herbert Warren Wind, has gone as far as to write: 'It was the sternest examination in golf I had ever taken.' That may be going too far, but it does ask for very good driving. You must always be reasonably straight and there are numerous carries from the tee over dunes and gorse. Sometimes these are blind shots, which doesn't help the confidence.

The club was founded back in 1889 when, like nearly everyone in those days, they got Old Tom Morris over from St Andrews to design the course. All the courses were outdated almost overnight by the development of the wound ball early this century and in 1908, the year that County Down became 'Royal', the great Harry Vardon, an infrequent architect, revised the original layout.

Royal County Down doesn't follow the traditional out-and-back links pattern. In fact there are two loops, each of nine, and each gets you conveniently back to the clubhouse. The first lies closest to the sea with the second being slightly more inland in character.

The first hole, a par 5, is helped by the prevailing wind, although the green presents a narrow target. You next have two stiff par 4s to play. The 2nd requires a drive over sandhills and your next shot then has to contend with a small green, with pot bunkers to the left and ground falling away to the right. The 3rd is rather a savage test, even with a kindly wind. This long par 4 is more than 450 yards with a green well protected by bunkers and formidable sandhills both left and right short of the green, with a few fingers threading across the fairway as well for good measure. It's the first of seven par 4s over 400 yards.

The 4th, at over 200 yards, whatever the result of your tee shot, which may well be over a sea of gorse, is played directly towards the Mountains of Mourne.

The next par 3, the 7th, is very different in character, just 133 yards from the medal tees. But care is needed, for the green is small, rather domed, and with gorse and bunkers to right and left. All in all it's just as easy or difficult, depending what you make of it, as the Postage Stamp at Royal Troon.

With the 8th and 9th we're back to fairly severe par 4s. The first of these requires no extreme precision with the drive but the long second has to be played through a neck to a narrow green with the ground falling away to either side.

The 9th, at one time a par 5, as it remains from the championship tees, is an excellent two-shotter. In fact the uphill and blind drive must be rather good to give you much chance of finding the green with your second shot. Once you've cleared your marker post, the ground falls very sharply away to a flat fairway. From there, you've only to rasp your iron uphill to a plateau green.

At this point the best of County Down is behind you. The sandhills are less towering and you're that little bit further away from the sea, which brings a perceptible difference in the terrain.

Soon you'll come across the easiest hole on the course, the 12th, quite a short par 5, but nevertheless calling for a firm drive to carry a depression.

The 13th is a most attractive banana-shaped hole, not quite a dogleg right, threading through a valley with heather in plenty to either side. The further right you are with your tee shot, the more trouble you must carry with your second shot.

The 15th is the most difficult of the remaining holes. Here your tee shot is blind (for the last time), with the second having to be played to a shelf-like green, cut into a dune.

After quite a succession of long par 4s, the 16th can provide light relief. It's certainly quite drivable with the wind behind you, being basically a hole played from one hill to another.

Although the 18th is a par 5, as it is played into the prevailing wind it isn't an easy home hole. It's perhaps the most heavily bunkered stretch of the course and the approach has to be particularly accurate.

Yes, it *is* a difficult course, one that could leave a 16 handicapper wondering if he'll ever break the magic hundred again, but on a good weather day where you've been, more than how you played, will remain long in memory. Perhaps you'll even have had a hole in 1. A certain Eric Fiddian did that not once but twice in the final of the 1933 Irish Amateur Championship – and still lost.

County Down might well be an Open Championship course, except that it's undeniably old-fashioned in the sense that there are several blind tee shots or approaches where the green is at least partially obscured. This can be forgiven of St Andrews but I doubt that the R and A, Sandwich excepted, would introduce a course on to the rota which did not give the player at least a reasonable view of the fairway and a clear view of the flag after a good drive.

Royal County Down has seen seven British Ladies' Championships, however, while Michael Bonallack completed his hat trick here in 1970 in the Amateur Championship, as usual putting like a man possessed.

£ £25, £30 at weekends

M none

✗ lunch during the week

🚗 take the T2 from Belfast through Ballynahinch to Newcastle, a distance of about 30 miles

---

ROYAL PORTRUSH

Bushmills Road, Portrush, County Antrim
☎ *Portrush (0265) 823780*

Ranking courses in order of merit is a popular golfing pastime. Portrush turns up on nearly all such lists within the top fifty not only of the British Isles, but of the world. The great golf architect Harry Colt considered it his masterpiece.

One of the oldest clubs in Ireland, Portrush was founded in 1888 and received its 'Royal' prefix a few years later. The course soon achieved championship status when Lady Margaret Scott won the British Ladies' the third time the event was played.

The 1951 Open, won by Max Faulkner, was held here – the only time the championship has been played outside England or Scotland. The Amateur Championship has also been to Portrush and produced another famous victory, when Joe Carr, an Irishman born in Dublin, crushed the American Bob Cochran by 8 and 7 in 1960.

The championship course, the Dunluce, is built amongst the dunes on two, and sometimes three, levels. The fairways are narrow and the rough severe, with plenty of heather in evidence. On most holes there's a view of the sea and the Antrim countryside often provides a backcloth. The quality of the turf and good drainage means that the preferred lies option does not come in during the winter. No two holes are alike, there aren't a large number of bunkers and the greens in general aren't heavily borrowed.

The first tee shot is to a wide fairway but with out of bounds either side. It is a not very difficult par 4, and is followed by a par 5 of 497 yards which can be reachable in two. However, the drive needs to be a long one if there's to be much chance of carrying the cross bunkers short of the green.

From the tee of the short 3rd, 159 yards, you can see the full spread of the links for the first time, with views over the sea. The 4th is the first really testing hole, a par 4 of 455 yards. The tee shot is very tight, the most difficult on the course, between out of bounds along the right and a well-placed bunker to the left. The entrance to the green, set amongst the dunes, is very narrow, with hillocks either side to catch anything at all off line.

The 5th is played directly towards the sea, a dogleg right, with club selection very important on the second shot because of the out-of-bounds fence and White Rocks Beach just beyond the green. The 6th is another par 3 with a demanding tee shot, a long iron. It's 198 yards and you must carry the ball all the way with deep hollows protecting both front left and front right of the green, which has many subtle borrows.

The 7th is one of the great holes and is 432 yards. The fairway is narrow and a good-length drive is needed or a wood will be necessary for the shot to the elevated green which falls away very quickly on the right and is fronted by cross bunkers.

By this time, you have probably become aware of the seclusion of the holes, with the middle section mostly played through their own valleys. The 8th is 'Himalayas' (I wonder how many holes in golf are so called?). It asks you to drive over hills with thick rough and then doglegs right with a pitch to a long narrow green.

Perhaps this will be a birdie opportunity, and the 9th, 476 yards, certainly is, particularly if you cut the corner of the slight dogleg. Even so, the armchair green is not easy to hit from long range and there are the penalties of a large hollow just in front, with rough close by on both sides.

The second nine begins with another par 5, again not long at 480 yards, where you need to clear a bunker on the right with your tee shot to ease the rest of the hole. Even then, you need a very straight shot, exactly weighted to avoid the humps just short of the green.

The 11th looks the easiest of the par 3s and perhaps it is, played from an elevated tee with the green well below. However, club selection can be difficult on this kind of shot and there are bunkers everywhere to catch anything short or off line. After two par 4s you must now meet the challenge of Portrush's most famous hole, 'Calamity Corner'. This is a par 3 of 213 yards, a terrifying driver shot into a wind. If you've got the length but are slightly off line, there's rough all around, and anything a little short will catch the far side of a chasm and tumble down to the bottom, about 50 feet below the level of the green.

The 15th is a far more encouraging hole, downhill for the tee shot and downhill again for the shot to the green, taking us from the duneland back to much the same level as the clubhouse. Bunkers cut into the green so the pitch shot at this 366-yard hole must be exactly weighted.

The 16th is where Faulkner at last began to stagger on his journey to the championship, hitting his drive very close to the fence on the left of the fairway. It's 432 yards with a large bunker protecting the green on the right and ground falling away on the left.

The last two holes, out of the dune country, are both par 5s, with the 18th being particularly flat. On both, strategic bunkering is the main feature.

There is another course at Portrush, the Valley, which is about 600 yards shorter than the Dunluce, at 6,278 yards, and lies closer to the sea for the most part. The turf is excellent and the greens are small and well placed. Despite the fact that this is also a links lay-out, only some twenty bunkers have been used in the design, much use being made of the shape of the land.

£ *£20, £25 at weekends*	**✕** *snacks, lunch and dinner daily*
M *a letter of introduction is preferred*	**▣** *snooker*
✉ *need to book in advance*	**🚗** *1 mile out of Portrush on the Bushmills road*

REPUBLIC
OF IRELAND

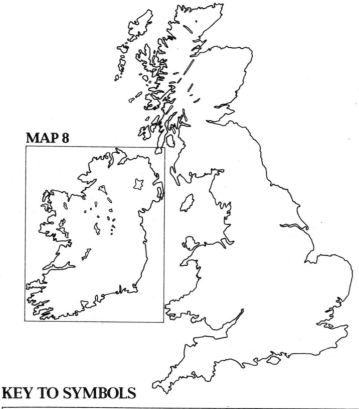

MAP 8

KEY TO SYMBOLS

🌳 PARKLAND	☎ TELEPHONE	✗ CATERING PROVIDED
LINKS	✉ NEED TO BOOK IN ADVANCE	🏨 ACCOMMODATION PROVIDED
MOORLAND	£ APPROXIMATE COURSE FEE	Ⓛ RESTRICTIONS ON LADIES AND/OR YOUTHS
HEATHLAND	M MEMBERSHIP REQUIREMENTS FOR VISITORS	OTHER SPORTING FACILITIES
DOWNLAND		
UPLAND		🚗 DIRECTIONS

BALLYBUNION

Ballybunion, County Kerry
☎ *Ballybunion (068) 27146*

·Most golf links are not quite as near the sea as one might wish. Very often, there are ranks of sandhills between the golf and the sea. It may be just a short iron shot away, but doesn't feel near. However, at Ballybunion, the towering sandhills come into play and don't separate the sea from the golf because they run across, rather than along the course. Several holes are right on the very shore. All this, and much else, is magnificent stuff, so magnificent indeed, that we're talking of one of the world's top courses. *Golf World*, for instance, ranked it in the top ten in the British Isles in 1984, while the American *Golf* magazine put it as high as fifth in the British Isles and thirteenth in the world. Several years ago the American writer Herbert Warren Wind wrote in the *New Yorker*: 'Very simply, Ballybunion revealed itself to be nothing less than the finest seaside course I have ever seen.'

Ballybunion has staged several Irish championships for amateurs and the Irish Professional Close Championship on three occasions, but it's not very likely that major professional events will come here. Situated on the west coast of Ireland near the mouth of the River Shannon, it's undeniably remote and· it could hardly be expected to attract large crowds.

However, possibly as the result of Mr Wind's article, it may be more famous among Americans than among the British. Thousands fly into Shannon Airport to home in on two targets, Ballybunion and Killarney.

The course can be stretched to well over 7,000 yards but you will be playing it at a lot less. You begin with a fairly short par 4, followed by two testing shots along the 2nd: a drive uphill to a narrow fairway, with a second having to carry a green cocked up on the top of a ridge. A long par 3 follows and then a couple of relatively dull par 5s well away from the sea; before the playing order was changed several years ago, these made rather an anticlimax of the finish.

The 6th green is set on a plateau and is a narrow target, especially if your tee shot is not on a good line.

From now on, you play with the Atlantic always in earshot and often very close indeed. The 7th runs along the shore for over 400 yards and is followed by a really good short par 3, played from a high tee in the dunes to a green amongst the folds and hollows below. The 9th is another long par 4 along the shore with a plateau green. The 11th is one of the most dramatic holes. Again, there's a plateau green and all the way you've the Atlantic on your right and huge sandhills on your left.

The 12th is a magnificent par 3, a wooden club for most, to a green way up there in the sandhills and into the prevailing winds. The 13th is the third of the four par 5s, with a downhill tee shot. Once more, the green is set up in the dunes. Then another par 3, the first of two in a row, a sequence frowned on by pedants. The first one is short, with the green well above you, while the second, at 200 yards, is very long, even if it is downhill, to a target that can seem ridiculously small. Of the last three holes, the 17th is the best, again along the shore and putting a high premium on accuracy.

I'm sure you'll be eager to set out once again after a pause for the Irish welcome in the clubhouse. You may, indeed, prefer to sample the New course, designed by Robert Trent Jones, but it is too demanding for a long-handicap golfer. When it reaches peak condition there will be many to argue that Ballybunion has the best thirty-six holes of links golf in the world.

£ *IR £30*

M *membership of a golf club*

✗ *snacks, lunch and dinner daily*

🚗 *from Shannon Airport via Limerick, or from Cork Airport via Mallow and Listowel. The course is off the L106 1 mile south of Ballybunion town*

KILKENNY

Glendine, Kilkenny, County Kilkenny, Eire
☎ *Kilkenny (056) 22125*

Situated just to the north of Kilkenny, the course gives views of the Johnswell Hills and the Blackstairs Mountains. The club is one of the oldest in Ireland, dating back to 1896; its course now measures 6,400 yards, with each half being fairly equally balanced for length.

There are four par 3s and three 5s but the pick of the holes is amongst the par 4s.

The 7th, just a yard or two under 400 yards, has out of bounds along the right and a horse-shoe-shaped bunker to the left. The 11th is more testing still, 436 yards with slight doglegging to the left and trees bordering the fairway on both sides. The 13th is another long par 4 of much the same length with the green set in a dip, calling for a particularly accurate second shot with a long iron. The 16th is a much shorter par 4 at about 380 yards, but it's tight all the way to the green with a wood on the left.

Although this is a flat parkland course, it's sand-based and good playing conditions can be counted on after wet weather. The club has hosted the Carroll's Irish Professional Matchplay Championship and the All-Ireland Mixed Foursomes were held here in September 1984.

£ *IR £10 and £12*

M *membership of a golf club*

✗ *snacks, lunch and dinner daily except Monday*

🚗 *leave Kilkenny city centre on the Castlecomber road and take the first right after passing the Newpark Hotel*

KILLARNEY GOLF AND FISHING

Mahony's Point, County Kerry
☎ *Killarney (064) 31034*

This course, dating from some fifty or so years ago, was the brain child of Valentine, Viscount Castlerosse, later fifth Earl of Kenmure, best known as writer of the weekly 'Londoner's Log' in the *Sunday Express*. It was, if you like, a gossip column, but one in which people strove to be included.

Castlerosse was a figure so much larger than life as to be almost a caricature, perhaps the only man ever to have the upper hand on Lord Beaverbrook, his employer. At the beginning of the Second World War, when his column was no longer in keeping with the spirit of the times, he went off to his ancestral home at Killarney, where he continued to interest himself in the development of the course until his death in 1943.

The club had started in 1891 with nine holes, with Vardon and Alex Herd later adding a further nine. However, in 1936 it was decided to move the course, partly to take the opportunity offered by a lake-side site at Lough Leane. Sir Guy Campbell designed the new course but Castlerosse made many alterations. Some of these were unorthodox to say the least. For instance, he had one fully grown tree planted in the middle of the 15th green and three on the 10th. He thought the outrage that followed would be excellent publicity. Disturbed by the time and labour involved in digging out deep bunkers, he attempted, without success, to persuade the Irish Air Force to come to Killarney for some bombing practice!

After the war important events began to come here, starting with the Irish Amateur Championship in 1949 and then the 1953 Home Internationals. Killarney became enormously popular with visitors, and got to be too crowded. It was decided that another eighteen holes were needed and these were completed by 1971 to produce two courses, Mahony's Point, 6,730 yards, and Killeen, 7,030. What you see today is basically the work of Sir Guy Campbell, Viscount Castlerosse, some say with a thought or two from Henry Longhurst, and Fred Hawtree, sometimes advised by Dr Billy O'Sullivan, the local golfing hero. The new holes were mixed with the old to form the two courses.

Killeen

The 1st has a tee set on a little spur projecting into Lough Leane and the hole then swings round, following the shore line, which comes into play if you drive too far right. If you go safely left, there's a tree to be carried. Only about 350 yards, it's a comfortable enough start. The next, a dogleg right, is some 20 to 30 yards longer and a stream eats into the fairway from the right but well short of the green, so it shouldn't be a problem. The 3rd, a par 3 of just under 200 yards, returns to the lakeside and your tee shot may have to be over the shore. Scrub short and right of the green is a more likely problem, however. Whatever your shot, the mountains make a superb backcloth. So also at the 4th, which swings right to left with the line of the shore. It's only some 350 yards but the fairway narrows between shore and trees on the left in the driving area.

The 5th is a splendid par 5 with two routes to the green. You can either play two straight shots and then turn sharp right with a little pitch, or drive down the right and try with, say, your 4-wood to cut the angle and carry a stand of alders on the right-hand side of the green.

The 6th is a very difficult 190-yard par 3 for the long handicap player. The large two-tier green is almost an island, with a stream close up at the front and at both sides, and a fall-away to trees and rough through the back. Be brave or play short and trust to a pitch and one putt finish.

The 7th is a 400-yard par 4 where streams come into play just as strongly. Keep left with your tee shot or you will run into the right rough and also have to play your second along the line of a stream. This one catches anything pitching short and right of the green. On the other side, a stream runs along the side of the green and part of the back also.

More water at the 8th, a par 4 of some 420 yards, played from an elevated tee towards the Macgillicuddy's Reeks and the Carrauntoohill Mountains with a road, trees and rough close at hand all along the left. A stream pushes out across the fairway some 25 yards short of the green.

On now to the 13th, a tough par 4 of around 450 yards. After a good drive, a little to the left of centre preferably, your long second is played through a gap in the trees and must carry a stream a good way short of the green. The ground falls away left of the green to encroaching trees. A bunker catches shots played too far right, in the search for a safe path.

Mahony's Point

At Mahony's Point the best holes are the last six. The 13th is a shortish par 5 of about 480 yards designed by Castlerosse and into the prevailing wind. There's nothing much to the tee shot. Give it a big bang straight towards the flag and you may get it far enough to be helped by a downslope. Your second shot will have to be a good one, for the green slopes away towards bunkers on either side and the road is close on the left. Even if you're playing a short pitch with your third, you'll have to be quite precise to hold the putting surface.

The 14th, another Castlerosse hole, 370 yards, is a dogleg left to a plateau green. There are big bunkers on either side and another short on the left.

The 15th is a tempting little par 4 of some 270 yards. As it's downhill for most of the way, with a slight rise to the green, there's a good chance of getting on with your drive, through a reasonably generous gap between the bunkers that are guarding the front on either side.

The 16th, a par 5 of about 520 yards, curves right back towards Lough Leane with Tomies Mountain beyond. A feature is the stream, which crosses the fairway some 70 yards short of the green, so you have to pause for thought before playing your second if you've hit a good drive. It continues along the right side of the fairway and passes close to the green, while there's another at a less menacing distance on the left.

The 17th, a 400-yarder, follows the lake shore all the way, but it's difficult to drive safely left because of a pine tree. There are no bunkers protecting the green, which is two-tier, but there is scrub through the back and to the right.

The finishing hole is one of the most photographed in golf, a par 3 of 200 yards, with the tee shot played over the edge of the lake. More of a hazard, depending on wind direction, are the bunker, road and rhododendron bushes to the left. It makes a fitting climax to golf in one of the most beautiful settings you could hope to find. The club declares: 'The scenic views of mountains and lakes are unequalled by any other course in the world.' It certainly has very few serious rivals.

💷 *IR £20*	🎣 *fishing*
Ⓜ *a handicap certificate*	🚗 *3 miles west of Killarney*
🍴 *snacks daily, lunch and dinner daily except Monday*	✉ *bookings should be made in advance*

LIMERICK

Ballyclough, Rosbrien, County Limerick
☎ *Limerick (061) 44083*

Here we're entering Woganland for it was here, so he tells me, that he was born though I believe he learned his golf on the other side of the Irish Sea.

Limerick is a parkland course on gently undulating terrain and has suffered, as so many of our courses have, from Dutch elm disease. More than a hundred mature trees have gone and there's had to be a re-planting programme, especially to replace the ones that were strategically placed according to the architect's idea of how a hole should be played. Other trees, as so often in Ireland, remain a feature, however: poplar, beech, birch, white beam, mountain ash, chestnut, lime and maple are all to be found, often profusely.

It's a good test of golf, thought good enough to host the Irish Professional Championship twice, and has produced Vincent Nevin, who won the Irish Amateur Championship in 1969 and played for his country in 67 matches.

Water hazards are well used, notably at the 3rd, a long par 4, where one confronts you about 25 yards short of the green. At the 6th there's a long carry from the tee over a ditch, followed by a tight second shot. Out of bounds comes into the scheme of things fairly often, as at the 7th where it's there all the time from tee to green along the left on a long par 4. The same is true at the 14th, a par 3 which is also closely bunkered around the green.

£ *IR £15*

M *membership of a golf club*

L *Ladies Day is Tuesday but play on other days can usually be arranged*

✗ *snacks, lunch and dinner daily*

🎱 *snooker*

🚗 *from Limerick take T11 for Cork and turn left at Raheen Church. Look out for the club on the left after a further 2 miles*

PORTMARNOCK

Portmarnock, County Dublin
☎ *Dublin (01) 332050*

Portmarnock is a really big course, over 7,100 yards from the very back tees, fully fit to test an Open Championship field – if it were in Britain. Oddly though, one British national championship has been played here, the 1949 Amateur Championship. Fairly appropriately, it was won by an Irishman, Max McCready.

Although it's very unlikely this event will return, the Carroll's Irish Open is a frequent visitor – every year from 1976 to 1982 and again in 1986 and 1990. The former Dunlop Masters was played here twice and also the Canada (now World) Cup in 1960, which was won by the USA, Flory van Donck of Belgium taking the individual title.

The links is set on a peninsula which runs north to south, but it isn't a typical out-and-back lay-out. Instead the course darts about and you never play more than two holes in the same direction with the result that the wind – and it does blow here – seems to come at you from all around.

As so often on the Irish coast, it's a fine place to be. The Hill of Howth and Dublin Bay are to the south, the islands of Ireland's Eye and Lambay out to sea, the Dublin Hills to the west and Drogheda and the Mountains of Mourne visible on a clear day to the north.

Just the right climate and lots of loving care have produced some of the best putting surfaces in the British Isles. Bernard Darwin wrote of them early this century:

'Perhaps the outstanding beauty of Portmarnock lies in its putting greens. They are good and true, which is a merit given to many greens, and they are very fast without being untrue, which is given only to a few, and is a rare and shining virtue. Even on a raw Easter time they demand that the ball should be soothed rather than hit towards the hole. I have read somewhere a story of a famous Scottish professional who declared that on his first visit to the course he arrived on the first green in two perfect shots, and had ultimately to hole a 4-yard putt for a seven.'

In writing about the course as a whole, I'll have to assume you're playing it on a reasonably still day, perhaps into the prevailing breeze. If the wind is really up you'll be facing the more or less impossible. If so, console yourself as you tot up your lamentable score by remembering that Henry Cotton, a very good wind player indeed, once finished 86, 81 on the last day in an Irish Open Championship of long ago and was still only a stroke behind the winner! When I played here in 1965 the tented village was destroyed by wind and gales.

The start is not too sternly demanding, and that's how it should be, three par 4s all less than 400 yards. The 3rd is the best of these, with a lateral water hazard to the right and an accurate shot needed to the well-bunkered green. Then comes a very long par 4, soon followed by a par 5 that could be very daunting indeed if you're frightened of numbers – 580 yards or thereabouts with the shot to the green being to the top of a little hill. It's a monster if played into the teeth of an east wind, but the wind's more likely to be a helpful westerly.

Soon, you turn for the clubhouse. The 9th is testing: the drive is over a ridge, and, if you are too greedy, there's a bunker in wait over the rise. The plateau green, very much a feature at Portmarnock, is hard to hold.

Further plateau greens follow at the 10th and the short 12th. The 11th is an apparently dull hole and can be very difficult to club because of its flat green. The short 12th is a delight, only 130 yards or so long, with a very small green up in the sandhills and close by the sea. If you're short, you'll catch the sharp upslope; further problems are provided by the bunkering and higher ground to the right.

Now comes another very long par 5, about 560 yards and likely to be played into the prevailing wind, with another soon to follow, the 16th, 520 yards. In between is one of Portmarnock's famous holes, the 380-yard 14th, which I've heard Henry Cotton rate as one of the greatest holes in golf. It plays towards the sea and the fairway swings left to a plateau green with two bunkers set into the upslope. The humps, slopes and hollows all around shrug away many a good iron shot.

The 15th is the best of the short holes. It's played with the sea to your right to a green that's rather small for its 190 yards, with nothing to help you get near the hole. Most members reckon this the hardest hole on the course and move on happily enough with a 4 on the card.

The last hole is an exciting one, a bit like the 16th at Deal. It's a touch under 400 yards and you won't often get any help from the wind. The green is again a plateau, with bunkers set into either side of the rise. If you've driven well, there's the thrill of sending an iron shot against the sky and seeing it plummet down towards the distant flag.

£ *IR £35*

M *membership of a golf club*

✗ *snacks daily, lunch Sunday only, dinner Monday to Friday*

🚗 *leave Dublin for Portmarnock and after about 9 miles turn right in the village just before the pedestrian lights. The course is about 1 ½ miles along that road*

ROYAL DUBLIN

Dollymount, Dublin 3
☎ *Dublin (01) 336346*

Royal Dublin celebrated its centenary in 1985 and must be the only championship course situated within the boundaries of a capital city. It's on Bull Island in Dublin Bay.

It is the second oldest club in Ireland (following Royal Belfast) and first played in Phoenix Park before settling on Bull Island in 1889. Over the years the course has developed to a little over 6,700 yards and is of real championship calibre. It has two very distinctive features.

The first of these are the close lies, which mean that very precise striking is always needed. Unless you're in a divot, you never seem to get a bad fairway lie, but the ball doesn't sit up well cushioned on grass, begging to be swept away with a fairway wood. The other strong feature is bunkering. Many years ago, John Low wrote of bunkers in general: 'Bunkers, if they be good bunkers and bunkers of strong character, refuse to be disregarded, and insist on asserting themselves; they do not mind being avoided, but they decline to be ignored,' and at Dollymount you ignore them at your peril. They are subtly placed and often gather the ball, particularly for shots into greens.

The links has been compared to both Hoylake and St Andrews. Like both, it's generally flat and has much in common with the Home of Golf in the very small acreage the course occupies. Both are out-and-back lay-outs, with the second nine at Dollymount being a bit of a long slog home if you're playing into a stiff wind as this half is the longer by some 500 yards.

The start is not fierce with a medium-length par 4 followed by a shortish par 5. You need to score reasonably here because the 3rd is more of a challenge, with good placement of the drive required to open up the second shot to a green which is very well bunkered. The 5th is rated stroke index 1 and is quite a long par 4 at around 440 yards. It's called the 'Valley' and is just that, with the fairway being only about 35 yards wide all the way.

Three of the four par 3s come in the first nine, and the best of these is the 9th, 177 yards. The second nine consists mostly of quite long par 4s and three par 5s. The 11th, 525 yards, is the longest hole on the course and can easily be three good woods when playing uphill into the wind. Here the green is set into a dell, as it is at the 13th, which is a longish 4 and stroke index 2.

If you are beating home against the wind and finding it very heavy going, there's relief at the 15th where you completely change direction and play away from the clubhouse. But back you turn again at the 16th, a clear birdie opportunity of little more than 250 yards.

The 18th is a famous finishing hole. It's a par 5 of only 482 yards and is doglegged to the right around the out-of-bounds 'garden'. You can go for the green on your second shot, with fair chance of success, but you'll have to trust your nerve to go for the big carry which continues until quite near it.

Christy O'Connor has been tournament and teaching professional here since 1959, and is still playing nearly as well as ever. He is one of the most natural golfers I've ever seen, still capable of putting on a show in a major event though he now appears only in the Carrolls Irish Open, held here in 1983, 1984 and 1985, pro-ams and, of course, the Seniors' Championship, which he used to win regularly.

£ *IR £27.50*

M *membership of a golf club*

✗ *catering from 10am until 9pm daily*

♪ *snooker, sauna*

🚗 *3 miles north of city centre on the coast road to Howth*

TULLAMORE

Brookfield, Tullamore, County Offaly
☎ *Tullamore (0506) 21439*

Situated quite near the centre of Ireland, this is one of the best inland courses in the country. It has a setting of trees and streams which feels remote from the outside world, with an occasional glimpse of the Slieve Bloom Mountains.

As you start your round, the woodland views of the 1st, 2nd and 5th holes are a delight, and the putting green is very much a feature, undulating and surrounded by shrubs and flowers.

After a start that won't test you too severely as the muscles loosen, the 5th, 460 yards, is the most difficult hole on the course. Your tee shot must be long and finish on the left half of the fairway to get a sight of the green for your second. This is played through a narrow tree-lined avenue.

267

The 9th, a 493-yard par 5, offers a similar challenge, again through the trees, and is very difficult to reach in two because of the accuracy of shot required.

The second nine begins with the stroke index 2 hole. This is a par 4 of 433 yards, severely doglegged to the right, with a lateral water hazard very much in play. The 17th is also particularly good; it is a par 4 a little under 400 yards, where you really must get a straight one away to find the narrow gap in the woods, which is quite a test at the end of a good or poor round alike.

Golf was first played at Tullamore as long ago as 1860 when just a few holes were laid out, the way so many golf clubs actually began. The present course has been in use since 1926 and measures just over 6,300 yards with four par 3s, and four par 5s.

£ IR £9   **M** none

X snacks, lunch and dinner usually available but the steward's day off varies

🚗 drive south from Tullamore for 2½ miles along the Birr Road and turn left at the first cross roads. The club is ½ mile further on the right

---

WATERVILLE

Waterville Golf Club, Waterville, County Kerry
☎ *Tralee (066) 74133*

This is a rarity in golf in these islands, a links course of recent design, and a remote one. As someone once said, 'It's so far south and so far west that you can see Boston on a clear day.' By car it's around 6 hours from Dublin, 3 from Cork and about 2 from Killarney.

Waterville is the creation of Irish American John A. Mulcahy. While making his money in the USA, he had the dream of building a course at Waterville. When he had the fortune he made his dream come true, giving designer Eddie Hackett a free hand as regards expenditure.

Hackett came up with a course that can be stretched to 7,234 yards, longer, for instance, than any course currently in use in the Open Championship. From these back tees, there are two par 5s of 587 yards and seven par 4s of more than 420 yards. The Kerrygold International Classic was held here four times in the mid 1970s and, when Tony Jacklin won the title in 1976, his total for four rounds was 290, one of his rounds being 79. Only two players broke 70 throughout.

However, don't despair; the tees are very large and from the forward ones it's a manageable 6,039 yards, with no par 4 more than 420. I shall discuss the course as it plays from medal tees, when it is 3,211 out and 3,410 back.

The Atlantic Ocean is on three sides of the course and inland the hills of Kerry form a backcloth. The fairways undulate quite gently, often winding between the sand dunes. There are many elevated tees, which often provide dramatic views of the hole you are about to play. The most dramatic of these is on the 17th. Set at about 250 feet above the ocean it is a vantage point for the whole course.

The greens are rather large and relatively flat, so putting should not often be a matter of exact judgement of borrow. Natural drainage burns run along both 1st and 2nd with grander water hazards at other holes; the Inny Bay borders the 3rd, 4th, 15th and 16th and the Atlantic the last two holes.

Two of the par 3s are fairly similar, the 12th and 17th, each played from a high tee to a plateau green with a chasm of dunes and knee-high rough in between. The 11th is a very attractive 477-yard par 5, aptly called 'Tranquillity' because it meanders amongst the sand dunes with the world blanked off.

The 16th, 346 yards, is very distinctive. The hole is crescent-shaped from tee to green and, to match, so is the tee!

John Mulcahy has made changes to his creation from time to time over the years and one alteration has been to uprate the 2nd from a fairly modest par 4 to one of 468 yards from the very back tees. If he wants to make Waterville the longest course in Europe, a couple of new back tees would surely do the trick.

This is not a course for a casual day's visit because it's a little remote. It's ideal for a short break, however, staying either at the hotel with reduced green fees or in the fishing village of Waterville. You'll have a warm welcome at either.

Amongst the members are an ex-president of Ireland, Gerald Ford and Bob Hope. Richard Nixon has been a house guest.

The modern clubhouse is set on a rise behind the 18th green with the ocean to one side. As the restaurant and bar are on the second floor the views are spectacular.

£ *IR £25, £30 at weekends*

M *a handicap certificate*

✕ *lunch and dinner daily except Monday, except in winter*

🚗 *when approaching the village, turn right at the church and right again on the road running parallel to the sea*

INDEX OF COURSES